*Partita* for Glenn Gould

Glenn Gould, 1956. Photograph by Jock Carroll

# *Partita* for Glenn Gould

## *An Inquiry into the Nature of Genius*

∽

GEORGES LEROUX

Translated by Donald Winkler

McGILL-QUEEN'S UNIVERSITY PRESS

Montreal & Kingston · London · Ithaca

© McGill-Queen's University Press 2010

ISBN 978-0-7735-3810-8

Legal deposit fourth quarter 2010
Bibliothèque nationale du Québec

Printed in Canada on acid-free paper that is 100% ancient forest free
(100% post-consumer recycled), processed chlorine free.

This book was originally published as *Partita pour Glenn Gould*, © Presses
de l'Université de Montréal, 2007. We acknowledge the financial support of
the Government of Canada, through the National Translation Program for
Book Publishing, for our translation activities.

McGill-Queen's University Press acknowledges the support of the Canada
Council for the Arts for our publishing program. We also acknowledge the
financial support of the Government of Canada through the Canada Book
Fund for our publishing activities.

Library and Archives Canada Cataloguing in Publication

Leroux, Georges, 1945–
Partita for Glenn Gould : an inquiry into the nature of genius /
Georges Leroux ; translated by Donald Winkler.

Translation of: Partita pour Glenn Gould (Montréal : Presses de l'Université
de Montréal, 2007).

Includes bibliographical references and index.
ISBN 978-0-7735-3810-8

1. Gould, Glenn, 1932–1982. 2. Music–Social aspects. I. Title.

ML417.G69L61813 2010      786.2092      C2010-904823-7

This book was designed and typeset by studio oneonone in Sabon 10/15

# Contents

# Preface to the English Edition

Since the initial appearance of this book in September 2007, at a time when Glenn Gould's admirers were commemorating the twenty-fifth anniversary of his premature death, our understanding of Gould's life and work has continued to grow. Important new studies and the ongoing publication of his correspondence have enabled us to fill in certain gaps. I have learned much from the recent contributions of scholars and artists who share my interest in Gould's aesthetic. Reflecting on their works, I have modified and refined my approach on a number of points, and have expanded my bibliography to take new developments into account. Chapter VI, "Scherzo," in particular, has been reconsidered since the French-language edition appeared.

To say that Gould is an icon of Canadian culture is an understatement. As I have tried to show, the more time I spent with Gould, the more meaningful that expression became for me. It is not simply a question of his environment and the places we associate with him, from his homes in Toronto to the landscapes of Georgian Bay. Even more important are his roots in Canadian thought, from Marshall McLuhan to Jean Le Moyne. But to say this still omits what is most essential: the freedom and generosity that characterize Gould's art and define it as Canadian. And so I am most happy to present my work to an English-speaking public whose appreciation of Gould has always gone hand in hand with a sense of its own cultural birthright.

I would like to reiterate my thanks to Gould's biographer Kevin Bazzana; he lives in British Columbia and I in Quebec, but we have enjoyed a constant dialogue. He had already helped me in the preparation of my essay, and since it first appeared in French he has accompanied me every step of the way. I would also like to thank my translator, Donald Winkler, who has brought both rigour and sensitivity to the work at hand. Crossing from one language to the other is very much a Canadian affair; he accepted the challenge, and I am most grateful to him.

# Acknowledgments

When I began writing about Glenn Gould in 1987, I never dreamt that he would remain with me the way he has. But he has never been far from my thoughts, thanks in part to the fact that my admiration for him has always been shared by many others. Several among them deserve my thanks. First, Ghyslaine Guertin, who has contributed so much to our understanding of Gould's art through her untiring work in publishing and translation. The two conferences she organized, in Montreal in 1987 and in Paris in 2003, set the stage for many productive discussions, and she has continued to inspire, both in Quebec and in France, our small community of French-speaking "Gouldians." Jean-Jacques Nattiez has long been a keen student of Gould the performer as well as of his aesthetics, and I am particularly grateful to him for our extremely rewarding exchanges. I am indebted also to Pierre Jasmin, *artiste engagé*, for his matchless perspective on Bach's work and the art of the pianist. I have never had the pleasure of meeting Gould's biographer Kevin Bazzana, but my reading of his work led me to contact him, and he proved to be a generous and enthu-siastic correspondent. He shared with me his encyclopaedic knowledge of the Gould archives, and provided me with a transcription of difficult passages from Gould's crisis journal. Without the aid and support of Ginette Michaud in preparing the text for this book, I do not think it could ever have seen the light of day. Not only did she correct what needed correcting but she helped me cope with my doubts and concerns. I owe her much. Finally, I would like to name Thierry Hentsch, who passed away on July 7, 2005. His conversation, when it bore on Bach's music and Gould's art, was luminous. I had hoped to make him a gift of these reflections, where he is everywhere to be found.

*Partita* for Glenn Gould

## Præludium

# Overture

## *Partita No. 1, in B flat Major*

Solitude is the prerequisite for ecstatic experience, especially the experience most valued by the post-wagnerian artist – the condition of heroism. One can't feel oneself heroic without having first been cast off by the world, or perhaps by having done the casting-off oneself.

*– The Age of Ecstasy,* 1974

From almost the very beginning Glenn Gould's art was intimately associated with our perception of his life. Or, to be more precise, our perception of the shape his life took. All who valued his art were impressed not only by the art itself, but also by his commitment as an artist, by his unique brand of asceticism, his ethic. It was not so much the biographical detail that sparked interest in his thinking and his idea of art – for what the biography comes down to is a total absorption of the life in the art – as the radical nature of his dedication to music. This devotion, from childhood until death, called for a commitment so intense and an asceticism so strict that we must, if we want to understand its nature and innermost dimensions, explore its connection with the art the interpreter bequeathed us.

Over time we have learned more and more about Glenn Gould, and as the accounts and biographies have proliferated we have not tired of what they have to teach us. But in one respect they are all consistent: apart from his crucial decision, in 1964, to abandon the concert stage, there was no dramatic turning point in Gould's life. His entire existence was bound up in the music, which demanded that the artist as a private person disappear, blending into his art. Gould's conversations, the reports of his recording sessions, his relationships with his producers, collaborators, and friends, his ironic exchanges with an eclectic assortment of correspondents, few of them intimates, all paint the same picture: a way of life in which the renunciation of life itself became the necessary condition for art. There is nothing mysterious in this formulation, even if it exposes a paradox that cannot be ignored: to live without living, is that still living? Or is it another kind of life? And who can say what this life is without access to its essential core, where it is rooted in art as a free and sovereign form? Everything suggests that this mode of life was vital to Gould's access to music itself, which perhaps explains our ongoing fascination with it. What constitutes a life's shape, and what the shape of any life implies in the ethical domain, is a question to which we will return. For now we need only note that Gould himself spoke in these terms.

There are a number of reasons for our interest, not the least of which are Gould's character traits, and what they can teach us about his genius; what is central here is the question of style, and a vision of the world that distinguishes one interpreter's work from all others. If we are to express the relationship between style and life, we need to find a language that allows the moral attributes of transparency and purity, the most obvious qualities of Gould's piano playing, to find their correspondence in a way of living and interacting with the world. In what respect, we might ask, does the purity of a performance shed light on the purity of the life? And how does the latter, if only by giving us the language we need, shed light in return on what we admire in his art? These questions, in their perfect reciprocity, are rooted in a life so uniquely lived, while being so utterly beholden to the sovereignty of art, that we might ask if it is appropriate to seek anything in

Gould beyond a pure symbiosis of art and life: the whole life in the art – the entirety of the art in the life. If we did not know Gould, if there were no images of him playing, if we did not have Bruno Monsaingeon's marvellous films, would we hear his art differently, would it be diminished? If we are deeply touched by his gestures and rapt expressions, if we pore over pictures from his adolescence or his mature years, can it be because we ourselves have thoughts of embarking upon the same road that he travelled? Why are we so fascinated by the tics and obsessions his biographers so often present as neurotic or narcissistic eccentricities, if it is not because we sense that what was behind Gould's art inhabited his life as much as it did his style? Why, finally – and this question is as persistent as all the rest – do we favour him with what we refuse to most artists, a keen interest in the sum of those declarations, however dogmatic or chaotic, that he scattered to the winds wherever he went? Their sometimes rebarbative nature does not faze us; we see it all as privileged discourse, and we look there for insights into the works that come from the same intelligence that played them.

This book is intended for those whose interest in Glenn Gould's art makes them want to go beyond the classic polar stereotypes habitually trotted out for artists caught between art and life: the ascetic and the madman, the hermit and the provocateur, the preacher and the mischief maker. Behind these caricatures of an artist seen as a slave to his excesses and his rhetoric, there is a man who chose to live differently. To reflect upon an exceptional individual, as I propose to do, is an indirect way of looking at what makes artistic freedom possible, and at what it can teach those who, though not endowed with the artist's gift, want to share in its beneficence, not only in contemplation of a beautiful offering, but in the marrow of their bones.

I have lived with Gould's art all my life, ever since the blessed moment in my adolescence when a school friend gave me his first recording of Bach's *Goldberg Variations*. It was 1960, five years after Gould had played these *Variations* in Montreal on 7 November 1955, four years after the dazzling recording that made his name was released, and four years before he left the concert stage following on his last recitals in Chicago and Los Angeles. I have noticed that all those who love Gould unconditionally, that is with an admiration beyond what one customarily accords an artist, are eager to tell you just when he appeared in their lives, as if that moment constituted an encounter beyond compare. I am one of their number. I can date the first time I heard him, and can also plot my first sighting, since with him one cannot separate what is before one's eyes from the act of listening. Above all, it is to my everlasting regret, even if I am ashamed to admit it, that I never heard him in concert. He often played in Montreal and I might have done so.

The *Variations*, along with the *Inventions*, the *Partitas*, and all that followed, became for me a single score, an unending counterpoint, each portion of which manifested a distinct emotional impulse, a contraction and a dilatation, an anxiety and a joy – the threshold to another world marked again and again by the same phrase: the cantilena, *Aria*, which opens and closes the *Goldberg Variations*. Like a traveller who has reached what he assumes to be the summit but happens on a path that will lead him even higher and farther, I embarked upon this road, not knowing where it would take me. There was always a balanced structure within sight, and a harmony that called out to me, beckoning; but there was also a story out of my past. One of my brothers studied piano, and in the basement of our house I used to listen to him practising the *Italian Concerto* over and over again. How many times, as I grappled with Homer's verses telling of Patroclus' funeral or Calypso opening her arms to Odysseus, and he struggled with the many difficulties of the concerto's final movement, I asked myself why this precious apprenticeship had been accorded only to him.

How often, too, from the silence of my room, as the slow movement rose up from our old Willis, I begged my brother to play it again, just as I was to do years later, hearing my younger daughter perform it with such grace.

Would it not be worthwhile, I wondered, trying to shed some light, if only for a moment, on this store of admiration – an admiration both unconditional and apparently disconnected from Gould and his art, and its debt to both? Accustomed as I was to the world of philosophy, so unlike that of music, or so it seemed, I did not fully appreciate what this undertaking would entail, or what it owed to the great figures I admired. Of course, I came up with rational explanations, even historical ones, as when I read that the theory of counterpoint had revived the Neoplatonic quest for a doctrine of universal harmony; passed down from Plotinus, through Saint Augustine and Boethius, this concept had inspired Bach's predecessors. But that was not, I knew, what counted most, even if it appealed to my own scholarly predilections. It took me a long time – several decades – before I saw that this admiration was a function of my intense interest in Gould's life and the shape he gave it. I read him as much as I could; I immersed myself in his terse, modernist discourse which, with its many certainties and its few moments of doubt, was not far from a theology. His turning his back on being a flesh-and-blood presence, his proclamation of a new media age, did not jibe with my own convictions, but I made the adjustment, and behind it all a voice kept speaking to me. I kept listening, and I set out to follow it. The more familiar I became with it, the more its art was revealed to me and the more sympathetic I felt with what I thought I understood of it. I began to ask myself, "If you knew nothing about him, if you did not know his aesthetic, if you did not even know what he looked like, would you appreciate his art in the same way?"

Later I came across a remark by Wittgenstein that seemed to address this question. It was written in 1931:

What does it consist in: following a musical phrase with understanding? Contemplating a face with sensitivity for its expression? Drinking in the expression on the face? ... Or to play it with understanding? Don't look inside yourself. Consider rather what makes you say of *someone else* that this is what he is doing. And *what* prompts you to say that *he* is having a particular experience?

I had often wondered if one had to play music in order to understand it, but I had never given much thought to that understanding itself. Perhaps Wittgenstein's way of putting things was mistaken. Is a musical phrase really a phrase, as in language? It seems hard to deny if we think of the *cantus firmus* in counterpoint, and yet ... The analogy of gazing upon a face merits a lengthy study that might, for instance, impress on us how important it is to watch someone play music in person. More precisely, how important it is to listen with one's eyes, as though Wittgenstein's proposed equivalence between the face and the musical phrase was urging us to go beyond what we hear. Not to look into oneself, does that not strike one at first glance as an unsettling demand? I remember a conversation with my friend Thierry Hentsch, himself a pianist, and a constant remembered presence throughout the writing of this book. It was after a concert by Piotr Anderszewski, who had just performed the *Partita No. 6*. We were asking ourselves if a limit can sometimes be reached in the interpretation of a work. Who could hope to bring anything new to the sixth *Partita*, after Gould? He replied: "The limit was not reached for him, nor for you." To listen is to know he was right. An interpretation is never more than a moment along the way, our contemplation of a face forever in flux.

To think about listening leads to a reflection on a life's shape. Because a musical composition is infinitely open-ended, because it is always unfolding while being interpreted in the present moment, it is elusive. That experience of the present tense ushers us into the presence of life. As with all meditative activity, silence is constantly under threat, especially from the thinking process, which plays havoc with art and interferes with our receptivity. Music never exists in a vacuum; it interacts with our thoughts, our concerns, even when it is there at our behest. No one has a magic wand to purify our inner space and conjure up the silence a work demands and deserves. An effort is always needed. I have often asked myself what would be the perfect listening experience, and I think it would be comparable to the way a plant receives the light. Ah, the obstacles thought puts in our way when we want the machine to slow down and it will not! We forget that mystics spend years learning to be at rest, to suspend animation, and here we are asking a piece of music to transport us there instantly, in simple obedience to our will. Give me this *Partita* and lead me to the waiting god! But thought, any thought, is a hindrance and can only lose its disruptive power if it is made accountable to a direction in life: can I be made better by music? Even if beauty is only contemplated, may it not, through that very contemplation, have a moral impact? Certainly, starting with our coming to terms with the anxiety inherent in the passing of time: peace resides in our keeping violence and egoism at bay; and if music gives us access to joy, our confidence in time will be renewed. Is the experience of the giver irrelevant to the impact of the gift? No, because what the giver gives us is the confidence that he found first in art. And so there is a preliminary threshold to contemplation, a kind of gateway, an exercise in welcoming: it is the moment when we realize that we would not be so troubled if distress found no host environment within ourselves. Is music not the first antidote to this distress, the first step on the way to serenity?

I realized that I could not provide a simple answer to these questions, even if Gould himself had proposed answers of his own. Already, looking at his repertoire, we can see where his preferences lay, but Gould was also crystal clear about the history of ing in an aesthetic quest for the sources of beauty. That gulf is the realm of transference, where the writer and thinker can be emotionally involved with his subject. This is not the philosophy that disdains affect and firmly resists the idealization of beloved figures. I would agree with those who divide philosophers into two distinct groups: those for whom thought is an ongoing analysis that must rely on transference in order to proceed, and those who discount their feelings because they regard them as an impediment to their search for truth. Here I endorse a kind of overt emotional empathy, I incorporate it into my reflections, and I accept this transference, taking upon myself all its demands and uncertainties. Beyond that, when I can, I offer my own interpretations.

One life is not enough to take the measure of the world of music, as it boasts an infinite capacity for repetition. Unlike a friendly conversation, different each time and impossible to duplicate, the act of listening to music often involves being taken by a desire to relive and reproduce an ideal emotion, a wish to go more deeply into a work, as if it could be possessed, absorbed, and might open the door to eternity. It's an illusion familiar to many music lovers, who are regularly at a loss as to whether they know the work they claim to love, or have only been resurrecting a landscape out of their childhood, a piece of their own story. There is also a paradox in the fact that while every hearing is unique, it incorporates all the others. While it may be said that friendship is a conversation without end and that it entrusts to time its deepening and its self-transcendence, only love can transcend time as such. Music, whether in the work or through the interpreter, can function on both levels. It provides a unique and different access to beauty on every occasion, but as we wish to escape from time – and as this is what we most want from art – it is no surprise that we lend particular importance to repetition and to the recurrence of an emotion. We see ourselves, then, all the more, as detached and eternal.

And if an exceptional artist seems to be telling us that this detachment is possible and that his own life bears witness to that very possibility, then we want to follow him forever. He is not only a friend with whom we hope to reconnect, he is a loved one freeing us from time's anguish. The attachment to an idealized figure generates its own models; through his asceticism he lends our lives meaning simply because we would like to emulate his as much as we can. And even if we can emulate nothing because we have neither the courage nor the resources, the very fact that we can aspire to do so is enough to reassure us. This realm is open to all; it will never again be closed off. It is never easy to free ourselves from an enthralment and look on it from a distance, especially if we have been seeking a form of truth, an overview or an explanation such as we find in the risky ventures of scholars compelled to seek certainties in art. We can understand them, but there are occasions when we would choose a modest, appreciative approach over the impulse to master and grasp.

I should emphasize that I make no claim to providing a biographical truth or a limned likeness that would explain or shed light on every archive or personal account. Even if, or perhaps because I may go some way in this direction in the act of transference, I will still not depict the person. I do not propose a life of Gould. That, his biographers have given us, each in his own way. I have read them; none is completely true, none could ever be so. I honour those who have kept their distance as much as those who have worked at close quarters, and I have learned from them all. Fine distinctions and plain speaking have both brought their rewards. Life is always elusive, however, in its aims as much as its accomplishments, and I have chosen to write in full cognizance of that fact. What I do envisage is to study the shape of a life as it is reflected in acts and words, to view it in the context of music as an art, and to take the measure of its generosity, since that is what has impressed me the most. And so I am presenting a range of perspectives on an artist who has been with me always. No other has ever taken his place, or such a place – which is not to say that I love and admire no other artist; I admire many, and could name them. To do so would likely reveal that they all bear, to borrow another image from Wittgenstein, "a family resemblance." But I have never loved or admired another as I have Gould, going beyond what I hear and see to what I understand as the choice he made in shaping his life, its ethical character, and ultimately the *devenir philosophe*, the growing into philosophy that became, following Thoreau's formula, his ideal of solitary independence.

From where I stand, can I possibly defend myself against the objections of those who would say I am mistaken or that I exaggerate? To be frank, I see this meditation as an exercise that shies away from the demands of truth, without abdicating from them entirely. I will broach subjects about which I know little, with an assurance, however, that is fitting when dealing with questions of a certain gravity, and I only ask that my remarks be received as a dispatch from that realm of transference to which I have alluded, in a spirit of idealization which I want less to distance myself from – why would I, when it has given me so much – than to grasp, in its workings, its bases, its language. If an artist exposes, in all his vulnerability, the inner workings of his life, and if he does so with a generosity and a simplicity that betrays no reserve, no camouflage, but on the contrary a consistent desire to live through his confrontation with the work and with the world, why reproach someone who would emulate this unbounded generosity with the sole intent of drawing fully from its reserve of goodness and peace? For these reflections all I seek is a benign reception, and what I offer in return is a way of seeing that has grown with time to be a source of inspiration, a call for each to embark on his own pilgrimage. And so, if speaking in terms of philosophy may grant me some protection by giving prior notice of the excesses to which such a call may be prone, then I consent. Let us just say that in this colour and its own scent. He knew them inside out, and he admired the fact that "the contrapuntal stance in the *Partitas* is immaculate." Gould seemed to be referring mainly to their rigour, but we could long reflect on the association between what is immaculate and what is immutable, or what we might view as a solemn promise that makes no compromise. Had not Bach's predecessors already likened strict counterpoint, in its own world beyond any musical embodiment, to the soul in its separation from the body at the time of death? This is something we shall return to. In the course of the interview, Gould asked himself the following question: does the succession of dances that makes up each suite represent a rigorous conceptual unity, given the single key, or could one imagine playing a new partita, patched together from movements picked out from one or the other? "I'd love to try it, it's a marvellous idea," was Gould's spontaneous answer, but one would still have to preserve the unity of key and above all the sequential rhythms and expressiveness generated by this new combination. Every *partita* is in effect like a series of characters or episodes that take the stage, each with an identity appropriate to the rhythm of the sequence and to its place in the counterpoint. Gould was impressed by the richness of the modulations, and the idea of redistributing the airs was, he thought, a promising one. The lengths, the relative textures, all could in fact be rearranged with as much freedom as the slow or rapid tempi and the execution of the repetitions. Sequences and themes recur, and all the pieces are carried along by an *élan* that is proper to the *Partitas* – a clean forward movement through time, a dynamic unfolding that anticipates the sonata. The progression is neither arbitrary nor perfectly systematic, since in listening we can construct for each series a narrative to parallel its development; at the same time unsuspected freedoms appear between the sections. The passage from piece to piece is crucial, and Gould felt that each exerted an influence on the following one, especially on their range and expression – not an absolute influence, however, as everything is open-ended. Because most of the pieces are not fugal, we might assume that the *Partitas* do not have the same gravitas and austerity as the sequence of preludes and fugues in the *Well-Tempered Clavier*. In my view that would be an error, for the very creation of open-ended suites made possible instances of thought and feeling that inspired Gould's own inventive descriptions: a courante that is "flighty and gibbering," for example, or a sarabande that is "elegant and perfumed." Joking, he claimed that were he to present an imaginary partita in concert, critics wouldn't even notice. Two things follow from what he said: the suite's rigour and its potential for fantasy.

I therefore took this idea seriously, to the degree that it has allowed me to associate each of my chapters with a particular movement, in a sequence that corresponds to no existing *Partita*, but which respects all of them. I have chosen to compose my *Partita* in a minor key, but as Gould suggested, one must make allowance for each piece to be transposed, should it one day be played. I have made my own the names of each piece, their forms, and even their keys, in order to match them with my argument, and I have taken the liberty of repeating some themes along with some variations. Bearing in mind my commitment to reflect on the shape of a life and on its music, I felt I could do no better, in reconstituting a score for Gould, than to assemble the decisive moments of another *Partita*, this one to be set down on paper as the score of his art and life.

I have divided this *Partita* into seven sections, each inspired by an existing *Partita* and closely associated with it in feeling and style. This overture constitutes a sort of preamble, akin to the *Præludium*, taken from *Partita No. 1 in B flat Major*. Here I introduce my subject, present a number of themes, and express certain concerns that I would like the reader to bear in mind throughout: negotiating the heights, not involving oneself in aesthetic philosophy other than as a guide for shaping a life, not resisting an idealization that would usher in a reflection on the nature of the gift. In the first piece, for which I have chosen the *Toccata* from *Partita No. 6 in E Minor*, I concern myself with the difficulties encountered in the course of a career, in particular the paradoxes of withdrawal and authenticity, but I propose no answers at this point; we remain on the threshold of a score that embodies an entire life, with all its enigmas and anxieties. The minor key seems appropriate for this first piece, where the inner life seeks an uneasy equilibrium with all that impinges on the artist from outside and contributes to his withdrawal.

The *Allemande*, taken from *Partita No. 2 in C Minor*, deals with the question of genius and represents a deeper probing into the paradox of art and self-expression. Because romanticism, and his rejection of it, was key to Gould's reading of the repertoire's history, we have to understand how he himself dealt with its demands. Unlike the saint, the genius cannot be emulated, he can only be admired.

In the third piece I have associated a reflection on Gould's pianism – in particular on his hands, his arms, and his shoulders – with the *Courante* of *Partita No. 3 in A Minor*. My hope is that the minor key might echo this intimacy with the performer's body, the artist's remoteness and uneasiness in the company of others, and his suffering within a physical entity that was so often intractable. Here we grapple with the concepts of distance and proximity, and with the indisputable role of the body in music.

From the *Air* and the *Sarabande* of *Partita No. 6 in E Minor*, which I pair, I have borrowed what everyone expects from a sarabande, a kind of movement that accompanies the world's onward flow and embraces the rhythms of everyday life. Here I return to the tension between aesthetics and a sense of purpose in the company of Natsume Sōseki and George Santayana, who introduce us to Gould the reader. As with painted screens that slide open to reveal new vistas, I try here to view Gould's extra-musical tastes as indicators for his inner life.

The fifth part is a *Sinfonia*, taken from *Partita No. 2 in C Minor*, a piece whose harmonic richness serves as the model for a solitude assumed and shared, a realm that is home to a community. Here we encounter the *Solitude Trilogy*, a radio triptych whose subject is Canada's distant population centres. It is a masterpiece – not only a paean to the Northern landscape but the incarnation of a religious ethic, seeking a workable distance between the nostalgia for community and modernity's assertion of individual identity.

With the *Scherzo*, taken from *Partita No. 3 in A Minor*, I return to Gould in his retreat, in his withdrawal. I study this solitude and this approach to life, which I view, even in its commitment to asceticism, as a decision informed by joy and not the product of traumatism or pathology.

I conclude, as do all the *partitas*, with a *Gigue*, taken from *Partita No. 6 in E Minor*. In this last section I evoke Gould's true landscape, a realm he inhabited from his youth and that from the outset gave him the raw material for his dreams. Here we come upon a few voices, such as that of Petula Clark, a few images, and a few portraits, especially the one Gould favoured, in which he is wrapped in his winter coat and wearing his cap. We find this portrait on his recording of Beethoven's popular sonatas, and François Girard recreated it in one of his short films. Is he moving away from us, as he did on the fateful day of October 4, 1982, or is he coming toward us, forever, as I sometimes think I see him, alone in a nondescript crowd? This imaginary *Partita* was written twenty-five years on to mark his disappearance, but it only has meaning if it can be played and replayed to celebrate his coming among us.

# I
*Toccata*

## Art and a Life's Shape
*Partita no. 6 in E Minor*

The truth of the artist is the truth of art: no work can surpass in range the limits imposed by the artist's own experience; no work can reach frontiers that the artist has not attained in his own life experience. An artist who would risk a lie by donning a mask that would misrepresent his relationship to the world could only produce inauthentic art, a simulacrum. There is nothing more palpable than inflated emotion, the makeshift, the formulaic. Even if authenticity has its own risks, starting with the fact that there is no self-knowledge that can absolutely guarantee the validity of a desire for truth and beauty, it remains an ideal more worthy of our trust than all the cynicisms that invite us to treat it with suspicion. No one would claim to be able to measure authenticity, and yet everyone embraces it as the only true standard. While art must expose the depths of a wound, of how it feels to be alive in this world, the artist himself cannot control the suffering this wound causes him – even less the pleasure he derives from what he observes. And if he tries to distort them through exaggeration or by playing down their importance, such manipulations will ultimately affect the legitimacy of his art, and it is he who will be disfigured. In the same way, if the role of art is to restore a moment of joy or of absolute union, and if the artist imagines that he possesses it rather than being possessed by it, then he will deform the very thing he hopes to convey.

This principle of authenticity would be crystal clear and utterly compelling were it not for the obscure motives that guide an artist toward creation, and the difficulty of grasping them all. Those who have tried, mistakenly identifying the artistic enterprise with an understanding of the motives behind it, have been faced with the paradox inherent in their quest for truth: the struggle to express what one wants to achieve and the reasons one is attempting to achieve it can never be equated with the task of actually working out a formal aesthetic, even though the distance between the two is small. In fact, we often see it crossed without any formal mention or philosophical justification. An artist who believes he is tracing the progress of his own personal desires finds himself, with no apparent transition, giving advice and laying down laws; thinking he has arrived at a universally applicable position, he misconstrues his own limits and overlooks the fact that he is merely himself. Another, who thinks he is only shedding light on what relates to his own feelings, launches into the promotion of an experience that can in no way serve as a criterion for others. If he persists, he could soon be embracing Kant's *Observations on the Feeling of the Beautiful and Sublime*, not realizing that if he were true to his own reasoning he might be taking up arms against it, opting for, abandoning himself to chaos. Kant claimed that the sublime was the realm of solemn emotion, and beauty the realm of smiling charm, but what artist can endorse such a distinction, however plausible it may appear on the surface? No one wants simply to divert and charm; everyone thinks his entire life is engaged in his work. Artists are both imprisoned by their experience and obliged to transcend its specificity.

It is as if truth in art makes itself known simultaneously on a number of levels. The artist's life is the murkiest level, given how

hard it is to understand just what, at the core of an individual existence, prompts the decision to become an artist. Beyond pain and
uncertainty, intention and calculation, the entire weight of life
clears a path toward something new that is nourished by the material of life, its suffering, its joy. To go into the studio, put the
writing table in order, tune the instrument, is to set off freshly each
day on the road that will make one's life an art, make an art of
one's life. The constant renewal of this decision, which is a decision to create, gives the artist's work its authenticity; all of life
defers to it and we cannot pretend otherwise.

The Greek thinkers, who placed the good life at the centre of
their ethics, paradoxically ignored artists; if they had granted them
any importance, they would have put them in the same category
as the contemplatives, who devoted their lives to *theoria*. But the
work of the artist itself stood in the way; the Greeks esteemed
most highly a life without work and they would not have grouped
artists, whom they saw essentially as producers, with economists
or politicians. But the *bios*, the concept of a shaped life, has
remained with us, to describe the choice we make of what will
govern our life, what its determining influence will be. Even if the
artistic work itself never materializes, even if it remains suspended
in an everlasting limbo, the shape of a life survives, for it embodies the expectation, the resolve to open one's arms to whatever the
work may offer. An artist who produces no work is not incon-
ceivable – his life is compatible with the very ethic of creation; a
work with no artist, on the other hand, is an absurdity. We expect
the concept of a life's form to help us reach an appreciation of
what is authentic, and what is not.

But we must also take into account another level, the reasoning
process, and ultimately the rational status of the art that a given
aesthetic produces. Here the commitment to a certain life matters less than one's access to guiding principles. It is not enough
to be authentic, to be resolute and sincere in one's artistic options;

one must also be able to clarify and bring to light what in the artistic experience contributes to a particular goal, whatever it may be. Not all artists seek to explain their work in this way, but all know that if their art is to be authentic it must have a rationale, and that a new work may, often with the support of others, succeed in formulating it. No artist will say, "My art has no raison d'être, I do not know where it should be situated, I do not care about its truth, I am indifferent to its purpose." On the contrary, he will say: "My art is sincere, I tirelessly pursue its goals, and although I do not know where it is leading, I want it to reach fruition and would be grateful to those who might help me uncover its true language. In the midst of darkness and duress, my only concern is not to stray from my path, not to abandon the work."

In his novel *The Three-Cornered World,* a text that Glenn Gould saw as particularly meaningful both for himself and for the entire modern period whose creative project he embraced, the Japanese writer Natsume Sōseki portrayed the inner world of an artist in search of a work that eludes him, constantly slipping from his grasp; nothing measures up to the perfection of the moment, nothing can be captured in time to fulfill his quest for beauty. From beyond his reach, the work throws the artist back on the life he has chosen, sends him back into his thoughts, and tests his resolution to live in and for art; he has to recognize that what he seeks is not so much the artistic work, which he now sees as a product of his thoughts which is of little interest, but the rational underpinnings that make the work possible. In pondering on why he wants to paint a particular landscape, Sōseki's artist is led, almost against his will, to question a way of thinking that has forged his ecstatic link to the world and to his longing, always fragile and precarious, for a realm beyond his immediate cares and concerns. Temporarily seduced by Lessing's effort in the *Laocoön* to define painting and poetry in terms of space and time, he loses touch with the concrete experience that took him beyond appearances, he allows himself to be tempted by aesthetics, and he lets slip the opportunity to realize the work. But he is rewarded with the conviction that he is on the right road: this ecstatic relationship is the necessary precondition for an authentic work, and this authenticity will provide him with an ethic, the only one that will sustain the kind of life that, come what may, he is resolved to pursue. His pilgrimage has taught him that art encompasses all these dimensions, and that he could, however paradoxically, live the artist's life even if he does not paint.

Glenn Gould had a kind of veneration for this novel, and the reason is implicit in the distinction I have just sketched out. The artistic quest monopolized his life, and even if the principles he established for himself provided the basis and the means for attaining the self-knowledge that alone can show what makes art essential for certain lives and not others, for him these principles were not what was most at stake. What took precedence was the life of the artist as revealed through his art, beginning with his decision to commit himself to it absolutely. The artist represents this dedication to the sublime; he is only that. There is no part-time artist, no artist who will disown the sovereignty of art over his life; there is only an unflagging commitment to the quest for this "state of wonder," which for Gould was at the core of his experience and his thought.

᳐

Glenn Gould was born on September 25, 1932, in a peaceful Toronto neighbourhood called the Beaches because of its proximity to Lake Ontario. His father, Russell Herbert Gould, and his mother, Florence Emma Greig, met in the Uxbridge countryside and settled in Toronto after their marriage in 1925. In this traditional milieu, the Protestant values of austerity, industry, and benevolence permeated all of life and were at the core of education.

When, later on, he vaunted the merits of George Santayana's great rite-of-passage novel, *The Last Puritan*, Gould was doubtless looking back on the ethic of upright behaviour and moral rigour that had typified the Protestantism of his childhood, along with its distinctive emotional reticence and the characteristic reserve traditionally associated with Puritanism. Santayana's hero was certainly not an artist, but as a man he represented devotion to community and the sacrifice of personal self-interest – including, if necessary, the sacrifice of all pleasures – that Gould admired in his parents. He had chosen a life of service, and Puritanism embodied its basic ethic. In praising this model, Gould could recapture the personalities of his childhood and acknowledge that they had stayed with him all his life.

Glenn Gould's youth was deeply marked by this ethic, and yet his education cannot be entirely identified with it. He was certainly as pious as his parents, both of whom were ardent believers, but not in the same way. In the fragmentary memoirs he wrote toward the end of his life, he spoke of his feelings on Sundays in the parish church, during the service. He remembered the evening light filtering through the stained glass windows: "So those moments of Sunday-evening sanctuary became very special to me; they meant that one could find a certain tranquility even in the city, but only if one opted not to be part of it."

The need for such a withdrawal and the fact that he found it in that sanctuary so early on perhaps together explain why he never rebelled against the Puritanism in which he grew up; where many others were inclined to reject its austere demands, he accepted them so profoundly that they never came into conflict with the requirements of his art. On the contrary, they seem, by providing a framework for his desire for solitude, to have nourished it in a very real way. His choice of the artistic life presented itself to him when he was very young, and he adopted all its rigours and responsibilities.

When we read the accounts gathered by his biographers, we cannot help noting how this formation, even though in no way intended as such, left ample space and freedom for his genius to be recognized. For those near to him very soon realized that Glenn not only had an exceptional talent for the piano but also that he was an exceptional child. In the schoolyard he was neither a fighter nor a conformist, and he was repelled by violent acts and words. His stay there was short-lived, and the story of his musical training, first with his mother, herself a musician, and then with his teachers in Toronto, was characterized by an unusual tension between the constraints of a milieu little inclined to accept the exceptional, and the demands of a talent soon evident to all concerned. Should we not try to understand how such freedom could flourish in a world so hemmed in by convention? For Gould's genius is not, and cannot be limited to its being that of an extraordinary talent at the keyboard – he was not alone in this – rather, it consists in his capacity to go beyond bounds, in his daring to undertake a quest that, at its farthest limits, could be transformed into a radical pursuit of the new.

And so Gould knew at a very young age that he was an artist, and early on he accepted the consequences of a decision that would engage his entire life. He also knew what role the artistic experience would play in that life. Because he was gifted – he always resisted the idea that he was a child prodigy – from the age of fifteen he was acquainted with the demands of the concert hall and the rituals involved in public performance. His first professional recital took place on October 20, 1947, at the Eaton Auditorium in Toronto, but it had already been preceded by several concerts and recitals, especially at the Conservatory. He must also very soon have realized that a life of performance was not really for him, but it took several years for him to decide that he had to bring it to a halt. In a 1962 text, "Let's Ban Applause," he takes the concert hall to task for its theatricality and stakes his claim for silence. I would like to quote this passage in its entirety, for in it we find the strongest expression of what will become his artistic ethic. I regard it as a declaration of principle that under-lies his entire aesthetic, and I will return to it often:

> I am disposed toward this view because I believe that the justification of art is the internal combustion it ignites in the hearts of men and not its shallow, externalized, public manifestations. The purpose of art is not the release of a momentary ejection of adrenaline but is, rather, the gradual, lifelong construction of a state of wonder and serenity. Through the ministrations of radio and the phonograph, we are rapidly and quite properly learning to appreciate the elements of aesthetic narcissism – and I use that word in its best sense – and are awakening to the challenge that each man contemplatively create his own divinity.

We should not be too quick to equate this state of wonder with the kind of ecstasy Gould often refers to elsewhere. What is implied here by "wonder" is both an ecstatic contemplation and the perplexity of one who is astonished and in a state of ques-tioning when confronted by beauty, finding himself suspended outside his day-to-day life of care and calculation, in a transitional state that leads to an experience of transformation beyond his ken. I introduce this frequently cited passage here only to conjure up that ultimate goal of art, "wonder," but it will also appear in all the variations to come. Every word in this declaration is important, essential, vital. What is the meaning of that "aesthetic narcissism," the ideal whose "best sense" Gould is careful to emphasize? In this withdrawal and turning in on oneself, in the creation of this divinity, we can hear the same affirmation as permeates Sōseki's entire aesthetic. I will return to this enigmatic writer and his aesthetic of separation, which for Gould was the perfect embodiment of an aesthetic of inwardness, in the section where I bring together the *Air* and the *Sarabande*. I will also have something to say about the seeming disjuncture between an elitist withdrawal and a commitment to modernity and communication, which Gould must have associated with an open and generous style of life.

In this book I want to reflect on the meaning of this sense of wonder and this sovereignty of the artistic life, and also on the factors that limit the experience. I also want to look at the transcendence of a work of art and the sway it exercises over a life, even in its persistent elusiveness. My assumption is that these limits are pushed outward day by day, and I am tempted to see there a parallel with holiness. I would not recoil from speaking of the holiness of art, if by that one means the absolute, uncompromising commitment to a style of life. We would not revere a saint who did not give of himself freely; nor would we admire an artist who took no risks. The demands of art are such that it claims life in its entirety, and that is the price of authenticity. Self-interest and personal motives have no part to play, while authenticity corresponds with a form of life that is perfect and pure. I speak here of purity and perfection less in relation to a work, than to the resolve to live in a certain way, and every artist's life demonstrates the tremendous struggles he must undertake in order to maintain his integrity. Like the saint, the artist is only too aware of how real and costly his weaknesses are, but he assesses his work strictly in terms of its own demands. For all that, the everyday world continues to make its demands felt, and if an artist's motives for choosing a life committed to art should turn out to be, a priori, only reasons to take flight from the world, to flee its confines and the suffering it imposes, he could, like the saint, risk being transported to a sphere where he loses sight of what is essential. This, however, is the smallest risk of all, for art in the guise of with-

drawal is first of all a gift, not only – nor even – chiefly a pleasure
to be enjoyed in isolation. That, Gould could read in Sōseki's initiatory text, but he could also put it to the test in his own art.

As with the choice of a saintly life, one may embark on a life
in art for the wrong reasons, skewing its fundamental altruism:
such are the limits of authenticity for those who lack the resolve
to stay the course. These limits concern the feasibility of withdrawal, the reality of separation, and the mirages of narcissism, all
obstacles that crop up on the path of genius. Not to mention the
lust for wealth and glory, which can corrupt the best of us: these
vulgar demons can sap the wills of the purest, the most generous
of artists, and I personally could not continue to admire any artist
whom I found to be cowardly or vain. My admiration for a work
would not be extended to the artist, or to the artistic virtues
embodied in the shaping of a life. The work itself could even be
affected. But this is a difficult question and I suggest leaving it
aside, since it is irrelevant to Gould. I will always, nevertheless,
favour an artist whose life is committed to his work to the point
of becoming indistinguishable from it, an artist who pushes his
resolve beyond limits. Take Joseph Beuys, for example, with his
embrace of poverty and his commitment to the democratization of
art. Or René Char in his *Leaves of Hypnos,* with the bond he
forges between beauty and political rigour. I am speaking here of
the artist who represents an entire world and responds to the
world's moral demands. "The genius," wrote Max Scheler, "is
actively alive in his work." Nothing seems more true, nothing has
greater consequences for the way one who hopes to receive its
blessings approaches art, and that is the reason I have no hesitation in speaking of a sanctity in art.

The artist's resolve, however, brings him no solace, certainly
not in the realm to which he withdraws, where, as for the saint,
one would wish him peace and repose. To think it did would be
to underestimate the tribute demanded by the world from those

who would remove themselves from it for reasons not of the world, reasons they choose to lodge at the heart of their asceticism. Even in his cell, the holy man who wants to distance himself from the world thinks back on the community of all those who, in their agitated state, are deprived of solitude, and at this very thought, wants to include them in his prayer. He is never alone, and his prayer becomes a benediction for all those who remain with him in his retreat. There is no need for him physically to attend to the lepers who are in his thoughts; their stretchers and the stench of illness are already present in his chapel. War and violence reach him even while, in the silence of his morning prayers, he works for the peace of all, bringing peace to his own heart. This mystery seems so remote that, in the eyes of the world, it has become a kind of madness, and yet is it so different from the mystery that animates an artist's whole life? Is it not comparable to the artist believing, mistakenly, that opting for solitude is in itself the one and only precondition for a form of life grounded in withdrawal, and that his work will stem from it alone? Is this not how he discovers that his solitude has been peopled from the start by those whose suffering art can alleviate, and that the will to contribute to that healing is as central to art as the resolve to create?

One of the most striking characteristics of Glenn Gould's art and life was his absolute commitment to a life in art and his recognition of the restraints imposed by the shape an artistic life must take. To be more precise, he was aware of the essential oneness of withdrawal and giving, because the more complete the withdrawal, the more generous one becomes toward all those from whom one thought to separate oneself. We might call this thorny paradox that of the hermit preacher, or the media-friendly artist-orator. Exhausted from the demands of the concert hall and the touring life, the pianist, already at the height of his renown, gives up performing before an audience. Among the musicians of his century, we can point to no comparable instance of such an ascetic

renunciation of rapturous fame and the frenzy surrounding public appearances. Gould explained his decision dozens of times, but
he soon tired of its being regarded as essential to his aesthetic. In
a celebrated conversation, in 1978, with Yehudi Menuhin, who
urged on him the joy, and almost the necessity of live performance, he confidently exposed its artifice, and briskly denounced it
as an illusion, as much for the artist as the audience. His decision,
in its uniqueness, still remains something of a mystery. Was it for
him just the solution to a series of ailments, with the promise of a
cure? It is his property, it carries his name. Gould as in the refusal
to perform, Gould as in the abdication of public appearances and
the rejection of compromise.

To trivialize the decision would stand in the way of our understanding the ultimate paradox to which it led. Not because the
reasons put forward by Gould might be considered inauthentic,
but rather because they were for him so certain and so clear. Gould
gave up the concert hall in the first instance because it made him
suffer. We cannot say that he sacrificed the pleasures of public performance, as if that were his experience. No, the concert hall made
him sick, and he distanced himself from it; but he also renounced
it because he thought the public transformed the artist into a
circus animal, and that the experience of music ought to be
something authentic, should play itself out far from a virtuosic
spectacle. This first reason, which is essentially a critique of public display, remains, however, somewhat superficial. We cannot
understand Gould's decision unless we shift our focus toward his
more fundamental motives: on the one hand, the artist's quest for
a space, an environment that the clamour of the world cannot
touch, and on the other hand the possibility of and the conditions
for a generosity that completes the withdrawal by reversing it.
These motives are those that guide the ascetic toward perfection,
the perfection of art and the perfection of life. Gould's biographers
have described the simplicity of the places where he chose to live,

the disorder of his papers and books, his scribbled scores, and the more we read their descriptions the more we see that Gould, wherever he was, chose to live in a studio. Or in a broadcast booth like the one from which he listened to a concert in Berlin conducted by Herbert von Karajan, when he could easily have joined the public in the hall. He claimed, however, to cherish an indelible memory of this concert.

In a 1980 interview Gould stated: "I can honestly say that I do not recall ever feeling better about the quality of a performance because of the presence of the audience." There was nothing egoistic in this statement, and if it seems to deny the audience any role in eliciting a beautiful or apt interpretation, it is because it sets as its standard a different sort of receptiveness, that of another, higher audience, virtual, universal, moral. The same artist who declared that he detested audiences and refused to be hijacked by the public would devote his life to producing recordings and preparing radio and television broadcasts for that same public. Concertizing, as a life, was a quest for performance above all else, but performance had nothing in common with the life of art. Gould's demand for solitude resembles the pilgrimage of Sōseki's painter: it is a matter of departing in order to break away, withdraw from a world of contingency that represents an obstacle and a limiting factor to the desire for serenity, itself a necessity if the artistic work is to be authentic. But if pursued only for its own sake, this requirement for solitude would remain an egoistic project with no redeeming ethical content. It would be purely a quest for satisfaction and would disqualify itself. And so this first requirement must be followed by another, that of giving truly: Gould's life is the embodiment of such giving.

The conditions necessary for such giving continued to concern Gould for the rest of his life. How to understand this? The gift of art occurs when a gaze that has been buried within oneself for a time is redirected towards a community. Because this gaze never becomes so insubstantial as to lose a sense of others, all others, it is transformed into generosity. The idea of a reclusive artist who sees his work as embodied in his own inwardness is as absurd as that of a saint whose vocation did not include any act of charity; this would be an artist who is utterly redundant and deprived of grace. The work is of course never the property of the artist and need never carry his signature, as its recipient body is infinite – the pure and unadulterated other. There is then some meaning in positing a form of inactivity that imposes renunciation on the artist, an infinitely recurring abandon. The artist shares with the saint this relinquishment of the work, since the quest for the work is from the outset part and parcel of the giving. Imperfectible, unattainable, the work breaks free and becomes pure gift. As soon as it exists – and this very existence counts as one of the most difficult enigmas to resolve for a life in art – the work reanimates the cycle of solitude and withdrawal, at the same time addressing itself to all those who await it and for whom it is destined. The hermit becomes a preacher at the moment when, measuring the worth of the work, he feels ready to give it up. He will not rest until the trail toward what he himself has achieved is blazed for others.

In the famous interview of Gould by Gould written for the magazine *High Fidelity* in 1974, ten years after he had left the concert stage, Gould restated his views on the primacy of the inner experience of music. His humour is light-hearted, as if he were hamming it up in print, and he plays with his own stereotype: to the "interviewer," who would like him to talk about music, he replies that he would prefer to discuss the political situation in Labrador or the rights of native people. Urged to explain his thinking about his withdrawal, he shows himself reluctant to see his decision as a "radical" gesture; it was only, he says, an attempt to solve a problem. Gould then makes the following objection to himself: if this decision had been shamelessly narcissistic, would it not then be deserving of criticism? Would it not be at odds with

the moral stance he habitually took? Why indeed, he replied, sacrifice the individual gratification to be derived from one's contact
with an audience if not because it was only experienced as a sense
of power? He then objected to himself that this moral renunciation
prevented him from experiencing "the naked fact of [his] humanity ... on display, unedited and unadorned." Gould was fully
aware of the scrutiny to which the body *qua* body of the artist, as
presented to the public, was subject, when it came to its presence
or its withdrawal. He was also aware that a sophisticated narcissism can be at variance with another, perceived as banal. Gould,
it is well known, did not really like Horowitz; he harboured a kind
of ill-tempered competitiveness toward him that was rare for
Gould, but we might suppose that what he detested above all was
Horowitz's love for concertizing. What to defend in its place? His
reply deserves quoting in full:

> I simply feel that the artist should be granted, both for his
> sake and for that of his public – and let me get on record
> right now the fact that I'm not at all happy with words like
> "public" and "artist"; I'm not happy with the hierarchical
> implications of that kind of terminology – that he should be
> granted anonymity. He should be permitted to operate in
> secret, as it were, unconcerned with – or, better still, unaware
> of – the presumed demands of the marketplace – which
> demands, given sufficient indifference on the part of a suffi-
> cient number of artists, will simply disappear. And given their
> disappearance, the artist will then abandon his false sense of
> "public" responsibility, and his "public" will relinquish its
> role of servile dependency.

To break the conventional pact of the concert hall, then, is first
and foremost to free the artist from the public's demands; but it is
also, perhaps, to turn the public back upon itself, to give it too its

undreamed-of freedom, a space where it will not be subject to the narcissistic will of the spectacular, authoritarian, dictatorial artist. For the artist, in the conventional pact, is "still, however benevolently, a social dictator." He gives and provides, while the audience only receives and absorbs. Can this dynamic be reversed? Gould thought so. He liked to talk about a "creative" audience. But he did not for all that renounce the responsibility that part of him considered fallacious, as long as it could be transformed into a mission addressed to an open and responsible public. Gould never shied away from giving moral expression to this mission, first as non-conformism, then as an ethic. Art must have a redemptive vocation, even if it is at times destructive. The challenge in contemporary art is to substitute for inner violence a force capable of compensating for its own "obsolescence." Faced with the violence of history, art must seek out the wellsprings of the beneficence it has to offer. Where to find them if not in a dedicated life, a life shaped by withdrawal? As long as the world does not understand that all forms of violence are one and the same, the artist has the right to withdraw to a place where he may reflect on the beneficent virtues of art, its powers of resistance, its spiritual action. He will be subject to doubts, will grope for a response to those who insist that he return. Even if he has withdrawn to free himself from the world's sufferings, ought the artist to return to the world like the philosopher of Plato's cave? That could constitute a kind of martyrdom, which Gould contemplated with a certain serenity: if he had to consider a return to the lion's den of the concert hall, he said to himself, "there could be no more meaningful manner in which to scourge the flesh, in which to proclaim the ascendance of the spirit, and certainly no more meaningful metaphoric mise en scène against which to offset your own hermetic life-style, through which to define your quest for martyrdom autobiographically." But the real Gould did not feel ready for that; the refuge of the studio had too many advantages.

No sooner had Gould abandoned the concert hall than he undertook, concurrently and with the same determination, the quest for musical perfection, which was his vocation, and the exploration of all possible ways to communicate with the public, which was to be an ongoing project. Recorded music took pride of place, but he also generated radio and television broadcasts, assorted writings – everything that he could draw upon in his endeavour to break down, after having built them up, the barriers surrounding the impermeable studio that was the ideal setting for his withdrawal. Separated from the world by a glass wall, he could enjoy the benefits of his isolation: not only the absence of stimulation from the outside world but, even more important, the moral separation that freed in him the desire to explore new paths. A critic like Charles Riley saw in this studio-bound asceticism the yearning for a technological environment, a yearning he shared with other ascetic artists like John Cage in his cell of silence (an artist whom Gould ironically did not much like), or Jasper Johns. Idealizing clarity and structure, these artists committed themselves to an ascetic life and embraced its religious roots, at times even its monastic heritage. Asceticism was their means of doing so, and even if many among them refused to see their withdrawal from life as an attack upon it, they did seek out difficulty and complexity, sometimes to the point of torment. Their bodies could virtually disappear, so much did they subject them to the demands of renunciation. I do not know if this description applies to all the artists Riley saw as modern saints; I believe, however, that Gould would not have disavowed it.

There are plenty of accounts, leaning one way or the other: those who knew Gould and loved him have tried to provide a balanced picture of this tension between a withdrawal which, with its compulsions and idiosyncrasies, sometimes made life difficult for others, and his exhaustive efforts at communication, his eagerness to explore all the resources of technology to disseminate not only his work, but the thinking behind it. His quirks were only ever criticized by those who did not like his art; and we must not underestimate the generosity of a love that alone could rise above a fascination with eccentricity, a love that came in the long run to constitute clear evidence for his authenticity and his quest for a pure and unconventional style of life. I will speak of it in due course as a kind of sovereignty, where freedom and communication made common cause. As for his urge to communicate, one well served by his exceptional energy and humour, it irritated only those who could not see in it the first signs of a new media culture. Gould, who was depleted by touring to the point of illness and depression, found in this new culture a source of inexhaustible energy.

Gould's turning point is worth a backward look. He experienced serious health problems all through the 1957–58 season, which led to the cancellation of a number of very important recitals. The record of these difficulties, in particular the correspondence with his impresario in which all the illnesses are noted and described, presents the picture of a man unhappy in a life that gave him no respite and above all deprived him of what he most desired – the peace to work, the serenity of art. Gould derived no satisfaction from his fame, and even less from the pleasures of travelling and the human contacts involved. With time, the very act of moving from place to place seemed an even more unbearable ordeal than playing in front of distracted or noisy audiences. He knew that depression lurked just around the corner, even though several of those concerts, such as those in London with Joseph Krips, gave him the opportunity to renew ties with an artist who shared an aesthetic that focused on the inner life.

Back in Canada, he was invited by two directors from the National Film Board of Canada to participate in a pair of documentary portraits. *Glenn Gould Off the Record* and *Glenn Gould On the Record* were released in 1960, and together they anticipate the changes afoot in an extraordinary way; this Gould is astonishingly happy and relaxed. We see him walking around Lake Simcoe, and playing Bach's *Italian Concerto* as if he were all by himself. In a letter to Gladys Shenner, a journalist who wrote an interesting article on him, he confessed: "This movie-making has done more for my morale and indeed enthusiasm for life in general than anything else within memory." If we compare this statement with what I have just quoted concerning the live audience, we can only come to one conclusion: Gould was looking for another kind of audience; he wanted to give in a different way. He did not want to withdraw just to withdraw, as he could quite legitimately have done. In September 1959, he was to return to Europe for a new tour which would begin in Salzburg; as luck would have it, he fell ill and had to cancel the engagements. He postponed the concert for two weeks, following two recitals recorded for British radio. Still under the weather, he had a high fever when he played Bach's *Concerto in D Minor* under the direction of Herbert von Karajan. He cancelled the remaining concerts, returned to Canada, and never again left America. Between his first recital on foreign soil on January 2, 1955, and the last in 1964, only nine years had passed, in the course of which he had given 256 concerts, a very modest figure compared to the schedule of other artists in his category. The contrast between his misery on tour, so obvious in his correspondence of those years, and his joy in working with the various media makes the outcome self-evident. Four years were to elapse before his final concert in Los Angeles, but the issues were clear and the decision was now only a matter of time. If, in 1974, he still spoke of Salzburg as of a martyrdom, it is because the memory remained a painful one.

In either case, withdrawal or communication, the mystery remains: we know of no one who has followed in Gould's footsteps, no one who has gone as far as he did along this road; and his commitment was radical, even if he did not like the word. The traditional persona of the concert pianist, an elite figure with a conventional following, must conform to certain rules, as much in his performance as in all other aspects of life. Alfred Brendel's severity vis-à-vis Gould reveals the true nature of what is at stake: the pianist, he wrote, must not put himself in a position where he stands between the audience and the work; he must serve it and stay in the background, but at the same time he must lend himself to the concertizing game, he must be willing to offer himself up to the spectators. For Brendel, Gould, in seeking refuge far from the concert stage, positioned himself front and centre. Far from achieving the anonymity he claimed was essential for his art, he had inflated his public persona with a large dose of helium, creating a figure more tyrannical than the virtuosos he denounced. But this criticism did not cut much ice from Gould's perspective, because for him a virtuosic performance was just that – a performance, a ritual that required an enormous sacrifice. Brendel felt that the artist had to accept that sacrifice; the audience takes pleasure in our mistakes, our hesitations, awaits them expectantly, but at the same time offers support to its hero through its mute encouragement, before even applauding. Brendel is the perfect example of the model he promotes: a great Mozart interpreter, a bourgeois artist, severe but ironic, posing willingly before his country house, but very discreet, and, all in all, perfectly colourless and submissive to his festival public.

On the other hand, as Kevin Bazzana so aptly remarked, Gould's interpretations were not simply readings of the works, but constituted a testimony to his vision of the world, and this vision implied a moral mission, a service to humanity in and through art. The artist must remain in the background, certainly, but he is the link to the work, and the work he does is inseparable from the interpretation: it is an appropriation of the work that carries his signature, a commitment that derives from an authentic experience of art, from the shape of a life. Gould was in some sense

entrapped by his decision to withdraw; he could not have foreseen that it would hit the impasse of the classical concert so close
to the bone, mercilessly exposing its inexorable decline, which we
are witnessing today. He could not have foreseen that he himself
would become the hero of an evolving new culture and that there
would be no escape from the cult already forming, with himself at
its hub. No pianist followed Gould's extraordinary example: none
broke so completely with the conventions, none withdrew from
the fray so uncompromisingly; none addressed the public so ami-
cably and with such intelligence as the man we see in Bruno
Monsaingeon's films. No one was so faithful to the precepts he
enunciated in choosing the form his life would take; none distanced themselves so completely from any compromise. None,
finally, could subject themselves to a critical gaze as honest and
joyous as his own in the 1974 interview. He was alone in that, and
he remains so.

There was nothing ordinary about this uniqueness. It could of
course generate a cult, and that did happen, but its most important consequence was to discourage imitators. Gould did not
really have a dialogue with anyone, and his exchange with Yehudi
Menuhin, despite the fact that it was grounded in real friendship
and constituted a genuine confrontation between diametrically
opposed points of view, in essence paints a picture of everything
that separates an artist who plays the game from one who wants
to opt out. When we listen to the conversation, filmed in June of
1966, and when we read the transcript, *Duo with Yehudi Menuhin*,
in John P.L. Roberts's anthology, we feel that Gould with all his
heart would have liked Menuhin to share not only his love for the
Viennese twelve-tone composers, but also his passion for communication and his predilection for a life apart. We cannot help
noting, however, that he becomes a more and more isolated voice.
This isolation was the price he paid for his convictions as much

as for his genius, and it conferred on his character a quality that distinguished him from everyone else: his determination, his obstinacy, and his refusal to compromise. Unlike the solitude of a saint, which distinguishes itself through actions and virtues, that of the artist can only be understood through the resolve to lead a certain kind of life to the limit, regardless of what may emerge in the work.

Friedrich Schiller distinguished the noble from the ordinary soul by saying that only the former takes into account what it is, not what it does. This distinction may not be enough to account for what separates the artist's life from other uncompromising styles of life, as the saint too is ultimately remembered in terms of his being. The excellence of virtue is inherent, even if it has no opportunity to express itself. What could a Saint Vincent de Paul do in a society where everyone was rich? And yet all his life he would remain the charitable soul whose aspirations he strove to fulfill, working to establish the necessary conditions. Is not the real difference, as Max Scheler realized, to be found in the artist's solitude rather than in his work, as the saint, too, can become inactive. The saint is never completely alone; he depends for his actions on others and performs them for others, and he evolves within a community of people who want to emulate him and will think back on him with mystical fervour as a much-loved exemplar. The artist may never see his work recognized, and the goal that represents the focal point of all his energy can constitute his life's most impenetrable secret; it is no less real for all that. Even his generosity, were it as absolute as his resolve to lead a free life, could remain hidden from all but himself. He cannot propose this resolve as a model for anyone, and we see clearly in the conversations between Gould and Menuhin how these two giants, in that context, could only relate as two solitudes separated by the lives they had chosen to lead. They did share a reciprocal admiration, but Menuhin, it would seem, was perplexed by Gould's radical marginality, and Gould disappointed by Menuhin's cautious adherence to convention.

In the eyes of many, a temperament so unusual could only imply a kind of madness – benign, certainly, but madness all the same. Peter F. Ostwald, who knew Gould very well, and was both a musician and a psychiatrist, wrote a book on him that is full of affection and admiration. He recalled that Gould experienced some critical episodes toward the end of 1959. He heard voices and thought he was being spied upon. It was possible, Ostwald thought, that these signs of paranoia were caused by an abuse of medication, because they never recurred; Gould's solitude, extreme when one considers the austerity of his material life, and the rigour, especially, of his chosen way of life, could have led him along difficult, more dangerous paths. He was spared that, though not the physical troubles of all sorts, real or imaginary, that afflicted him, and of which I will speak in due course. Ostwald was the first, however, to suggest that Gould might have suffered from a form of autism, Asperger's Syndrome, a possibility examined more recently by several psychiatrists. The fear of certain objects, a shortfall in empathy, extreme isolation, and in general, behaviour patterns revealing an obsession with rites and control – all these are consistent with the syndrome. I will not pursue the matter; I am not really interested in assigning a pathology to what for me is a radical commitment to a life that will both keep one separate and offer protection.

That Gould might have had tendencies favouring a form of autistic withdrawal would not in any way exclude his having sought out this separation and protection for more fundamental reasons. The depressive aspects of his personality, certainly less prominent than his manic attributes, are they not typical of artistic melancholia? The angel's view of the world is always that drawn by Dürer, and like the feeling of the sublime, it touches first and foremost on what is solemn and primary. Gould was a solitary individual, but one whose solitude constantly served the work at hand. If something in his life were to be described as a symptom, it is not his isolation or his obsessions, but his compulsion to work, to play music, to record. And so I would speak rather of a fixation on work at the heart of an overarching idleness, in the Buddhist sense. He never seems to have experienced, where his work is concerned, a dark night of the soul, one of those critical periods described by mystics when the void beckons, when the divine presence is lost, when there is a repudiation of all language. Sōseki's painter would have experienced it through the constancy of his quest, but not through the fear of losing the work, or the despair at not being able to achieve it. Even during his difficult crisis of 1977–78, recorded in a diary about which I will have more to say, Gould's artistic activity did not slow down, and his projects continued apace. He was always involved in his work, always driven to produce.

Another way of trying to get close to Gould's personality is to speak of genius, even if one must for that introduce a concept whose romantic associations would doubtless have displeased him. The genius also withdraws – he is first and foremost one who relies on no rules, who breaks them all; so says Kant in his *Critique of Judgment*, seeing genius first and foremost as a refusal to imitate. Nothing that can be learned may lay claim to genius; it is by definition beyond all that. "Genius is the talent that gives the rule to art." It goes hand in hand with another significant trait, an obsession with death, because genius never has enough time and is confronted at every instant with a work's finitude. To describe Gould's life from the point of view of genius is to insist on its exceptional nature, on its accompanying solitude, and perhaps above all on the freedom that made it possible. It is also to reflect on the sense of urgency that characterizes it: had he not set his fiftieth birthday as the end point for his pianistic career? He died during the week that followed. Can an interpreter be a genius in the same sense as a painter or a composer? Kant refused to claim that a philosopher can be a genius, since he does not create a work or invent knowledge. He seeks the conditions for knowledge, but he does not overstep their limits. Does the interpreter create a work? In answering this question I would invoke once more the artist's solitude: it is his choice of this form of life, more perhaps than the work he has produced, that confers on him his pure individuality. In that respect an interpretation in no way differs from a work itself, because it incorporates the choice an individual has made for his life, one that also finds expression, though differently, in the work. Thus it can transgress fully and be creative; it can give art its rules.

No one can listen to Glenn Gould play without acknowledging that the transcendence of a work, its pure abstraction, its mental existence, is brought to life beneath his fingers in a way that marks it with a special stamp. But no one can doubt, either, Gould's recognition that this uniqueness, the distinct character of his interpretation, opened up the whole question of fidelity to the historic work. For him, the act of creation authorized one to extend the limits of interpretation; the issue was never that of fidelity to the work, but of revealing its transcendent, idealized potential. His readings of Mozart's sonatas were convincing to almost no one, and yet he insisted right to the end that they represented a window onto uncharted territory. The same was true of his interpretation of the Brahms *Piano Concerto in D Minor*, performed under the baton of Leonard Bernstein, who took the precaution of publicly dissociating himself from it. Gould later claimed that he had musicological reasons for his slow tempo, but that was not what was most important to him. In adopting those extraordinary *tempi*, he again wanted to open up new territory where meaning could assert itself. These questions impinge on the whole subject of aesthetics, to the degree that they revive the debate about the autonomy of a work as much as its incarnation as an ideal. There is no reason to dwell on this, other than to show how Gould found in these interpretations the opportunity for a singular freedom –

as singular as that which culminated in his withdrawal, and, essentially the same. It is in this fundamental sense that we can speak of his genius and, in a way that casts light on it, of its primacy.

Gould was persuaded that a work of art exists in its own right and that it contributes to the world's spiritual reality, but he similarly thought that a work's greatness consists in the interpretation it solicits, and that this greatness reveals itself in its capacity to inspire in the interpreter an understanding that opens the work out, making possible a wide-ranging reading that adds to what is already known. When we reread what he wrote on Bach or Schoenberg, we see that for him it is first and foremost this strength in a work that makes it sublime: its poetic capacity to open the mind to unsuspected meanings. This opening is more than poetic, since it includes an essential moral dimension that is intrinsic to a work's formal attributes. The work adds to what is good; it does more than enlarge the scope of what is perceived and felt, it also expands the moral realm of what enthrals us, and, as he wrote, it frees up the divine that can be found in every human being. And so Gould's aesthetic is not averse to genius, and his stubborn determination to argue for the appropriateness of an interpretation, or for its freedom – which for him often meant the same thing – constitutes the clearest proof of his belief in the power of interpretation to create, to open out, to transcend, and not simply to imitate or to reproduce.

Even if the dark side of Gould's temperament, in particular his obsession with controlling and explaining everything, seems inconsistent with the tempestuous fieriness and deep-seated irrationality of the romantic genius, we would be wrong to dismiss this aspect simply because it seems to exclude the intellectuality that Gould always held in such esteem. This intellectuality was, on the contrary, what for him defined a work – its performance as much as the discourse on it. In that, he was more rigorous than most, reproaching himself in an exaggerated fashion for any excess in the expression of feeling, and pushing the analysis of everything, whether it be his illnesses or the works in his repertoire, to astonishingly rational extremes. That he saw Bach's contrapuntal music as the high point of art only confirms this aesthetic partiality, which led him to criticize romanticism so harshly and to favour harmony, clarity, and transparency above all. But we will see that this bias was not so complete or so rigid that it led him to exclude lyricism. In the ten broadcasts that he produced on Schoenberg for the Canadian Broadcasting Corporation, he navigated between the formality of serial music and the nocturnal beauty of *Transfigured Night*! Of all the categories with negative connotations for Gould and his art, romanticism is the most complex, and I shall come back to it. It is not so easy in fact to define romanticism, whether in the context of a reflection on genius, in the lyricism of performance, or in the aesthetics of creation.

Is what is dark necessarily romantic? Does the solitary individual automatically belong to that brotherhood, he who seeks nothing more than to free himself from the world of shadows and demons that beset him and that he wishes to master? Withdrawal in itself has nothing romantic about it, especially if its purpose, as was the case for Gould, is to create the conditions for technical mastery of a work and provide the starting point for an unending communication. But we cannot so easily dismiss a description that affects so many other aspects of Gould's life. In regard to his work, we would be right to emphasize everything that goes against romanticism, such as the importance of light, clarity, and grace. But if that must involve our seeing Gould as an artist who is a cold technician, we would upset the balance, for we would at the same time be neglecting the lyricism that is inseparable from all the rest. This artist who, all his life and despite so many obstacles, found the means to avoid dejection, and who was able to reach an ecstatic state that, in his mind, was accessible to all, must have been able to draw on both precision and emotion, technique and lyricism. From the depths of the studio to which he withdrew, he addressed the world with an artistic production that was perfectly mastered, rigorous, exemplary, and at the same time fully committed to its own feeling, to its unique brand of ecstasy.

All his public personae – the outrageous humorist, the farcical characters, the impersonator channelling his own struggles – attest to the freedom of which he was capable. What other artist could take the risk of making such emphatic and often incomprehensible declarations as he made on his notorious Silver Jubilee album? He could do it, and even had to do it. He could perform the contrapuntal masterpieces he revered with the greatest of rigour; he could explain their principles, and give chapter and verse on their science. But he could also use this repertoire as the perfect point of departure for his own abandonment to the lyricism in which it abounds, making no secret of the stock he put in the sublime. His admiration for Schoenberg, more even than his love for the music of Bach, illustrates this balancing act where he sought perfection, and every time he defended Schoenberg it was to draw our attention to the intensity of that tension. Otherwise he would probably have not permitted the publication of those images that were soon reproduced everywhere, where we see him in a state of rapture, bliss, almost in a trance. His self, his body, all his being were given over to the sublime.

But at the same time, as if he wanted to show that he was not just the angel Jock Carroll so admirably photographed, he varied his roles and showed himself to be more of a social animal and more contemporary than the stereotypical members of society to whom he was preaching his gospel of renewal. In his interview with Jonathan Cott, first published in two parts in *Rolling Stone* in 1974, he attributed the pleasure he derived from his dramatizations to the freedom they gave him to express himself in a different way: "I, for instance, was incapable of writing in a sustained humorous style until I developed an ability to portray myself pseudonymously." This joyful, ebullient discourse belonged to a sort of *Doppelgänger* who accompanied Gould throughout his life, a vaguely anarchistic rebel, mischief maker, and gadfly to the bourgeoisie. The cast of characters he incarnated reveals an unusual sense of the burlesque, at the same time as it illustrates his capacity to understand the points of view of others, including those whose aesthetic views he did not share. We need only cite his parodies of the great British conductors such as Sir Thomas Beecham or Adrian Boult. We think also of his invented psychiatrist, Doctor Wolfgang von Krankmeister, who doubtless served to exorcize the voice of authority – even the threat of castration – that made itself heard on the frequent occasions when it was suggested he might be mad. One of his favourite characters was a hippie pianist, Theodore "Teddy" Slotz, whom Gould created after an encounter with a New York taxi driver in 1966. Slotz became his most colourful critic, while at the same time representing a youthful generation to which Gould still wanted to belong. There was no derision here, just a desire, from deep in his withdrawal to the studio where he continued to work, to belong to the everyday world and to continue speaking out. We can only imagine the heights his prolixity might have attained had he come to know the freedom of the Internet.

We mustn't forget his portrayal of the young actor in biker's garb, worked up to introduce a musical broadcast; it is one of the funniest things I have ever seen, but also one of the most tragic: Gould knew that his life had distanced him immeasurably from street culture, and he badly wanted to show that he still had connections to it. And what to say about Myron Chianti, this double of Marlon Brando, a coarse and powerful character Gould went so far as to have leaning on his piano? When he compared Petula Clark to Webern, he showed to what extremes he would go to assert the range of his experience; his withdrawal allowed him to be incomparably generous. After all, the biker had doubtless been in his Toronto schoolroom; one has only to read his friend Robert Fulford's account of their young years to see this. Gould was quickly isolated from the everyday world, first by his mother, then his teachers, and finally by the life he himself chose. The characters he invented reflect a nostalgia for a unified society where art could take its place simply, without exposing the artist to the imposed discipline of withdrawal.

For me, there is nothing trivial about these games. Behind their clownish façade, they are an inversion of Gould's own life choice, tragic and generous. Alfred Brendel would never have done such a thing; he would never have taken the risk, not the man who sipped tea in Salzburg salons and wrote ironic, painful poems on the suffering of an artist doomed to observe conventions and seek release in derision. There is nothing artificial about the energy generated by Gould's portraits. On the contrary, they were nourished by what seems to have been a joyous and mocking approach to life. There is an innocence in them that prevents us from seeing these performances as pure buffoonery, and the accounts his biographers have culled from those who enjoyed his company are all consistent: Gould was neither gloomy nor morose; he seemed always on the outlook for a good joke, an outrageously absurd expression. In him, the buried adolescent was forever seeking an outlet.

Was this frenetic approach to human relationships designed to avoid a deeper, more substantive and direct connection? Did he want to short-circuit all threats from the realm of the serious and the intimate? As I said, we cannot allow this question to obscure what he was most consistently, "the quintessential nice Canadian boy, at heart a man of decency and integrity." This description by Kevin Bazzana deserves a moment's pause: first, for the expression "boy," which evokes a man who was eternally young, a bit airy, offhand almost, as if he remained always the young Glenn of youthful brilliance and rapid-fire iconoclasm. I think there is truth in this. It highlights his joyful freedom, his elegant haughtiness, and his constant search for approval. Gould would also have approved of his being presented as essentially "Canadian." As Gilles Marcotte noted, he would not have appreciated the fact that in Thomas Bernhard's novel, where he appears as a fictional character, he is presented as "Canadian-American," as if being Canadian were not enough to distance him adequately from Europe. No matter if the Austrian writer intended Gould's character to be a kind of noble savage, an antidote to Salzburg decadence, he was never anything else but Canadian – and not American. I will address his love for Canada in the section devoted to his documentaries on solitude; it is a very special Canada that Gould loved, much in his image. Gould was so Canadian that his name has been carved into a Toronto sidewalk, and his bronze likeness erected at the entrance to the theatre that bears his name at CBC headquarters. We can see this statue in Bruno Monsaingeon's last film, *Glenn Gould: Hereafter*. It shows Gould sitting on a bench wearing his overcoat and cap, making conversation with passers-by. But what does being "Canadian" mean? Is it to love Canada, its open spaces and its freedom, as embodied and lauded in his *Solitude Trilogy*? Is it to relate oneself to Canadian culture, as he so often did, evoking A.Y. Jackson's painting or the humour of Stephen Leacock, who had been, even though he never met him, his neighbour at Lake Simcoe?

My own feeling about this question is complex: the Canada of Glenn Gould's personality was first and foremost the immense territory stretching from the West of the Mennonites to the solitude of Newfoundland, and Gould described this land as a realm of solitary communities, a land of solitude where a solitary person could be happy. He seems not to have read *Two Solitudes* by Hugh MacLennan, the novelist from Nova Scotia who settled in Montreal. This book, published in 1945, would have instructed him

Gould was a unique figure, a figure of solitude whose entire life was ruled by weighty choices to which he remained faithful. In this *Toccata* I have tried to express and come close to what this figure owed to these choices, how he drew from them a form of heroism in art that was realized in the shape he gave his life. Not without its paradoxes, his was a life that was reconciled to the tension between withdrawal and communication, between life and art. If neither genius nor sainthood could ever account for it entirely, it is because in its radicalism it paved the way for an exemplary art, and it is in the art that we must seek the understanding that will now be our concern.

## II

*Allemande*

# The Paradoxes of Genius
*Partita no. 2 in C Minor*

Glenn Gould's lifespan was brief, only fifty years. Although his youth coincided with the Second World War, nothing ruffled the waters of his first years as an apprentice to the piano. With Canada at war the country was praying for its soldiers, and the young Gould's recollections of those years were of feeling distant and on the margins. Similarly, the beginning of his concert career coincided with the 1950s, when Europe was rebuilding and America was enjoying unprecedented prosperity. There too he lived against the grain, not sharing in the post-war frenzy at all, other than to flee its excesses. Nothing approaching a political observation finds its way into his correspondence, which is totally given over to shaping the life he has chosen. Like Oliver, the young hero of George Santayana's novel, *The Last Puritan*, Gould committed himself to achieving spiritual goals that set him apart from society, while at the same time putting himself at its service. Gould so much resembled the American philosopher's protagonist that, were it not for his artistic genius, the novel's moral tale might have been his.

He wasn't one of those romantic cads who want to experience everything. He kept himself for what was best. That's why he was a true puritan after all. His puritanism had never been pure timidity or fanaticism or calculated hardness: it was a deep and speculative thing: hatred of all shams, scorn of all mummeries, a bitter merciless pleasure in the hard facts. And that passion for reality was beautiful in him, because there was so much in his gifts and in his surroundings to allure him and muffle up his mind in worldly conventions ... For that reason you and I loved him so much. You and I are not puritans; and by contrast with our natural looseness, we can't help admiring people purer than ourselves, more willing to pluck out the eye that offends them, even if it be the eye for beauty, and to enter halt and lame into the kingdom of singlemindedness.

Gould must have seen himself in this portrait. He could only have admired the constancy and the scrupulousness of a hero so entirely devoted to his community. He valued austerity not for its own sake but for what it made possible in the search for an autonomous style of life. He never rebelled against his puritanical education; its demands were consistent with the discipline he associated with his art, and Gould adopted very early on, well before leaving the concert stage, a solitary way of life in which this discipline could manifest itself invisibly, without his having to give it any philosophical foundations. It was only after his withdrawal in 1964, with the avalanche of questions from his critics, that he found it necessary, as in his self-interview of 1974, to speak of "puritanism" as the fundamental moral stance he had chosen.

But, to go back to the question I was raising: how is it that such freedom might come to be in a world so rife with conventions, so dominated by middle-class Toronto's Protestant tradition? If genius is characterized by audacity and the power to propose new rules, perhaps there is an explanation. Santayana devoted an entire novel to exploring the prospects for virtue in the midst of an ambitious and hypocritical world. He never took the purity of his hero at face value, but the more he investigated, the more puritanism impressed him as an irresistible fact, a kind of miracle at the core of a society that rejected it *a priori*. It was a miracle of goodness, the gift of virtue. In an important epilogue, Santayana reproached himself for his own idealization of his character; after all, did his hero not lack strength, power? But his answer was one that Gould might have endorsed: if "he required a lot of time to mobilise his forces," it was because "they were very great and drawn from a vast territory." This response brings genius into the moral realm. Gould would have been pleased.

But was this the right answer? Can Gould's genius be explained? And what do we mean when we speak of this unusual way of being that he in so many ways embodied? To approach these questions, we must first look into what fascinated Gould himself to the point of obsession: interpretive genius, a genius that left no room for anything less than perfection. At the same time, we must relate interpretation to the way genius wants to portray itself; Gould always felt that he belonged to a tradition he admired, and that he could not only understand it but also shed light on it and expand its bounds. Doubtless he would have liked to compose more than he did, but the axis along which he had undertaken his research, a line of thought that led straight from Bach to Schoenberg, did not tolerate many detours. I will have occasion to speak about his string quartet, but clearly his quest for perfection was not to be found in composition; he chose, rather, to seek it within established tradition.

No pianist has written or recorded as many musical commentaries as he did, and none has violated as many conventions in analysis or performance. Since his childhood, and despite the fact that his puritanism ought to have taught him respect, Gould persisted in what one might call his excesses or exaggerations. He continued to take chances with his genius, exposing it to risks that could have had him spinning out of control, with ruinous consequences. If he had not decided to ignore so many conventions, both before and after his decision to abandon the concert hall, his genius might not have been so clearly defined, or so plainly seen. For in all his efforts, and above all in the constant and sophisticated analyses of his preferred repertoire, Gould tried to articulate the meaning of a quest and a style that would not otherwise have been evident. And so he subjected musical tradition to the same critical analysis as he did his own performances, to a meticulous dissection that was consistent with his attempts to transcend convention.

No pianist was so willing to live with such a scrim of personal idiosyncrasies interposed between himself and his public. Gould could not have been unaware that all the eccentricities he chose not to conceal tended to monopolize his coverage in the press, but he always seemed totally comfortable with the good-natured narcissism he displayed, to his own amusement, from the very beginning. Such casualness signalled a deeper indifference to everyday life, routine, the vagaries of the ordinary world; consider his ill-fitting clothing, his choice of diet, his nocturnal life in the silence of his apartment, the disorder that seemed central to his existence. Consider also his phobias, and everything his style of life seemed to imply: an eccentric inability to adjust to the simplest of demands, a congenital incapacity to adapt which the puritan, on the other hand, would see only as a refusal to accept the norm.

And yet there was nothing maladjusted about Gould. All his life he juggled numerous projects, he carried on a wide correspondence, he spoke out frequently, and he remained faithful to the fundamental ethic of devotion to his art, an ethic that had shaped his life since his childhood. He was meticulous and obsessive, capable of working both very slowly and in great bursts of energy. No one who worked with him, none of his technicians or producers, ever spoke of him in terms of his being dysfunctional.

To what do we attribute, then, this reputation for unhealthy eccentricity, if not to his strict resolve to lead a free life in perfect harmony with his ideals of austerity and perfection, making no concessions to worldliness and appearances? In short, it may be ascribed to the alignment of puritanism with genius which set him apart from all other artists of his day. I shall return to the subject of Gould's solitude in due course, but it should be said at the outset that eccentricity is also a form of solitude, a desire to protect oneself from the world's rebukes, a protective screen set between the artist and the world in order to give precedence entirely to art. This style of life is at the heart of his aesthetic. Gould could write: "Solitude nourishes creation, and collegial fraternity tends to dissipate it ... I separate myself from contrasting and conflicting notions. Monastic seclusion works for me."

His friend Peter Ostwald spoke of how this isolation did provoke periodic episodes of distress, a kind of neediness that led Gould to seek out the conversation of friends, even distant ones. Ostwald first met him on the way out of a recital in San Francisco on February 28, 1957, and he was astonished that Gould became attached to him so quickly, despite the distance between them. Gould called him frequently from Toronto to tell him about his projects and his concerns. Many have told stories about his late-night telephone soliloquies, when he had stopped work and wanted to talk to someone. Like his letters, his conversation was friendly and cheerful, and Gould never complained of anything, other than his many physical ailments and afflictions, real or imaginary. In the last analysis, his eccentricities were simply the consequence of such an unusual form of autonomy that they tended to be interpreted as a sort of flaw, a kind of weakness. The opposite is the case, however: Gould was an austere artist who in all things chose poverty, and who derived from it a higher freedom. Kevin Bazzana speaks of him as a Spartan. The term is apt even though I doubt that any Spartan would have tolerated such non-conformism. If he was Spartan, it was mainly in his day-to-day life; in all else, he was Santayana's puritan and nothing else.

Perhaps we should acknowledge now that it was the strength and the seriousness of his puritan convictions that made possible all the transgressions that are proper to genius. For one of the central features of puritanism is the priority it grants justification: what is right, even if it is far from the norm, may be justified, and Gould very early claimed the freedom to say what he thought, as if he had a kind of mission to establish the conditions for the acceptance of what he created. This freedom was never characterized by resentment or revolt, and to the extent that we might speak of an urge to transgress where his interpretations are concerned, it is always in the sense of reaching beyond, of furthering the quest for the rigour and purity required by art and life. He proposed nothing on the basis of a random feeling or an arbitrary judgment; he gave reasons for every change, justifications for what was new. The bulk of his writings, interviews, and commentaries are consistent with his performances in this respect: nothing is affirmed solely for the pleasure of virtuosity or personal taste; on the contrary, everything is matter for a discussion in which the most clear-cut judgments coexist with an exceptionally rigorous reading of musical history.

Here, I find myself in fundamental agreement with Kevin Bazzana when he notes that as an adult Gould embraced a heightened version of his parents' values. In other words he rejected none of them, but rather carried them to their logical extremes. It is worth looking into this assertion, which is so pertinent to Gould's art as well as his life. The isolation he chose had nothing in common with the modesty or discretion of his parents' life, and yet it was the same thing on another scale, a form of austerity, of severity. To understand it we must, in a sense, incorporate his genius into the representation he fashioned for himself; we must try to view all these exaggerations and eccentricities as aspects of the very language through which he sought to convey what he was searching for. His obsession with the perfect interpretation was much in the same vein; it required an extremely complex technique whereby musical sequences were recorded separately and then joined together end to end in a collage. It suggested a mania for control, perhaps, but above all a stubborn determination to go the limit in his quest for rigour and perfect order. That same perfectionism, in the philosophical sense proper to this term in ethics, guided his art and his life; the quest for the good was grounded in something real, not just in subjective appreciation.

We who have his recordings in hand, and can place them alongside the body of his analyses, can follow the path laid out by Gould himself. We don't have to put ourselves in his place; we just have to listen. Very early Gould was conscious of his gifts and set out in search of the conditions required to manifest them, and an understanding of the demands they would make. He was puritanical perhaps, especially in his constant emphasis on knowledge and reason in dealing with what otherwise might have emerged as uncontrolled emotion. What we hear in his art is never contradicted by what he worked hard to say, and conversely, his explications are never contradicted by his art; we find the same values in both, and an extraordinary consistency in the way he approached his accounts of his research and experience. In fact, there is no difference between the stance that enables us to conceptualize genius and the relationship between the wonder of art and the language that embraces it.

As a child the pianist already knew that his art could transport him to a rarefied and exclusive world. But he also knew, just as surely, that the artist can try to communicate the mental processes that are guiding him toward this state of wonder, and set forth the criteria for reaching it. The truth of the experience belongs to the artist alone, as only he can say where his art has led him, toward what state of ecstasy, toward what serenity, what sense of the absolute. This is the privilege his authenticity grants. If he risks saying anything about it, for example by associating a form of the sublime with a moral predicate such as rigour or purity, then he sets off on a path with no return. The experience of the state of wonder inherent in the work, which he proposed as its supreme goal, is only possible in terms of the truth from which it springs: the artist's achievement is an authentic and truthful manifestation of what he seeks, and to that he bears witness. Similarly, he alone can risk expressing the meaning of a work in words that constitute a "supplement" to the truth. I say "supplement" because Gould the interpreter knew that the truth of a work resided first and foremost in the transcendent spirituality of the work itself, and that it was only revealed or made manifest in the interpretation. It was in fact no more accessible to language than to musical interpretation; it existed beyond both.

We find this supplemental truth everywhere in Gould's art – an expression in another form of the genius that was alive in him first and foremost in his playing. Even though this parallel text is at times obscure, we can draw on it to help us penetrate the veil of representation and gain new access to his work as an interpreter. Many critics have found Gould's elaborations verbose and unbearable; I suggest, rather, that we recognize how deeply imbued they are with his puritanism. The sublime is not unrestrained excess; it can be expressed, and that was his conviction. We may regret that he wrote nothing systematic and that he showed no desire to restrain his power of association; his writings for the most part chart very oblique paths. But if we give them the attention they deserve, they will always yield the charged moment when Gould expresses his most deeply felt convictions. That moment is always the same, whether the subject is *The Art of Fugue* or Richard Strauss, whom paradoxically he very much liked; it is the moment when the beauty of the work finds expression as a virtue. Gould never ceased expounding this principle; he was forever searching for the concurrence of a perfect interpretation with an essentially moral validation.

This, in any case, was Gould's own prescription, expressed in a multi-faceted ensemble of writings: aesthetic judgments on the history of music, musicological analyses, aphorisms, ascetic formulas, pronouncements for the media, philosophic reflections on performing and listening. The author of these texts was not first of all a writer or scholar; but he was an artist committed to his work and dedicated to his quest for the sublime, someone for whom writing and speech were an outgrowth of the interpretive practices that constituted his genius. What Gould sought for himself, but also for the universal audience he always addressed, was a clarification of his principles and – always – a demonstration that they were well founded. He did not philosophize, and rarely indulged in dialectic; he was, rather, quick and decisive. We can only dream of a conversation he might have had with a thinker such as Peter Kivy – a shared reflection on pure music and the genius that makes it possible. All his work was directed toward the formulation of an aesthetic; however, he remained far from reaching any overarching statement, circumstances most often preventing him from moving beyond the rationale at hand. When he did risk a generalization, he most often went too far, caught himself, and fell back on humour on the following page. He did not suffer from any shortfall in intuition, only in patience.

My aim here is to reflect on this relationship between interpretation and elucidation, bearing in mind that Gould's work involved an explicit and elaborate mediation between the two. The decision to withdraw from the concert hall would not have been the unique gesture it was had his energy not immediately been reinvested in recordings and in communication. What is astonishing is not so much the courage it took to make this decision, since for him it was a liberation, but its imperfect or paradoxical nature. Once retired from the concert hall, Gould felt free to replicate himself, and he did so freely, speaking out while allowing himself to be filmed from every angle, and impersonating a variety of characters, some frankly comic, all of which enabled him to recapture through his public voice what he feared he might be denied by concert goers. Which was what, exactly? I would say, tentatively, and subject to what may emerge from what follows, a way of ensuring that his work might continue to serve a certain idea of music. What does it mean, in fact, to justify something? It is to offer the best possible reasons for making a choice. Gould knew how to make an argument, but it is not so much his talent for doing so that impresses us as the energy he expended in order to convince. The puritan rarely doubts; he is flush with certainties that feed his perfectionism. For Gould to like the music of Robert Schumann, for example, was an impossibility. Even when Peter Ostwald undertook to devote a book to him, which appeared in 1985, Gould dismissed the composer and advised Ostwald to concern himself with "a more serious musician." This was in the course of their last meeting.

I am tempted to push the inquiry further by evoking the Glenn Gould of before 1964, when the burdens of the concert hall weighed on him every day and, as his correspondence confirms, he was struggling to fulfill his obligations. In particular, we can look at the images captured during his tour of the Soviet Union; not only did the concerts strike a responsive chord with a demanding audience that recognized his genius, but they were also the occasion for exchanges and lectures in which we see him already seeking a rational understanding. This reciprocity between performance and thought in the context of the artistic experience is very telling. Even then it was not enough for Gould just to play the piano, however joyously, in performance; he had to go further – to think, to understand, to explain, to justify. The success of the interpretation itself already seemed no more important than the challenge of elucidating the history of the music, the challenge of judging it by criteria as strict as they were moral – and holding to them. All this, puritanism helps us understand.

We can go further by looking at the novel the Austrian writer Thomas Bernhard devoted to this paragon of freedom. It is a strange piece of fiction, at an awkward angle to Gould's biography, but nevertheless rich in its implications. Its narcissistic bent has long intrigued me. What exactly was Bernhard trying to grasp hold of, drawn as he was to an ethic of pure solitude, and provocative in his own way? Perhaps a model that would help understand how a pure work of art, through its own genius, may earn the right to an eccentricity of presentation. The taste for provocation divides these two artists more than it brings them together, but the obsession with a pure and justified mode of expression is common to them both. This fiction presents us with a Gouldian character that Gould would no doubt have appreciated, having himself assumed roles embodying moral and aesthetic temperaments that could express hidden facets of his thought. Appreciated, but not entirely, as Bernhard's Gould has forgone too many social ideals, has given up defending them; cloaked in his genius, he holds sway in sadness. But this narrative frees us to probe Gould's representation of himself, to expand upon it, to open it out; here, breaking free from the life of a concert pianist, mute and magnificent, Gould becomes a teacher, something in real life he declared he would never want to do.

Mind you, that's what he always was, and from the very beginning he was able to mesmerize his audiences for hours, expounding on the subtleties of the works he performed. In his novel *The Loser* (*Der Untergeher*), Thomas Bernhard, himself fascinated by the demands of genius, pushes to extremes the impact of musical genius on one's experience, and undertakes, from the perspective of music, an inexorable analysis of all life as decay and decline. At the same time, he reaffirms music as redemption and salvation. In constructing his fiction and seeking salvation through it, Bernhard only reaffirmed the idea that Gould himself had never needed to be saved. He placed him in a position of complete sovereignty. Gould appears in fact as a luminous genius, but his power shatters the lives of two of those near him, who also sought success as musical artists. One is Wertheimer, who represents the august personage of Ludwig Wittgenstein, also a musician; the other is the writer-narrator, himself an exceptional pianist. But neither can aspire to the transcendent state of grace conjured up by Gould's playing. Each must recognize his own inadequacy and lay down his arms. Wertheimer shifts his focus to the humanities, succeeds only in amassing fragmentary notes, and ends by killing himself. Gould dies as well, from Thomas Bernhard's pulmonary illness, an obvious indication – perhaps too obvious – of the author's admiring identification with him. The narrator is left alone and creates a memorial: the novel we have been reading.

Although it could have been partially inspired by Gould's writings, this portrayal of genius depicts a transcendence so lofty that the character is heedless of the gulf separating him from those who remain below, doomed to insensitivity and mindlessness. Here is where Gould differs, and radically, from the Austrian writer, for one never finds in him this sort of contempt for those who are unable to raise themselves up and are irremediably bogged down in their misery. An artist brought face to face with such a reality would be plunged into a state of suicidal despair. Genius must pursue its radiant, solitary path, joyful in its discoveries and serene in its judgments. Of Gould's genius Thomas Bernhard retains, in fact, only the attributes of confinement, isolation, and distancing – dark and imperious features that best correspond, in fact, to his own Salzburgian vision of a yawning abyss between the aura of genius and social mediocrity. Gould would not have recognized himself in this arrogance so bent on excluding others, he who wrote that any distinction made between an artist and his public would be anathema to him were it to introduce a hierarchy isolating art in a position of superiority. Of course, he would have applauded all the scathing criticism of the Burgtheater bourgeoisie, but he would not have taken it so seriously.

Similarly, Thomas Bernhard's novel turns its back on all the openness in Gould's narrative, on all that is welcoming and gracious, and that points the way for each and every one toward beauty and the sublime, while formulating arguments to encourage their pursuit. Even if these efforts come down to a deep-seated invitation to solitude, they remain an authentic exercise in communicating the virtues of art and a call to share in them. Such communication comes close, in fact, to being an exhortation. In a 1971 letter to John P.L. Roberts, Gould spoke of the therapeutic value of art, its power to heal: "For me all music which lacks that ability to isolate listeners from the world in which they live is intrinsically less valuable than that which manages the feat." A solitary genius is never truly solitary, or he would imperil the very authenticity of his project. In his solitude he is as troubled as the saint in his concern for those who suffer.

In dealing with these paradoxes, we must approach them in light of the motives and rationales I touched on earlier. Thomas Bernhard represents the outer reaches of how Gould's genius was received, accentuating oppression and exclusion, a stance that I find indefensible because it marginalizes what Gould himself came to value above all, universal access to the quest for the sublime in music. Bernhard's character, the reader may have noticed, is yet another "impersonation" in the vast gallery of Gouldian figures, and this solitary genius, an arrogant and charismatic master, might have found his niche among them, on one essential condition: that Glenn Gould could make fun of him, and that this celestial and tormented personage could be mocked, by for example the leather-jacketed biker, Myron Chianti, actor by profession, whom Gould placed centre-stage in a 1974 television commercial promoting his radio work. Thomas Bernhard would neither have understood nor accepted this, for the simple reason that he was always so serious and dramatic, so tormented. That was not the case with Glenn Gould. Those who considered him arrogant had it all wrong; he was certainly a bit authoritarian and pompous, serious in the moral sense of the term; but there was nothing in his nature that resembled scorn or distance, despair and cynicism even less. On the contrary, we find, as with Santayana's hero, only a compassionate will to facilitate the attainment of a goal, to give in order that obstacles may be surmounted.

Even on this point, it is far from clear that the very idea of genius, so difficult to grasp, really applied to Gould. That genius represents the transgression Kant observed, especially in art, one can easily accept, but if this transgression leads to complete disconnection and arrogance, then we withhold consent. The models Gould revered within the musical tradition set an example of gift giving and community, starting with the northern masters like Dietrich Buxtehude and Jan Sweelinck, whom he particularly admired. But he also discerned this moral ideal in his favoured musicians, Johann Sebastian Bach and Arnold Schoenberg, and if he seemed reluctant at times to speak in terms of genius when discussing the tradition whose high point these composers represented, it is simply because this concept was for him irreparably compromised by romanticism, whose share of obscurity and irrationality he refused to include in his spiritual conception of art. If we refuse romanticism's irrationality, as he consistently did, then we must also refuse to revive the romanticism implicit in the notion that art reserves for the artist-creator – and the interpreter – an inviolable domain where he might attain both an absolute that transcends representation and an ascendancy over convention. By contrast, the genius of the northern masters and the custodians of that tradition linking Bach to Schoenberg, was not an obscure and exclusive genius, but rather a spiritual transcendence brimming with generosity toward the communities they inspired.

Of these two signposts of genius, the first, the transcendence implicit in any representation, is the least open to view. But it is the most important, for genius, *a priori*, is self-evident, as Kant contended with such conviction. All of the artist's struggles to explicate it can bear no comparison to the absolute to which he has gained access. To explain, as Gould did, the sublime nature of the *The Art of Fugue*, is an impossible task, even for a confirmed perfectionist. Yet one must apply one's life to that task. Genius has nothing to "express," and yet Gould never stopped making that effort. The other signpost, freedom from convention, is the most time-honoured signature of genius – the capacity to break with a conventional paradigm, transform it, lay bare its entrenched norms, and then surpass them (this is the second phase of Kant's argument). Drawing on this power, genius pushes back the boundaries; they are surpassed and their lines redrawn. No accomplishment, no performance, no demonstration is needed for this to take place; genius can stake out its territory with incomplete, perfunctory – even hasty, inchoate – indicators. To follow Gould to this far frontier, where, for instance, he alters the interpretation of the *Goldberg Variations*, is to recognize both the hold that conventions can exert and the genius that can overthrow them.

To study Gould's piano playing one must go beyond what musical criticism can offer. Kevin Bazzana, who is not only Gould's most accomplished biographer but also the best authority on his work as an interpreter, has modulated his approach in such a way as to avoid slipping into judgments based on personal taste. Great critics, such as could be found in years past in the pages of many European and American newspapers, sketched a portrait of Gould that was not without merit, but that placed inordinate emphasis on his personality, and did not describe his performances with sufficient rigour. More is needed, and there is work still to be done. Gould himself set the standard by which any discussion of his work should be judged, and it must be acknowledged that the historical record of how his concerts and recordings were received is not, barring a few rare exceptions, very glorious. To like or not to like – Gould demanded that more be said than that, and he was the first to show the way in his liner notes as far back as 1955. The analysis of the scores, the work on rhythms and timbres, the historical discussion of forms, all require, following on the rich contributions Bazzana has made to our view of Gould the interpreter, careful study. We don't have to delve very deeply to see that Gould's interpretations were anything but arbitrary caprices.

Here again the puritan ideal can be our guide, to the extent that Gould's creative genius never stood in the way of his intense effort to understand. If we were to present him as a romantic rebel, we would immediately lose sight of his inventiveness. I have at times taken the step, the better to grasp their arguments, of itemizing his critics' lexicon (fascinating, stupefying, iconoclastic, brilliant, exciting, irritating, inspired, etc.): the list is long and redundant, with few critics even coming close to a discourse appropriate to Gould, one whose starting point would preferably have been a respect for his rigorous research. Were his interpretations apt and justifiable, where did their truth and power lie, how did he establish what they were able to contribute to the reading of the work? Even moral descriptions, so important when they associate an ideal of purity and transparency with the discipline of counterpoint, demand something beyond intuitive empathy. Most critics preferred, and still prefer, to talk of taste. But Gould, as it was with virtuosic brio, wanted nothing to do with taste and never talked about it, even if he was unsparing in his harsh judgments and his use of hyperbole. If he risked a judgment based solely on his own personal appreciation, one came to expect a lengthy dissertation to follow concerning forms and principles, and it never failed to materialize.

This way of posing the problem of genius raises again the question of recognition: who recognizes genius and how does one recognize it? Being wholly pragmatic, such an indicator is as important as those already cited; the capacity of genius to make its reality felt by directly compelling our recognition of the sublime surpasses any attempt to demonstrate its existence through discourse or its departure from convention. Traditional models can certainly be shaken to their foundations by analytical writings, but nothing can replace the intuitive apprehension of genius in and of itself. The more refined these analyses become, the more they circle it from the outside, isolating the inner life of genius, which demands another language. Genius exists only to the degree that it affects me, although it must be supposed that it is touched by itself as well and involves a process of self-discovery. This reflexive nucleus where the genius realizes both his own limits and his own sense of the absolute becomes the model for the way Gould will subsequently portray himself. He set the pattern for this continuum in the firmness of his convictions at the keyboard, in his writing, in his correspondence. He could find precedents in Schoenberg, and even in Thomas Mann's creation of a character imbued with self-knowledge. His familiarity with the writings of Theodor W. Adorno was limited, but there are many affinities between the two, even if what was key to Adorno, a kind of tragic pessimism, would certainly have given Gould pause. He could also have evoked the genius of Beethoven, whose sonatas and concertos he knew so well, and whose anxiety in the face of public recognition he shared. How not to think of the *Heiligenstadt Testament*, a declaration written by Beethoven in two stages on October 6 and 10 in 1802? This text marks a unique moment in the history of music: in his solitude Beethoven assumed the responsibility for entrusting his legacy to others, he accepted the burdens imposed by popular recognition, and he accepted that he had a duty to pass something on, all of which served one purpose: to free himself from despair, and above all to assure himself of his identity, to confirm his genius. He was doomed to lose his hearing, but before God he could attest to the goodness of his heart and the authenticity of his art. He knew the extent of his talent, and he took the measure of its fate in the isolation imposed by his tragic condition.

To set down in writing an anguished testament is of course consistent with the idea of a genius imbued with a dark and melancholy romanticism, but the example Gould set shows that there are other possibilities: an unstinting rapturous certitude need not always, in its expression, be shot through with gloom; it can on the contrary result in joyous and serene communication. This offering of thanks is key to Gould's genius, I would suggest, and his language is far from melancholy, at least on the surface. Perhaps he fought dejection so fiercely that everything he said was cleansed of it. This all coheres with his knowingly anti-romantic accounts of his interpretations, but the interpretations themselves do not always reflect what he said about them; they are often, on their own, highly lyrical. We should bear in mind, however, that there is no contradiction here between lyricism and strict counterpoint; the one is the fulfilment of the other. The interpreter's goal is serenity, a state of being beyond the pale of romanticism's chaotic melancholy. In general, the pleasure and inventiveness of Gould's playing, his departures from convention, are so powerful, so sharp, and above all so constant – the most striking example being his readings of Mozart's sonatas – that the very idea of time, so married to melancholy, evaporates. His preferred repertoire was far removed from traditional romanticism, and from the great pianistic tradition. When Gould wanted to denigrate an interpretation, starting with his own, he said it was "pianistic." But this does not dispense with the question of romanticism as such, and its unfailing link with lyricism. I shall return to this point in my discussion of Gould's piano playing.

And so our task is to study the convergence between motives and justifications on the one hand and interpretation on the other; and the tension between a model, which exists outside of time, and is so idealized as communicated through his writings, and an interpretation, whose role is to guide us to the same harbour, but is constrained by time and exists apart from language. Through this disconnection, more keenly felt in Gould than is generally thought, we may grasp the relationship between genius as will and genius as an absolute.

This tension is abstract because it corresponds to a transcendent vision of the work that Gould always situated a fair distance from the interpretation itself; it is also fluid and mobile, since each interpretation can be reviewed and radically reconceived; and implicit in this potential for returning to the work again and again there is a polyglotism that puts paid to the very notion of there being one true interpretation for all time. Gould rarely recorded the same work twice, and when he did, for example with the *Goldberg Variations* in 1955 and 1981, at the beginning and the end of his career, he felt compelled to defend in detail the changes he made. There was nothing spontaneous about them, nor did they reflect a natural process of maturation. Rather, they sprang from very considered decisions. The transcendence of the work, to which genius has access, implies an infinite reservoir of meanings that he alone can deploy; it is not a fixed essence, however sublime. And so it is not just the displacement of a convention that is a sign of genius, but also the fact that such changes are hard to pin down, and that this very mutability is a defining factor. We will find little in Gould's writings to confirm this radical theory of interpretation, perceived as the infinite power of genius to construct and deconstruct the work with the same inevitability; but the great majority of his commentaries do move the truth or universality of interpretations along in a constant headlong flight. Gould perhaps hoped that this pursuit of an ever-receding perfection would discredit once and for all the idea of genius with all its objectionable attributes, in particular its unreasonable outbursts, its unfounded ardour, its recalcitrant fervour; in fact it resurfaces as the absent signature for all his, in appearance, anti-romantic work. If the idea of genius plays no essential role in Gould's writings, it is because the romantic view of it makes it unacceptable, and so it is suppressed, along with all the dark embodiments that have traditionally given it expression. It becomes just one more convention whose boundaries can be pushed back and reconfigured by an intelligence seeking another sense of order.

And so our interest in the way music is portrayed shows us a side of genius traditionally kept out of sight; the non-melancholy side of Gould, which manifests itself as much in his aesthetic judgments as in his defence of radical interpretations, and sets itself up in opposition to the romantic definition of genius, associated with power. Gould would have agreed with the criteria proposed by Kant, and above all with the rational endeavour to define the rules that art confers on nature. As Kant said, posting a victory over melancholy is in itself an accomplishment of genius, and it is in the transcendent act of reaching beyond melancholy and the contingency of day-to-day life that Gould's asceticism and mysticism realize their artistic goals. The ecstatic serenity achieved is neither melancholy nor gloomy; it suffers no loss, but attains, on the contrary, to fullness.

This point accentuates the depth – despite its incompleteness and its non-conformist position – of the portrait offered by Thomas Bernhard, a sombre genius, subject himself to melancholy and depression; by choosing Gould as a model, he presents him as both oppressor and liberator. The pianist of genius crushes the mediocre musician, annihilates him; he exposes the immense gap between ourselves and the transcendent, non-romantic otherworld of genius. Virtuosity being murderous, how could we expect from it a surfeit of goodness? But at the same time it frees up new forms of representation, including the art of the narrator, who becomes "a philosophical worldview artist." What makes us all the more susceptible to this hydra-headed phantasm inspired by the Gouldian genius and spread over three separate fictional characters is the fact that Bernhard in his youth was a virtuoso musician, and that all his work is an upward climb through literature in search of a spiritual state worthy of the music of his childhood, freed from bourgeois stupidity, the violence of Nazism, and any shortfall in technical mastery.

In this fictional representation, which we can contrast with Gould's writings, the most compelling idea is that Bernhard's Gould is inhabited by a depression that he has repressed. Bernhard's "depression" contrasts sharply with Gould's serene joy, his assurance, and his confidence in a declared goal that is free, apparently, of all guilt. We need only hear him discussing his work with Bruno Monsaingeon to be persuaded of this. Gould did not believe that his talent destined him to an unending, oppressive isolation, but Bernhard's narrator writes: "When we meet the very best, we have to give up." The meeting in question, imagined by the author, takes place on Monk's Mountain, at a spot called Judge's Peak, and in his symbolic rendering of the Gouldian genius, Bernhard takes care to submit the hermit's ascetic destiny to a dispassionate judgment. To his mind, and at some obscure juncture, melancholy and the struggle against melancholy become one and the same: both are symptomatic of a struggle lost. This paradox deserves clarification, because, it must be emphasized, Gould would in no way have seen himself in this light.

If we return to Gould's genius as revealed in his writings, we will find this same association of asceticism with serene judgment, analytical and assured. Everything is expressed in such a way as to downplay the genius's isolation, keep him in contact with others, strip him of all arrogance; Gould wanted everyone, through him, to draw near to what is sublime in the work, and this heartfelt desire is found everywhere in his writings. That is how I interpret what so many critics reproached in him: his murmurous singing while performing a piece. What is this unsettling song if not a message, a compassionate signal designed to draw in to him those who might risk feeling excluded? Here again we find the young Protestant musician in his local parish, and his association with an imagined community. Gould himself wrote that puritanism tended to view art as "an instrument of salvation," but this communal ethic more than anything else lent his approach its deeply humanist moral vocation. He would explore that concept more fully in his work on isolated communities in the *Solitude Trilogy*. There, his puritanism manifests itself most overtly as an appeal to the community for a shared and elevated discipline. How else to view his admiration for music that carries a moral message and a potential for elevation, music that, through its purity and rationality, has no relation to performance and entertainment? Peace for the community is what such music can provide – a form of serenity where uncontrolled expressivity plays no part; this is the puritan ideal, embodying a desire to contemplate, and a desire to share this contemplation with others.

It would distort my argument to see it as a psychoanalytic exercise portraying puritanism and anti-romanticism as morally rigid. The genius of Gould's interpretations is perfectly consistent with the pragmatic concept of genius as opposed to a romantic one: first comes the absolute mastery of an interpretation imbued with ease and fluidity, and then a power of renewal combined with a perfect command of convention. Where the two dimensions of the Kantian analysis take on a different meaning from that implicit in romanticism, is in the fact that for Gould they bear no relationship to any subterranean or irrational darkness: for him, everything unfolds in the light of day, and the transgression of convention is natural. His idiosyncratic attributes, seen by some as provocative, are secondary, and in no way interfere with the inventiveness of a sensibility guided by its own standards, the most important of these being clarity. In this clarity, which embodies and expresses almost Gould's entire aesthetic, the tormented aspects of the romantic genius are explicitly rebuffed: no trace remains of complacency, simulation, or bogus suffering, and in their stead one finds certitude and sharpness, which Gould will elsewhere represent as an ascetic approach. And so precision grows out of an aesthetic that is anti-romantic from the start. And Gould quite simply spurned that repertoire that was impervious to his asceticism, whose lyricism, for example, was infused with suffering, as in Schubert and Schumann. The fact that lyricism continued to play an important role in the works he favoured is in no way at odds with this practice. Indeed, it resolves the paradox I referred to earlier: the aesthetic of clarity in no way excludes lyricism, and it is Gould's preferred repertoire alone – formal in nature and giving priority to structure – that accounts for his reputation as an "intellectual, cerebral" musician. Had he applied himself to Schubert's *Impromptus*, he would probably have taken the same approach as he took to Beethoven's most romantic sonatas. He would have isolated, sparely, all the structural lines, but he would not have shrunk back from what makes them sing.

Everything in Gould's explanations of his options and his motives militates against romanticism, but what attracts us most in Gould's playing are the hints of muted melancholy that show through an exquisite lyricism accepted on its own terms. We like this restraint, we are sensitive to this resistance to romantic genius, and we set great store by whatever shows it to be trivial, common, even banal. After all, Gould cut his iconoclastic teeth on this terrain. But we would not esteem Gould, as he would not have esteemed Schoenberg, if he had opted to entirely exclude lyricism in favour of dry technique. That is not what we hear when he plays, and it is not what Gould heard when he performed Schoenberg.

Of all the key aspects of Gould's thinking, the most animated were certainly his discussions of the recording process, his with-drawal from the life of a concert pianist, the value of technology, and the importance of the media. These are all pertinent topics whose pertinence was very much of their time. They obscure, how-ever, the demystification of genius that was clearly vital to Gould: his marginalization of the romantic, melancholy artist. What strikes us first in Gould's opting against performance is his deter-mination to trump the melancholy of the concert hall. No music would be more appropriate than that of Bach for such an endeav-our. Later I will speak about the aspects of Bach's music in which this conviction is grounded; already Philip Spitta, in a now classic work, was able to affirm that Bach had purified music of its expres-sive, melodic elements, to return it to a form of chaste austerity. Gould was close to sharing this judgment, which gave priority to form over expression, but he would never have concluded, from his puritan premises, that melody had to be purged. An excessive and purposeless *legato*, yes; what sings, no.

Thus it is that one view of genius, that of Bernhard, comes head to head with another, that of Gould. If the struggle against melan-choly becomes an obsession with melancholy itself – its symptom as well as its source – it is because, for Bernhard, its apparent absence only means that, being unable to transcend it, one cannot admit to it. Bernhard in his approach is fascinated by Gould's example only because he proceeds from a position that is its polar opposite; far from resisting melancholy, he commits to it utterly, steps into it over his head, going so far as to denounce the genius he holds responsible for his despondency. Paradoxically, in the depths of solitude, Bernhard rediscovers a serenity that would appear to be a property of genius alone. That is perhaps the most telling meaning of the novel's enigmatic title, *Der Untergeher*: he who plunges to the depths, he who goes beyond appearances, and not he who is shipwrecked, he who sinks to the bottom. Thomas Bernhard died on February, 12, 1989, and he died in anger: nothing in the anguish that had assailed him since his bastard childhood – his hypocritical education in Vienna, his pulmonary illness, his failure as a musician and an actor – had found consolation in his writing. With time, his derision and cynicism turned against him. One can only imagine an encounter between the writer and the musician, in a world infused with art and morality. I foresee no reconciliation, just perhaps a hand held out in greeting.

All the paradoxes of genius are there in this confrontation between the persona of Gould and European culture. Thomas Bernhard's portrayal very much displeased Gould's friends, and yet he was trying to express something truthful. We can only reconcile these paradoxes if we come to terms with the ways in which Gould's own representations, when set in motion, contributed to them. That is the reason why the entire edifice of justifications and legitimization built up by Gould must be deconstructed, in the very way that Bernhard tried to isolate what lay behind its force. This edifice rightly belongs to the work and its workings, and the very tension inherent in the relationship of a work to its interpretation constitutes an acceptance of art as a vital form of life, a moral and spiritual vantage point. The command of convention, the indisputable existence of an aesthetic inspired by a consideration of genius, can thus be probed by scrutinizing the tension itself. That is my present project.

Is it possible to come to a better understanding of what "to represent" really means? Following on the relationship linking Beethoven's *Testament* to his work, we can seek to understand Gould's intentional representation of his art and of himself as an offering that makes no demands. This expression belongs to Bruno

Monsaingeon, who culled it from the 1974 self-interview; it is very beautiful and very apt. Even the anti-spectacle of Gould's extraordinary pranks and character sketches is entirely free of derision. It is a consistent model of charity and intelligence, always shot through with laughter. Nothing could be further from the world of Thomas Bernhard, for whom contempt was the primary and the strongest form of the sublime. That, paradoxically again, is something that might be said to connect them, on the presumption that one can conceive of a rare and perfect inner life opening out equally on two paired possibilities – on the one hand the desire to elevate, and on the other, derision and the longing to take flight.

The withdrawal that fosters Gould's inner life and the art of representation may in the end be only provisional. When Gould wrote that he had excised from his musical life everything that was not cloistered, this affirmation in no way compromised his desire to give of himself through the most impeccable and the most elevated musical experience he could possibly render: an offering independent of any demand – made, in fact, despite the lack of demand. This attribute, more than any other, is what distinguishes the modern representation of genius from romanticism. For Gould, it is solitude in its purest state that guarantees the greatest sense of community. And so just as one paradox in art, in which interpretation and its explicative representation are pitted against each other, seems to be resolving itself, another appears on the scene in the overlap between isolation and communication. The arguments on which Gould drew in order to justify his retrenchment almost all dealt with the benefits of technology, and we are told they came to him from reading Jean Le Moyne. That is possible. All these technical matters must be approached in a similar way, with the focus on the listener rather than the artist himself. Even if we can speak here of a new "philosophy of music" that grants the technology of reproduction its own creative power, what is truly important is the way the artist and his genius work towards a shared experience.

Gould's endorsement of technology had two advantages. First, it constituted a protection from the concert hall, cosseting the artist's vulnerability, and presenting itself, overall, as a defence. The anonymous studio isolated the genius and sheltered him from the crowd; but in the technical instant itself this solitude opens itself to the world, offering itself in the reproduction of genius. Most of Gould's manic traits, whose outward manifestations belied any hint of melancholy or depression, may be laid at the door of his paradoxical "communication screen," where technology filtered out and repressed the romantic propensities of genius, while seeking modern ways of dissemination and a renewed community.

Thus it was for the editing of Gould's performances. By projecting onto the technological universe his quest for a perfect solitude that was sympathetic to artistic genius, Gould paved the way for a decisive deconstruction of genius in the romantic vein: his discontinuous execution, with the music chopped up, segmented, and re-edited in a succession of collages, was in radical opposition to a virtuosic performance carried out according to a prescribed ritual, on a stage, and within an indivisible time frame. This last repression of romanticism was the most extreme, because it excluded everything in romantic genius that was an impulsive reaction to circumstance, everything that embodied the headstrong present tense and a public presence. In that respect it resembled the aesthetic of Walter Benjamin and Theodor W. Adorno and its attention to the strength of the fragment and the power of parataxis. Juxtaposition outside time became the technique of choice for the new creation, replacing contingent time and projecting genius itself into a timeless realm where nothing romantic remained.

What was striking in the legitimization of this new musical philosophy was not so much the depiction of genius that it sought to uphold – that of the musician as engineer and communicator –

but the way in which it tended to camouflage Gould's inner life, as if to protect it. Here we have another paradox: the will to communicate and the impossibility of communication are one and the same. They are expressions of the same contradiction cultivated in withdrawal, and elicit in the genius an ineradicable tension between what he knows for certain from his own experience, and his resolve to pass that experience on to others – not just to communicate it, because that would be a modern way of bypassing the paradox, but truly to give, to make an offering. I return to Bruno Monsaingeon's formulation: an offering with no prior demand, a generosity that is unconditional and is without expectations.

It is just this paradoxical phenomenon – the very source of Gould's mannerisms – that makes it possible for the suppressed genius to resurface. This is the core of the matter: here we see how art functions as a gift and, in keeping with this generosity, how music evolves as a constant work in progress in an environment that is first a state of availability, a reservoir, and then an archive of the new. No other formulation can account for the distinct quality of Gould's writings, in which he tries both to explain and defend his unconventional options, and to propose a precise experience of art. He seeks a mode of expression independent of any expectations, something that from the outset, given the history of performance, makes him an apostle of rupture and renewal, free of all demands for recognition and special status, all desire for exploits and the spectacular. This approach is truly distinctive, and its tone is so profoundly non-German that we must set it up in opposition to the art of Thomas Bernhard, which is so tragic in its embrace of the impossible. But the *Allemande* of *Partita no. 2 in C Minor*, to which I dedicate this reflection on genius, is suggestive of my argument and my reading of the facts: Gould shouldered his destiny as a genius, but only in an unromantic guise; its tradition, for him, was to be found beyond romanticism, in another Germany – the one that nourished Bach and Schoenberg, and which along with them opposed irrationality and the excesses of temperament. It was also, as it happens, both Christian and Jewish.

Such generosity is abstract, pure. To borrow an idea of Walter Benjamin, it dislodges the aura of here and now in favour of a reality that is unsure, and yet paradoxically more certain. Unsure, because the experience of art loses its definition as a physical encounter in a specific time and place; the experience is deconstructed as an experience and becomes pure representation. The artist no longer plays on demand, he does not give of his genius in response to the invitational strategies of others and, contrary to what defined the romantic concert, he does not propose an emotional experience within a shared time frame. A great admirer of Arthur Schnabel, Gould wanted, like him, to offer a repertoire that was clean and dense, and like him he was prepared to defend it. Like Rosalyn Tureck, whose playing he evoked with such admiration, he aimed for a moral practice of interpretation. Far from the concert hall, the actuality of the experience also appeared more certain, for through the mediation of technology he was assured of a targeted community whose shared search for salvation went beyond particular circumstances. Each individual, alone, in front of his record player, found elevation and sanctification in this new community. With his withdrawal now a precondition for representation, Gould worked at his own annihilation, at his disappearance as a proper name, as is evidenced by his wealth of invented characters, his mocking dismissal of the heroic persona, and above all his earnest wish that each individual might make his own discovery of that beatific light filtered through stained glass windows, and a music that was pure and puritan.

Many signposts point in this direction: his facetious admiration of the Vermeer forger, his character comedies, and especially the many arguments he made in his own defence, always the same in essence, even in his self-interview: it is not me, but the other who is the truth in music. The obsession with clarity, like the constant recourse to a light form of *staccato*, may be correlated with a turning toward the listener that one may interpret in this way: his work seeks a polarity that will associate clarity with equality, or more precisely, a sense of the other. Gould's anti-romanticism emerges in his justificatory texts as being profoundly egalitarian in nature. It alone can overcome the heroic dominance of the virtuoso pianist. That Gould in his youth had romantic tendencies is undeniable; we may cite, for example, his passion for Wagner's *Tristan* or his admiration for certain flamboyant conductors such as Leopold Stokowski. His quasi-veneration for Schoenberg did not, either, exclude the lyricism characteristic of the great Viennese, and when we listen to the superb recording he prepared in 1964–65 of the six *Lieder, Opus 3* with the bass Donald Gramm, we see clearly that the atonal program was not rigid gospel for him. But these preferences were soon overshadowed by a structural and modernist approach to music, which led him to favour works that eschewed emotional dramatics and expressivity in general. In this repertoire the body is not stirred; rather, it recedes from view in the course of enlightenment – a distinguishing feature of this form of expressive lyricism.

In this purging of the personal components of genius, the idiosyncratic compensations have nevertheless garnered the most attention: the withdrawal from the concert hall compensated for by our recollections of the artist humming away on a recording, the departure from the stage compensated for by the television screen. Gould foiled in advance any approach to his work that would characterize it as vulgar aesthetic narcissism; he laid claim, on the contrary, to a higher aesthetic narcissism, one that was profoundly spiritual, and to the reimagining of oneself as a divine being, as he affirmed in the text around which I have organized these variations on the shape of his life. Time and time again he confronted his critics with a character he disavowed completely, a media personage, self-intoxicated, arrogant, provocative. His true position as a creator was, on the contrary, off to the side: in the art of representation that was his, it was the distance he maintained that generated the otherness that to him was essential. Only with a marginal positioning of this sort can genius be experienced with no sense of oppressiveness; it manifests itself quietly, free and self-assured, yet never indifferent to the fate of the community. Teddy Slotz, Myron Chianti, were in the studio with Gould always.

And so one paradox takes the place of another. In this progression there is a movement toward the centre, where we find an assumption implicit in Gould's work throughout his entire life: the prospect of being received, the reality of a welcoming, the certitude of equality. It finds expression in the performance and the interpretation, as well as in the writings. Of all the traits proper to the romantic genius, the one that is the most radically wiped from the slate is arrogance. The work is presented on the same level as it was conceived, as a model and ideal of equality; in its transparency, in its clarity, the approach is profoundly egalitarian. There is no privileged access, no zone of turbulence or mystery kept in reserve, no dark madness as a precondition for genius, no private property. And to say that it is not melancholy is to acknowledge such genius as a pure offering, made with open arms. One has to have seen Gould on television presenting the works of his choice for this to be confirmed, to observe how he was never on parade, how he wanted to lay the work out and offer it to all.

I think we may conclude that in a very real way Gould created an environment where this intention might be made manifest, but that he was reluctant to be more explicit. Where teaching was concerned, he opted out, not by saying that he could not do it, but that he would not. But this refusal was only a minor departure from his intense activity in propagating music through radio, television, and film. Gould gave us all that we might require to grasp the a priori egalitarianism of his approach, one that at first glance might seem to have run counter to the idea of genius.

This creative marginality implies a censuring of competition, of its corrupting power; the will of art is a will to transcend all that is injurious, destructive, sterile. Bernhard's interest in Gould was grounded in this quest for what the artist himself called moral righteousness, and which led to a separation from the world. But seen as puritanism, it maintained its integrity only if not cut off from a generous approach to the community. In fact we find here no rigidity, no contempt, no aridity, since we are dealing with a solitude sought with the gift and with joy in mind. These ideas are pursued metaphorically in Gould's depiction, prominent in his writings, of the Nordic latitudes, the white desert far in the Arctic. Of course, Gould gave these metaphors Ibsenist connotations consistent with his predilection for Sibelius's *Fifth Symphony*, a boreal music evoking Finland's forests, and this leaning gives us some sense of the romantic impulses against which he was struggling. But there is no melancholy in his interpretation of these Northern metaphors; the separation from the world, the monastic reclusiveness, corresponds to a "philosophy in the making," to a spiritual project that is preliminary to the ecstatic experience, the heroic condition. I shall have more to say about this in the context of his important triptych for the radio, his *Solitude Trilogy*.

I come back to the text I have so frequently cited. In 1962, Gould wrote: "Through the ministrations of radio and the phonograph, we are rapidly and quite properly learning to appreciate the elements of aesthetic narcissism – and I use that word in its best sense – and are awakening to the challenge that each man contemplatively create his own divinity." Thus, what he rejected in romantic genius was transformed into an ideal of spiritual egalitarianism in solitude. Gould also wrote that solitude bestows on us the gift of reconciliation. By leaving behind him the asymmetry that characterizes the concert hall, Gould not only broke with one more convention – not only worked to alter his own identity – but also reinforced the equality of those on the receiving end of the interpretation he offered. Such was the meaning of what this modern genius represented; such was the meaning of Gould's "aesthetic narcissism." Just as a book, in its infinite availability, embodies the very idea of egalitarianism, so the recording lends legitimacy to the unfurling of a boundless offering accessible to all, discrediting the illusion that a community was only to be found in a live and continuous performance. The modernity associated with Gould's genius does away with this disparity; it paves the way for an unconventional egalitarian world. Here all paradoxes are reconciled, and we are left with an infinite gift.

It is tempting to go further, since Gould endowed each of these paradoxes with an identical aesthetic theory: art, he said, is a transcendental experience for which we must guarantee the conditions of access. It is neither a game nor a sublimation; nor is it just something else to do, but rather the path to an intuited reality offered to one and all. The seriousness of the stakes is accompanied by a serenity corresponding to an ideal of spiritual perfection. In penetrating to the core of this ideal, I would take special note of how the aesthetic and the ethical are superimposed in determining its expression; this transcendental experience has as its goal a state where all judgment is suspended, or more accurately, suppressed. And so genius sets itself up in a realm where its representation goes beyond the sphere of art.

The mystical sentiments one might anticipate here seem relatively absent from Gould's writings, and the publication of his complete correspondence, which is said to contain a number of Adornian passages, would doubtless help to clarify this point. Still, I would like to give some thought to this desert of judgment – Gould's expression – where the experience of art is made possible. In his 1974 self-interview, he insisted on the need to suspend aesthetic judgment if one hoped to achieve spiritual perfection. This is not unlike the sound deprivation that John Cage saw as renewing music – an environment that is from the outset free of archaic conventions with their unconscious, judgmental incrustations. Beyond judgment, genius offers salvation and deliverance from this unconscious, at last transcended. In projecting the ideal of a subjectivity freed from the weight of judgment, Gould demonstrated the importance of his "impersonations," those imitations of known characters through which he sought to solve the difficulty of asserting, allocating, judging. Some paradoxical judgments may be associated with this purifying stance, such as, for instance, his unconditional partiality to Orlando Gibbons, or his love for Sweelinck's *Fantasia* or his veneration for the music of Jean Sibelius. On a number of occasions Gould gave voice to judgment's operative principle, one that for him was the driving force of aesthetic narcissism: to arrive, by means of differentiation, at a form, however fragile, of identity. Knowledge, he thought, was only possible in relation to the negation of what we are not: "The ability to portray ourselves in terms of those things which are antithetical to our own experience is what allows us not just a mathematical measure of the world in which we live … but also a philosophical measure of ourselves."

We see here into what deeps the paradoxes of genius and its representation have led us: I am what I am not. Musically, this formulation has considerable aesthetic impact: it rules out repetition almost entirely, it puts a damper on expectations, it vindicates the solitude that has made it possible. In his comments on Beethoven's *Opus 2* sonatas, Gould noted the consequences of such an attitude, including the diminished status of the strong sonatas such as the *Appassionata*, and an admiration for the more formal sonatas, such as those of *Opus 2*. I cannot, personally, go along with his verdict on *Sonata no. 29, the Hammerklavier, Opus 106*, which he thought a failure, and yet I understand what led Gould to see it as such, in particular the recapitulation with its classic structure.

In the text he read in June 1964 when receiving a doctorate *honoris causa* from the University of Toronto, "An Argument for Music in the Electronic Age," Gould encapsulated what he was aiming for: "a fantastically varied and subtle range of interpretive insinuation." This expression shows well that the paradoxical representation of modern genius is not animated by a project of reform, but by an ideal of sovereignty. By reform, I mean a perception making the case that something has for a long time been poorly comprehended and that it is time to revise our understanding. Gould's approach to the Brahms *Piano Concerto in D Minor* in a public performance disavowed by Leonard Bernstein because of its slow tempo, a performance that broke completely with the work's traditional interpretation, supports my argument; Gould did not think that the concerto had always been badly played; he only wanted to play it differently, outside of the convention, in that desert where judgment was absent. And so insinuation substitutes itself for judgment, and if one agrees to imbue oneself with an unconventional spiritual aesthetic, one may free oneself from judgment absolutely. Gould did not bar himself from making sharp verdicts, but the way he portrayed his art shows that he always had the opposite in view – the transcendence of judgment; seeking a transcendental experience, he wanted not to reform, but to open out. The *Hammerklavier Sonata*, from this point of view, too easily incorporated repetition; the structure was old-fashioned. For Gould, the long fugue that closed it was manipulative.

All the avenues I have explored invariably lead us to the idea of rapture. To do justice to a non-mystical given – which is to say an aesthetic experience that does not presuppose a supernatural reality, but is mystical "in the sense of Ludwig Wittgenstein or Thomas Bernhard" – we must view it in the context of a number of other elements that we have discussed since the beginning of our journey. On the one hand, rapture is a state proper to one who avoids the paradoxical formulas of modernity. Gould thought this avoidance possible, and he made it a goal worthy of being pursued. In the first broadcast from the series "Music in Our Time," which he called "The Age of Ecstasy," he spoke of the contemplative piece by Karlheinz Stockhausen, *Stimmung*, inviting his listeners to discover in it an inner voice that can shepherd us to the heart of the harmonic structure. The example is here as eloquent as the commentary, in the sense that Gould associated the process of purification and innerness implicit in harmony with a form of contemplation.

All this harked back, for him, to the influence of Schnabel, of Tureck, and even of Wagner. In a 1959 interview with Vincent Tovell, he recounted a childhood memory, when at the age of six he attended a concert conducted by Josef Hofmann. It may be summed up in one word: he was "enchanted." He played the entire orchestra, he became Hofmann. This rare recollection from his early life remained buried, smothered under the whiteness of virgin snows, surfacing only in 1955 when he recorded the *Goldberg Variations* for the first time; the cantilena opening and closing the work was for him like an ecstatic ballet, where all could be understood and recreated. Were not the two recordings of the *Goldberg Variations* the chiastic figure that opened and closed Gould's very life? Between these two cantilenas of enchantment, a life was contained. In reading his writings, one cannot long resist the temptation to transform these cantilenas into the very landscapes onto which Gould superimposed them, the northern solitudes of his Uptergrove countryside. Imprinted on my own memory, in the same northern guise, are his recordings of Bach's *Inventions* and *Partitas*, which enchanted, literally, my entire youth.

The suppression of romantic genius thus coincides with the depiction of another genius, a modern genius to which Gould was committed. What makes him important in our eyes is not that he struck out at all the traditional forces and conventions; that, another could have done in his place. More significant is the fact that in this representation of genius, what was deliberately intended to be set aside makes a return. The paradox of a genius affirming itself in the midst of denial, offering itself where there is no demand, and taking its place beyond judgment in a realm that in practical terms is beyond representation, impels us to inquire into both the author of the interpretation and the source, in the artist, of the representation itself.

One could look upon this phenomenon less generously. If one concentrated only on the idiosyncrasies and other obsessive aspects of Gould's work, on his choice of repertoire, on his desire to control things technically, on his approach to the instrument, one might tend to view this genius as a compensation for depressive traits linked to the inaccessibility of the ideal in art, of the perfect work: to the impossibility of attaining one's goal, of being adequate to it, of prevailing over folly and misfortune. The depiction of genius in terms of its idiosyncrasies could be a way of exaggerating the romanticism of the individual one wanted to discredit. With Gould however, these stagings were pushed so far and were so extravagant that they had the opposite impact – the dissolution of the self. This effect is relative, for we need to maintain the fiction of a person of genius in order to plumb Gould's art, to avail ourselves of its benefits; that in itself is just one more paradox that his genius faced – having to disappear in order to communicate. The more generous interpretation is that which reads into his obsessions not the quest for a singular and original condensation of the self but an authentic desire for retrenchment, a will to make an abstraction of oneself. Idiosyncrasies, from this point of view, do not structure the self; rather, they create a shelter for a destiny that is both spiritual and vulnerable.

In this reading of his genius, Gould provided a kind of pre-scription, conferring on technology the paradoxical task of buttressing solitude, offering a defence against what is malevolent, all the while seeking instruction for this solitude in the realm of communication. Thomas Bernhard set his initiatory contact with Gould at the heart of that paradox, and my encounter with the two of them could have unfolded from there, if that narrative had been amenable to such a point of departure. I began this meditation on genius with a German reference point, but it was a different kind of genius that I really had in my sights, one more serene, one that found in its zeal for equality a way out of the contradictions inherent in romanticism.

## III

*Courante*

# The Hands of Gould, the Body of Glenn

*Partita no. 3 in A Minor*

The mystery in a pianist's hands is their memory; their secret is the spirit that dwells within them. Tactile, physical, deeply material, this memory is a key factor in childhood exercises that bring fingers into contact with a keyboard for the first time, and in the end it is inseparable from the piano playing for which it is a constituent element. The pianist's art is the material memory of his style, and this memory provides access to a music that is non-material and self-sufficient. But the memory is also non-material, because it can just as easily hear nothing physically and respond only to what is written down. The hands recognize the keyboard without the eye needing to guide them, and at times without the ear even hearing the music it generates; imbued with the rhythm and the writing, the hands can work away in silence. We see teachers assigning exercises on mute keyboards and we see others who, to train the fingers, recommend practising on flat keyboards, where the position of the white and black keys is only indicated, without their yielding to the touch.

Fingers exercised in this way feel neither pressure nor traction, they simply repeat the abstract movements of a score. By incorporating the writing, they reproduce the itinerary of the score. The hands are only the most visible and complex component of a system that sets in motion the elbows, the shoulders, the entire body. Pianists who work assiduously at their fingering labour to apply it to the score, but performance memory involves much more than a decision to employ the index or the middle finger. The strength or lightness of touch is a response to the score's demands, and every pianist knows that his art depends on a bodily comportment that cannot be reinvented or reconceived each time; this attention to the body creates memory, the memory of art itself in its encounter with the work. It is in the body, it is outside the body. Hands and memory, the pianist's conundrum.

Glenn Gould liked to say that the music he played had a life that was independent and non-material. It existed, as it were, without his hands, on which he nevertheless lavished the most intense and exhaustive care and training imaginable. This was by no means the only paradox to be found in his thinking, but it was a persistent one, and very concrete; he claimed never to play a piece on the piano without having first memorized it completely. He even said that he could play and rehearse a piece without touching the keyboard. He memorized it by playing it with his hands, but mentally. It is difficult to understand how the memory of a work can be created without any tactile relationship having been established, if we do not acknowledge, like Gould, that music is above all a mental and spiritual entity, and that it is closer to a mathematical theorem than to the body in action, than to hands in contact with the instrument. All his life he referred to this mental image as the necessary precondition for his work, and when in 1977–78 he experienced a crisis he thought was fatal to his art, it was that capacity that he feared he had lost. He spoke often, in fact, of the need for a non-material image of music, a "non-tactile experience." He suggested that the best way to achieve this was to distance oneself from the instrument and to favour a purely analytical grasp of the work. Playing, he liked to remind us, is always a compromise, and even though this compromise seems inescapable – because one always wants to hear something aloud – one can lessen its impact by seeking to draw closer to a music that is ideal and transcendent. His memory for music was prodigious, as Bruno Monsaingeon confirmed. After a recording session with Gould, as they were returning home by car, they heard a string quartet on the radio. While listening, they tried unsuccessfully to identify it. The announcer informed them that it was Mendelssohn's *Quartet in F Minor*. The next morning, from memory, Gould played the entire movement they had heard in the car on the piano.

How to comprehend this closeness of music to thought? Not all music, of course, makes the same demands on the body, and when still young and studying with his teacher, Alberto Guerrero, Gould learned to favour the repertoire widely regarded as "intellectual." It was this great educator who taught him to know and love the music of Schoenberg, not to mention encouraging his predilection for Bach. Cerebral in nature, this music boasted the structure, the architecture, the musical lines that correspond to mental and spiritual phenomena. From there to declaring, as Gould did at the end of his life, that one does not play with one's hands but with one's mind, is not a great leap. Nevertheless, the question of the body remains something of a mystery, and no one would go so far as to claim that an intellectual repertoire is less likely to be inscribed in the body; even a simple song-like melodic line will make the body gently rock and sway, generating that twisting action that creates tension between what is lower and higher. On the other hand, the body's response to the very special lyricism associated with the contrapuntal repertoire and its quest for an elevated state, while being perfectly evident in all the filmed records of Gould, and quasi-perceptible even to the ear, is none the less ineffable, and his curling into a position both contracted and freed is something difficult to describe.

This intellectual aesthetic, akin to a form of sublime Platonism, led Gould to some extreme conclusions: the existence of a work is not only independent of the artist's body, but ultimately it doesn't matter if it is never played, as long as one can have access to it by other means. Can the pianist then truly play without his hands, with his mind alone? All who have heard Gould without seeing him know that his playing was unique in a number of ways, most related to this aesthetic of isolation and abstraction. It is best described, I believe, as an analytical aesthetic that gives priority to the clarity of every voice. Clarity, a precise line, and contrapuntal transparency command an attention that generates a style, and this style in turn dictates a repertoire that favours Bach and the English virginalists over classical and romantic works. One might almost say that Gould very early on chose music of the mind over music of the body, and that he never afterward wavered. This is confirmed by his childhood friend Robert Fulford, who notes that, for Gould, music became less and less material. "In Glenn's mind, music was becoming refined and bodiless, almost entirely separated from the physical. Sometimes he spoke of music as if it existed in some distant and abstract sphere, beyond physicality."

There is, however, something too facile in this picture; it is both true and inadequate. True where the aesthetic is concerned, to the degree that the principles of counterpoint are based on a theological doctrine of universal harmony to which music gives access; musical forms are in fact immaterial forms and, as Kant insisted in his *Critique of Judgment*, they alone may be judged beautiful. Material sound may be pleasant, but it is only beautiful if it is informed by the intelligible meaning and the structure that are the essence of art. This idea is not to be taken for granted; all music theorists have their own perspective on the notion of pure music, independent of sound. Is to describe music to understand it? And what sort of understanding is required to experience the pleasure of music? We have only to read the work of Peter Kivy to measure the complexity of what is at stake, but Gould seems not to have concerned himself with philosophical debates in which his cut and dried opinions might have involved him. He knew the history of counterpoint and its religious origins, certainly, but he never discussed the principles of his aesthetic, and would not have appreciated any philosophical opposition.

Still, this picture falls short where the playing itself is concerned. If we can say that Gould did not play with his hands but with his mind, and that his music derived from a firmly held idealism, we need only look at his many performances preserved on film to see something else. In the filmed records of his concerts, or in the many sessions with Bruno Monsaingeon, what we see is a body that is not just the simple, mechanical conveyor of thought, but a body at work, a body in action, a body absorbed in its art.

To describe this body is to grasp at an inner rapture and a voice that sings, an ecstasy in plain view, a voice that makes itself heard and exposes what is hidden in song. If we could not see this body, or even hear the voice that Gould refused to suppress – even in the recordings where he might have asked for it to be done, for in concert he could not do so – would we have the same perception of his playing, would we know as surely what he chose to play and to offer as an interpreter? This obsessive question is not meant just for him. In choosing a seat in a concert hall we want to be able to see the artist's performance; we want to see his hands, we want to see his body in relationship to the instrument, we want to see the artist. What would we say, for example, if the concert were given behind a screen that hid the performers? We would then be in a position to free our listening experience from visual distractions, but would we not lose something? According to Gould we would lose nothing, since that is what we do, after all, when we listen to recordings. But is he right? Another approach to this question involves images: why do they seem so important to us if they have no place in the process of understanding music's rapturous power over the body? How does music move us, and what is the body's role in that? What does it express when it rises up as if it wanted to leave itself behind and escape gravity?

In abandoning the concert hall, Glenn Gould wanted to hide his hands, and his whole body, from view. The reasons for this decision were very complex, from the need to escape the competitive world that turns the artist into a circus animal, to the desire to involve himself technically in his interpretations through his work in the studio. But one of the paradoxical effects of this decision was to bring Gould before television and film cameras and, while the concert hall had restricted him to a very limited public, to generously replicate his image. And so Gould withdrew his hands and his body, no longer offering them to the direct view of the public, but he gave them back through the intercession of the camera. Whether we look at Bruno Monsaingeon's admirable 1981 film, shot just before Gould's death, on Gould's performance of the *Goldberg Variations*, or his later work, *Glenn Gould: Hereafter*, in which he brought together a number of unreleased sequences, most notably a piece of Brahms that gives us access to a very rare expression of emotion, the conclusion is the same: Gould's hands, all the workings of his body, are not extraneous to what we hear; they make something heard while giving it to us to see. There have been critics, like François Delalande, who tried to interpret these gestures systematically; to give only one example, we often see Gould marking the beat with his left hand when the music is being played with the right. I don't know how far one can go in that direction, as there is always a good distance between the expressivity of the playing and the work at hand on the keyboard. But if we were deprived of this uncommon intensity coursing through the body, we would be denied a privileged access to the music as it is being played.

Why? In the first place there is an impact on our own bodies, which want to reproduce this movement while taking it in. More precisely, our bodies want instinctively to reproduce this movement in order to gain access to the same state of thought and feeling, the same sense of wonder. Here again, we find ourselves on the threshold of one of musical aesthetics' most lively philosophical debates: that which pits the partisans of knowledge against those of feeling. If music seems sad, is it because it stimulates that emotion in us, or because it possesses a formal property that is identifiable? Jean-Jacques Nattiez, with more clarity than others, has set out the conundrums of meaning and expression in music. He has also proposed a synthesis of Gould's aesthetic that lends importance to the question of temporality and the priority he accords structure. It has often been written that Gould's playing was beholden to structure first and foremost, to the detriment of expression. This way of viewing things stresses the precedence given to musical form and the contrapuntal balancing of voices at the expense of other aspects of music such as texture, but it unjustly leaves in the shadows, and as it were hidden behind a veil, the expressiveness sensed and felt in and by the body. For a theoretician these two levels are superimposed: what one feels while listening to a work as beautiful as the *Goldberg Variations* may be described in the first instance as a primary emotion intrinsic to the sound, but it will be better understood if it incorporates a knowledge of form and the intelligible beauty of counterpoint, as perceived in the unfolding of the lines and the balancing of the voices. I will not venture further into this aesthetic terrain; I want only to show how all of Gould's work inhabits it in a most direct way.

And so the paradox of Gould's thinking about music and the body is reflected in his decision to reduce his visibility by walking away from the concert hall, only to magnify it later in the filmed image. The picture of Gould seated on his famous little chair, low and rickety, forced into a tilting of his elbows and shoulders such as to almost bisect the line of his neck, is only the best known of all those available to us today. The chair had been built for him by his father, and even when it became uncomfortable, he did not want to be separated from it. It was part of his myth, like the Steinway CD 318, to which Katie Hafner has devoted an entire book. If we look at the photographs taken by his friend Jock Carroll when he was only twenty-three years old, we see the shift in his posture over time. It was like a protective embrace, whose main feature was the coiling inward, the refusal to be dominated. In this posture, the curvature of the back stood for everything in the body's movement that resisted a glorious elevation, a pure élan that would propel one upward. Gould at the piano was never triumphant; a conquering brio was not for him. Nothing was more foreign to him than Horowitz's body language, forever poised for the moment when he would bound up to acknowledge the thundering applause of his exuberant fans. Gould's body at the keyboard seemed to shrink inward with each bar and to anticipate, on the contrary, an infinite silence. He leaned over the keyboard with a kind of meticulous and exaggerated concern, his bent knees held at a striking angle; his face almost touched the keyboard, and one was left with the impression of an effort so concentrated that the rest of the body, the shoulders and torso in particular, were interfering with the hands and the face. Kevin Bazzana compared this posture to a fetal position, going so far as to affirm that Gould recaptured, in his contact with the instrument, a kind of uterine security, cherished ever since those hours when he worked at the instrument on his mother's lap. Gould was not yet born when Florence Greig Gould first exposed him to music. At the age of three he was at the piano, and it is said that he knew how to read a score before he could even decode the pages of a book. All of

*Goldberg Variations,* going over the entire piece in this abstract manner before its actual execution.

Persuaded that pianistic power originated mainly in the back and not in the arms and shoulders, Gould's teacher wanted to free him from tension in his arms. It is said that he applied strong pressure to his pupils' shoulders as they played, forcing them to resist by tensing their back muscles. Gould described, in his 1977–78 diary, to which I will later return, how he viewed the complex system that linked his limbs to his back. But he never questioned the theories – shall we call them physio-mechanical? – that he had inherited from his teacher, and which most certainly played a key role in the onset of the muscular problems that plagued him over the years. Gould was even drawn to elaborate physiotherapies based on ultrasound, despite the doubts expressed by his friend, the doctor Peter Ostwald, who refers to them in his memoirs. Such complex technology could only have consequences, but Gould seemed not to fear them. The idea of dipping his hands in hot water before playing is more ordinary. It seems also to have been the brainchild of his singular teacher, although the strategy is not that surprising for a pianist seeking a light touch, and who has had exquisite technique from a very young age.

We could doubtless hold these technical excesses responsible for everything in Gould's adult life that seems to have resulted from them, but that would be to ignore the many problems, some real, some imaginary, that compromised his health over the years. Here again we encounter a difficult paradox: for the artist, the body was a docile and perfectly mastered instrument, and the quality of the work right to the end seems to bear this out – and so this docility was priceless; for the man, this same body was a source of unspeakable suffering and constant torment, as is shown in the 1977–78 diary he kept while nursing his hands and his entire body in an attempt to recover the power and discipline he thought he had lost. His hands, especially, were for him a site of chronic pain. He almost always wore gloves, and his biographers were quick to blame all his pianistic idiosyncrasies on a hypochondria that played havoc with his daily life.

There is no point in delving into every aspect of Gould's rapport with his body, other than to insist that many of his "medical" problems were in no way imaginary. A serious back injury, incurred at the age of ten when he was launching the family boat on Lake Simcoe with his father, seems to have affected his spinal column, and all the doctors who treated him confirmed the pernicious effects of this accident. But was this youthful injury responsible for everything? Can it explain all of Gould's complaints? The incident doubtless inspired his self-created image of the body's perfection, of its indispensable docility, while at the same time exposing the fragility of what was for him, from a young age, a pure instrument and one he treated as such. It reinforced the idea that Gould was not his body, that he was, as it were, external to it, and could resist its resolve.

But Gould thought he knew this body well. He would itemize all his symptoms, and especially their diagnoses, in the most obsessive and objective way, drawing on the medical terminology he systematically acquired. His crisis of 1977–78, provoked in the first instance by his fear of losing control of his technique, represents the most painful episode of that kind. But he did suffer from hypochondria, almost from the very beginning. In a letter to his impresario, Walter Homburger, dated October 18, 1958, when he had just cancelled all his concerts for that month because of a persistent cold, and when he had taken refuge in a Hamburg hotel that he compared to the sanatorium in Thomas Mann's *The Magic Mountain*, he described the disturbing results of a chest X-ray, and reported a significant loss of weight. To read all the letters from this period, particularly those appended to his 1977–78 diary in the edition prepared by Bruno Monsaingeon, is to make oneself dizzy: Gould could describe in great detail complex pathologies, all of which, if we were to take his word, were playing a role in dramatic scenarios that would end badly. If we except the tour of Israel in this same year of 1958, the succeeding months found him almost always depressed and in pain, and it is hard not to think that it was the very life he was leading that made him so fragile. Whatever the source of this vulnerability, it was totally real, and we may regret that the accretion of such episodes was not taken more seriously by those who should have been able to foresee their later gravity. Or had they perhaps too easily given up on trying to convince Gould not to try and heal himself? His primary physiotherapist in Toronto, the chiropractor Herbert J. Vear, provided an overview of his symptoms, and showed how they had become chronic, especially around the neck and the shoulders. He blamed first and foremost Gould's posture at the instrument, but he perhaps neglected to look at his body in the wider context of the life he had lived.

Gould had a congenital fear of illness, and he seemed always to be living at close quarters with an organism in peril. He suffered from hypertension, but this problem seems to have been rapidly dealt with. That did not stop him from portraying himself as someone with chronic circulatory problems. His medical notes, in particular those he wrote before a consultation, are obsessive to the point of panic, and his hysterical relationship to his body seems to have set in very early. His biographers all make a point of his unhealthy fear of germs, which not only drove him to use all sorts of cleaning products, often toxic, such as Lysol, but also had him fleeing the company of people with an ordinary cold. Should this exaggerated hypochondria be held responsible for his bad posture, and more generally, for his uneasiness with others? Shaking hands was a painful experience for him, but as I will try to show further on, there were other reasons, also chronic, for the hard time he had living in a body and mastering day-to-day life, even as that body became over time such a perfect servant of art and its aspirations. Here Gould harboured such a confounding attitude that we might almost regret never having been able to confront him with it: when we list all those he consulted for medical care, we can't help being astounded at the range and variety of medical resources he felt he needed. Often, of course, he played one off against the other, hoarding prescriptions and thinking himself able to judge their compatibility and measure their side effects. But when we stop to consider the benefits he derived from all this, it would appear that he never found anywhere the serenity and well-being he craved. He considered himself the best qualified to know what he needed, and his biographers who catalogued his experiments have brought to light truly dangerous episodes, such as the acquisition of a diathermy apparatus that generated heat for the muscles with an electric charge. What would have done him the most good was a yoga master who might have persuaded him to adopt a healthy posture and to perform daily breathing and balance exercises. Instead, exasperated physiatrists and orthopaedists prescribed him anti-inflammatory medication such as *Indocid* (indomethacine), *Naprosyn* (naproxene) and phenylbutazone, in increasingly powerful doses, to the point that he thought himself afflicted with a severe arthritic pathology, and intoxicated himself by piling on his drugs. It remains that all the prescriptions he thought necessary to administer were prescribed for him by doctors. Like others, I have compiled the list of all these medicines, their commercial names, and their chemical composition; in its length and its sophistication it is a tragi-comic rhapsody that would fill several pages.

Gould manipulated this medical symptomatology with a sort of disabused fatalism, as if he were doomed to a medical destiny that would be his alone: nephritis, aponeuritis, fibrositis, none of the syndromes was dramatic enough to fulfill the role he demanded of it, to make it clear to the body that it was cursed. Doctors, as is well known, do not like patients who flaunt too much knowledge, but Gould, alas, fell into this exasperating category, and even his friend Peter Ostwald could not instil in him a calmer, more positive attitude. If his symptoms had been more severe, then he would have had the proof he sought that his body loomed as a powerful obstacle to his pursuit of genius. A real cancer might have saved him; he would at last have been able to define his illness, to seek repose for a time, like Hans Castorp on his mountain, and stop imagining that he was being invaded on all sides by aggressive pathogens. Instead, Gould multiplied his imaginary and catastrophic diagnoses, he continued to live an unhealthy life, he persisted in reinterpreting his personal history to show that he had in his youth suffered traumas so severe that his entire physical makeup had been irremediably damaged, and he fashioned descriptions, astonishing in their precision and their intensity, of his many afflictions. In short, he furnished himself with all the justifications he needed to continue on in the same direction, the worst possible.

One episode in this complex odyssey deserves special attention. Early in 1950, Gould found himself on Lake Simcoe. Incautious perhaps, he was walking on a part of the lake where the ice had not adequately hardened. He fell into the lake's cold waters, and was seriously frozen. I do not know when he recounted the incident, reported by Kevin Bazzana, but it has left me with a lasting and painful impression, even if I know little about the circumstances; I cannot help noting that Gould chose as his preferred picture of himself a photograph by Don Hunstein taken in January, 1970, in which we see him advancing over the frozen surface of a lake. He, who complained so often of the cold and so dreaded any chill that he bundled himself up summer and winter, would have experienced on that distant day an hour of terrifying distress that remained with him forever after, and that he could only exorcise through a protective image: his coat, his famous cap, his gloves.

His brutal end, when he was carried off by a cerebral haemorrhage, gave him no opportunity to elaborate further, but we cannot but feel that the tragic death lurking for a very long time in his blood vessels might have been avoided. The very idea of taking some good advice and adopting a healthier life style, not to speak of putting an end to his self-diagnoses and the concoction of his own pharmacopeia, seems never to have occurred to him. There is no reason to doubt that he suffered greatly; an inventory of all his symptoms, not to mention his complicated relationships with doctors and physiotherapists up to the very end of his life, would fill a book. The question is rather: why, where the life of the body was concerned, was his attitude so Manichaean, and so incoherent? Why was the very idea of health so unimportant to him, so secondary and so trivial? How to explain that he embarked on a downward spiral of sedatives, anti-inflammatories, and even barbiturates such as *Nembutal*, without taking into consideration the long-term effects? And yet his notes, filled with endless lists of medications and dosages, sounded the alarm loud and clear.

✍

Glenn Gould's body was physically linked to his instrument. On the Chickering piano of his youth, or later on the Steinway of his choice, the famous CD 318, Gould never stopped seeking the perfect touch – not only an adjustment of the fingers to a percussive mechanism, but an ideal continuity in the articulation and repetition of his keystrokes. Is there a contradiction between this quest and his professed idealism? Whatever he said about the remoteness of the musical idea, or the discrete identity of the work, Gould the pianist remained all his life technically married to his keyboard. He certainly thought that the work of his hands – indeed, his entire body – was beholden to what was ideal in music, but he also gave himself over completely to a physical exploration that would make him one with his instrument. The story of CD 318, like that of his chair, runs through most of Gould's life, and like the life, the instrument was the focus of an obsessive and quasi-medical concern for perfection. Gould talked about the mechanics of this piano as he talked about his own body. He recounted its mishaps – in particular its famously being dropped in 1971 while in transit, resulting in trauma reminiscent of his own in that youthful accident – and he described in detail its care and, dare one say, its physiotherapy, as administered by Verne Edquist, his technician. Almost to his death, Gould identified himself with the life of the CD 318, and he only replaced it when he no longer had any choice, when he was forced to admit that its time had passed. Could he have sensed that like this worn-out instrument, spent after so many displacements and mechanical interventions, he himself was nearing the end, and that it was time to loosen the bonds and let himself go? It was probably too late. His last records were recorded on a Yamaha, in particular the second version of the *Goldberg Variations*, but his ties to the instrument had lost their intensity.

In the pictures of him that are left to us, we see reflected again and again what he said in the passage to which I am continually drawn back, concerning the ultimate goal of the artist's work: how can the body involve itself in this infinite process, in this "gradual, lifelong construction of a state of wonder and serenity"? This little phrase, always the same, merits long and careful consideration, especially where it applies to the body, given its pertinence to Gould's keyboard aesthetic and his commitment to detachment. As his choice of repertoire makes obvious, Gould's playing was deeply involved in this quest for the ideal associated with contrapuntal perfection, but it was also a labour of the body seeking a form of dissociation, a goal beyond the nature of beauty itself. Wonder and serenity are not emotions per se, but attitudes, moral stances, forms of wisdom that all philosophy from Kant to Heidegger has tried to express in harmony with ethical ideals. The artist who chooses to give them pride of place in his art seeks not only the material perfection of his creation but also, and above all, the soul's perfection – beauty inwardly manifest.

I will talk later of how Gould found confirmation of this aesthetic in the work of Natsume Sōseki, but just seeing him at his instrument already gives us a sense of the depths to be plumbed. Gould's playing reveals him often, as I have said, in a state of inner transport, of a rapture bearing him away to another realm, remote from the world's contingencies. In that world his body is transformed, his hands and arms the embodiment of this rapture. The gaze is turned inward, the eyes are closed, and his fusion with the instrument is absolute. At times, and without our being able really to foresee it, Gould joins in, his singing voice soft, murmurous, but audible. All this behaviour is there from his very first concerts, and critics noted it with a mixture of admiration and irritation, as though these last traces of the body ought without question to be expunged. But who could – who would dare – differentiate those mannerisms and idiosyncrasies from the body's rapture under the spell of the music? Here too, Gould was the transgressor, for he revealed, by going far beyond it, how unbearably bourgeois the body's expressiveness was as manifested in the concert hall.

This intensity was not overtly emotional, because the repertoire more or less excluded that, a priori. Though emotion may be generated by the work, it cannot constitute its declared objective. By favouring works whose archetype was *The Well-Tempered Clavier* or *The Art of Fugue*, Gould set up a kind of symmetry between the perfect clarity of his keyboard technique and contrapuntal music. Only the coincidence of these two could create the conditions for that sense of wonder – otherwise something else would be at work. In the many instances where he discussed the nature of counterpoint and the fugue, he sought to shed light on what lay behind this coincidence, not so much in terms of a linear history of music, but rather with an insistence on the fundamental discipline of counterpoint. He certainly was familiar with the religious and philosophical background that led Bach's predecessors, Buxtehude and Kuhnau, whom Bach succeeded at Leipzig, to adopt a doctrine that viewed counterpoint as anything but just an exercise. Far from being an abstract or empty form, counterpoint was an art abounding in meaning, whose secret ambition was to reveal in tangible form the universal laws of harmony, the rules of the universe. Contrapuntal art is cosmological as much as it is spiritual or ethical. Those who study its genesis today, such as David Yearsley, for example, are reviving a belief widely held in a time that expected much more from music than just court entertainment. By studying, for example, the last choral fugue composed by Bach, an incomplete fragment, we see how his entire work was rooted in this contemplative tradition, notably in music designed to come to terms with death. *Cantata 106, Gottes Zeit ist die allerbeste Zeit, Actus Tragicus*, or *Cantata 54, Wiederstehe doch der Sünde*, which Gould presented on more than one occasion – notably in 1961 with the mezzo-soprano Frances Bible and in 1962 with the counter-tenor Russell Oberlin, and which he hoped to hear sung by Barbra Streisand – belong to this spiritual world where all music participates in the divine concert of the cosmos. Gould knew all of that; he had absorbed it during his Protestant childhood, he was aware of the importance of prayer, and he knew above all that Bach's sense of community could only be recaptured through a personal commitment to contemplation.

He explained all this in a number of essays, in particular in the text for the CBC broadcast of January 25, 1962, devoted to Bach. Discussing the advent of musical architecture in Bach's time, he insisted that the Cantor's primary preoccupation was spiritual: "Essentially, for Bach, art was a means of expressing that state of belief in which experiences could be natively guided, in which only the obstructions and temptations of the world could thwart the immutable totality of existence, in which, however,

almost last, at the end of a long history of keyboard instruments. In Gould's 1960 review of a study by Erwin Bodky of Bach's keyboard music, he does not hesitate to take the writer to task for an exaggerated interest in the melodic to the detriment of the more formal features, and he insists on the ascendancy of harmony:

> For Bach's counterpoint is harmonically centered counterpoint, and there is no aspect of Bach's style which is not ultimately mediated by harmonic considerations. The registration of his dynamic terraces, the dissonant twang of his ornamentation, the articulation of contrasting rhythmic figures – all are controlled by the steady pulse of harmonic movement.

It is this position, argued clearly and at length, that grounds Gould's approach in his playing. It shows why he preferred the piano to all its ancestors; only the piano can give us access to this pulsation in tonal harmony, the structural foundation of movement as universally conceived.

Such a judgment ought not to surprise us, as it is based on a historical analysis that Gould used to illustrate the slow process whereby the human body discovered in the musical instrument a form ever more complex, yet also increasingly akin to itself. Blowing into a bone flute made melody possible, and the instrument became an extension of breath and the voice; wind instruments are related to the materiality of song deriving from their recourse to breath – they are the first musical witnesses to life. Drumming on an animal skin allows us to express rhythms and intensities, and here the link to the body is different: by stimulating rhythm, percussion instruments accentuate the body's desire to pound the earth and free up all forms of dance. Strings represent an initial mediation, which places them some distance from the body's primitive gestures; with the strings, the body takes a step backward and entrusts the instrument with the responsibility for expression. Keyboard instruments have none of these direct links to materiality, but they have an advantage: only the keyboard in its perfect conformity to the structure of the two hands allows for the complete expression of polyphony. One need only observe the rhythmic movement of fingers striking and keys being depressed to appreciate the nature of the material adjustment involved in counterpoint and the workings of hands on the keyboard. One might even wonder how the octave scale, full-blown in musical theory before the invention of the keyboard, could have had the keyboard organized any other way than according to the principle of the five fingers. As to the history of equal temperament, it would also bear analysis from the point of view of the instrument.

When Glenn Gould said he wanted to distance himself as far as possible from his instrument, he was reinforcing yet another paradox: the more one's hands are adjusted to the keyboard in the practice of rhythm and polyphony, the more the line of the music is detached from its material incarnation, and the more it goes beyond its sound. This is how Gould conceived of the pianist's art – as an art that through its complete material engagement with the keyboard, succeeded in transcending it completely. He went so far as to write: "Part of the secret in playing the piano is to separate yourself from the instrument in every possible way." In the last analysis the instrument is but the extension of the hands, and like them it is at the service of the abstract score, of the musical line expressed in the purity of the writing. Gould never laid claim to a purely pianistic aesthetic based on the specific expressivity of the instrument. On the contrary, he thought that the resources of the piano were largely inconsequential in relation to what one might demand in the way of perfection from music written for the keyboard, which is the absolute beauty of a line developed in a contrapuntal motif. On one condition, however: that everything be utterly clear. One might legitimately ask what it was he heard when he played, since for him this detached perfection resided in a kind of absolute silence, in a serene contemplation accessible only through the form. But whatever he heard – and he certainly heard something – was transmitted to him by the rhythmic percussion of his two hands. In other words, what he heard was not a specific sound, but a distinct action.

This approach perhaps explains his choice of instruments of "translucent" sonority. He praised his old Steinway CD 318 by invoking its precise articulation and he referred to the piano of his childhood as an instrument offering a direct "tactile" purchase. The character of his playing confirms this preference for clear and precise instruments capable of sustaining a clarity of line, revealing the tonal structure, doing justice to the harmonic treatment. We can, however, go farther by suggesting, along with those who have studied his playing most carefully, that Gould always tried to reproduce an imaginary orchestral sound, so much did counterpoint strike him as the natural form for all music. It had to consist of voices, each one identified with a particular instrument. We see him, for example, in a film by Bruno Monsaingeon on musical interpretation, *The Question of Instrument* (1979), outlining the choices available to an interpreter of Bach by comparing the different voices to the workings of strings, as if their tonal quality could be deduced from the polyphonic writing. It has even been suggested that his interpretation of the *Goldberg Variations* was based on an analogical reading that identified the work with a string quartet. This instrumental analogy would not be of such great interest had Gould not chosen to present it in the context of a performance style that was monochrome and, as Kevin Bazzana put it, almost always "black and white" – totally absorbed, it seems, in the work of the hands and indifferent to the sound produced. The movement of the fingers on the keyboard remains, of course, responsible for the intensity of the percussion, and all these aspects of his playing have been studied, but nothing seems closer to his musical ideal than the working together of the hands in the service of counterpoint.

A pianist's hands can draw on the following powers: articulation, phrasing, a forceful or gentle percussiveness, the ability to press down or hold back, to go faster or slower, but none of these actions dominate the playing as much as the capacity to separate, to isolate, to orchestrate in time the various elements of what has been written. Counterpoint is a developmental technique that favours connection and progression, and its beauty derives not only from its quasi-metaphysical relationship with temporality but also, and above all, from the fact that it alone can transform pure temporality into song. All of Gould's art was grounded in this equilibrium, whereby the complementarity of the hands, identified with the voices, succeeds in supporting the writing of counterpoint while at the same time exposing it. Gould was never indifferent to musical expression, but the more his work deepened the purer it became, and if we listen, for example, to the recordings of Bach's *Partitas*, we see that with the passing of time he took the risk of playing, as it were, with naked hands, that is without bringing anything else to his playing but the work of his hands. He increasingly reduced the use of the pedal, which put more emphasis on the melodic line and on the voices. This approach coincided with his distancing himself more and more from the romantic repertoire. The beauty of the song was enough in itself; it had no need for any additional sonic artifices.

Returning to those pictures of Gould at the keyboard, we find ourselves sharing in what his devotion to art bestowed on him: his body in a state of transport, his hands deployed unnaturally over the keyboard, his face transformed, all inseparable from his interpretive style. In his seemingly tortured body, contorted through long practice into its awkward posture, we may trace the history of a discipline and the traumatic impact it has had, but what we hear is a harmony that belies this suffering. We consent to our own rapture, knowing that the music's emotion is non-material but that it courses through the body nevertheless, and that it can require of the interpreter a mastery that is more than just musical. The care Gould lavished on his hands and his body, his fear of cold as well as of physical contact, his conflict with the Steinway technician who gave him a friendly tap on the shoulder that he claimed would destroy his ability to play forever – an episode that goes far beyond the question of performance, and to which we will return – all these elements transcend the anecdotal and bring us to something else: behind the rapture there is a fear of loss and an anguish at the prospect of the void. Despite its immateriality and timelessness, the perfection of counterpoint must be heard: it is not given to everyone to read harmony like Gottfried W. Leibniz or Johann Mattheson, who communed with scores and felt no need for the instrument.

I do not believe that Gould went that far, whatever he said about the need to maintain a distance from the keyboard. He knew what a sensitive interpretation demanded; he had made it his life's work. Early on, he had become conscious of his genius, and he had had to accustom himself to a life that was out of the ordinary, that bore with it solitude and phobias of all sorts. For an ordinary man, hands are only hands; he is not afraid of their being hurt at any moment. For a pianist of genius, his hands are at once the repository of his memory and the material connection with the music of the keyboard, and through it, with the spiritual incarnation of harmony. And so it was not surprising to see the young Gould starting to suffer from pain and tension in his arms and shoulders, and becoming a chronic consumer of medications; even though he recognized the immateriality of music, and despite the fact that he was granted the gift of being able to hear a work without playing it, and that he was endowed, to his very fingertips, with perfect pitch, he was prone to all the afflictions, all the losses that affect those whose art depends on their body. That explains why, in the long run, Gould chose a life in which the work of refining interpretation could go on, autonomous, far from the concert hall; the act of imparting an interpretation to a recording, seeking perfection there, delivered him from the ordeal of imperfection and loss inherent in a performance before an audience in the fragile environment of an auditorium. There is no comparing pianists to writers – their hands attest to this – but Gould showed how vulnerabilities could be overcome for all.

The aches and pains that affected Gould's playing were all too real, and he kept a record of the serious crises that had interfered with his quest for perfection since his youth. He was probably the only one aware of this threat, because nothing of what was recorded on disc or on film points in that direction. But as of 1977 he kept a diary to which he imparted, anxiously, his observations. Bruno Monsaingeon, who undertook their transcription and translation, has drawn attention to the gap between Gould's painful perception of losing his powers and the apparent serenity of his playing, which he maintained right to the end. Reading this diary, which runs from September 1977 to July 1978, is an ordeal, and the account he gives of working on himself is doubtless truly accessible only to artists who have lived through such crises, and, to overcome them, have made similar ascetic choices. We find here, in particular, expressions so coded that it seems impossible to deduce from them a precise medical diagnosis. Gould's text, "both cold and breathless," in the words of its editor, is first of all an attempt to capture what it means to master the piano, but the artist is so engaged in his perception of the most secret linkages in his body, of the articulations and the muscles involved in his playing, that he ushers us into the cell where the musical ascetic persists in tormenting himself in an effort to recapture what he calls his lost image. I find no equivalent in literature, other perhaps than in the diaries of mystics recounting the loss of God's presence, the desertion by the beloved object. But for Gould this object was just an image, and not the object itself. Even if he had been utterly deprived of it, he would not for all that have lost contact with the transcendent music.

But what sort of loss are we talking about? I believe it is important to emphasize, as did Monsaingeon, the psychological dimension that pervades all his notes, a fear of losing the perfect synchronization between mental image and the workings of the body. The diary in fact shows us another Gould, almost his double, "a fragile and vulnerable Gould on which he is trying to get some purchase, and whose luminous projection, all he has left to us, barely enables us to divine its existence." Gould tried a number of strategies, combining the most diverse postures and exercises, to resist what he felt was an enemy lurking within, just waiting to surface and destroy him; but according to the diary these efforts were in vain. Vacillating between the euphoria of an anticipated victory and the most terrifying discouragement, the pianist first addressed his own discipline, his capacity to recapture the perfect synchrony of all his limbs. At times he thought he had pinpointed the source of his trouble, the height of his wrist or the coordination between neck and shoulder, for example. He noted the links with certain pieces in his repertoire, observing himself as if from an independent point of view. He exulted when he was able to pick out a trait common to all his difficulties, for example (on April 8, 1978), "the lack of constancy in shoulder elevation." He thought then to have recovered what he had lost.

The role of the image keeps on reappearing, insistent: "As 'image' had suggested, during preceding couple of days, elbow fulcrum nec[essitated] sitting farther back than was desirable, esp[ecially] in contra[puntal] textures, and substantiated impression of a higher than desirable center of gravity" (September 29, 1977). What image could this be, other than that abstract and idealized representation of the music that holds sway over the inner life of the performance? In his October 8 entry, he speaks of it as of an image of immense clarity. But several passages evoke, rather, an image of the body itself, as if the artist had access from within to a vision of the body's mechanism that he is trying to control. Perhaps the note of November 5 provides us with an important key: after three weeks during which he seems to have stopped keeping track of his exercises, Gould returns to his diary to relate two intersecting experiences. He reports that he has once again got behind the wheel of his Chevrolet Monte Carlo, "and that coincided with a restoration of control." He cannot then resist a direct association between the repair work on his old Lincoln and its replacement by the Monte Carlo, whose level of comfort seems intimately associated with the restoration of his image. We cannot help noting that this association is not unrelated to his position at the instrument, and that the nub of it all resides in the control of what, even though familiar and tried and true, had suddenly become recalcitrant and unpredictable.

Was this anxiety at losing what was most essential based on a real problem, on some difficulty that was more than a figment of his imagination? Did it have something to do with his ingestion of medications? At the time of this crisis, Gould's body was likely showing signs of exhaustion; Gould would die only five years later. He had abused it in every way possible, and if one had to throw back at him his precept of distancing himself as far as possible from the instrument, it would doubtless have been to suggest to him that he stop treating his body so harshly. The experiences related in his 1977–78 diary are so astonishing – some even implying that he might let himself collapse onto his keyboard or artificially block the articulation of his elbows – that we can only wonder at his perception of what a body, in general, could be. That he harboured a representation of his body analogous to the mechanism of his instrument, of which he demanded more and more flexibility, is not surprising; the

1977–78 diary shows to what extremes his identification with his old CD 318 had led him.

What is most astonishing is that, despite all these vicissitudes and all these torments, his playing – indeed, right up to the end – in no way changed. When he writes in his entry for February 13, 1978, that he is tired of the ordeal, we can only understand him in terms of that perception separating him from his imagined ideal: "Elevation at what price! 1≤ hr. (app[roximately]) were devoted to intermittent systems – none of which brought comfort or variety of dynamics. I longed for shoulder-pull release, which brought pain freedom, and an immediate cessation to right hand finger-tip nerve-tingle. But the penalty was a lack of that modicum of control which shoulder-pull systems permitted. There has to be a way." There was none – not, in any case, in the quasi-surgical realm where he had tried to exert control, and he had to give up, as he had given up on the CD 318.

The diary is cut short for no particular reason, Gould having exhausted his avenues of research. At no time does he seem to suspect that the loss of his image might have been taking place at a deeper stratum where it was always threatened with extinction. However, on April 8 he writes: "For one brief moment ... I <u>had</u> it; that gleaming, lustrous sound was back and I realized, more than ever, that <u>that</u> was the sound of control; I always realize, at such times, that the history of all these problems goes back to attempts (inadvertent or otherwise) to substitute other systems for it." Despite its cryptic aspect, this conclusion points us toward those realms of inner struggle where music, within the body, must wage all its battles. It also broaches, willy-nilly, the subject of the unconscious, but in the case of an artist for whom mastery was essential to art, how even to acknowledge its existence? If the body refuses to "participate," if the hands are painful to the point of his wanting to treat them with "burning compresses," how to comprehend this weakness, how to control those systems and to restore calm?

Glenn Gould died on October 4, 1982; he was fifty years old. The last pictures we have of him are of an adolescent body prematurely aged. In his youth, his mother had already reproached him for his languid posture, unsuitable for the physical demands of concertizing. She urged Jock Carroll, who went with him in 1956 to the Bahamas, to make sure that he got plenty of fresh air and sun. Looking at the photographs Carroll brought back, we see a Gould all bundled up, resisting everything the light and the warm sea had to offer. I wonder what his mother would have thought. She doubtless saw him as another Horowitz, but Gould had even then decided to live his life differently. Was his health already so fragile, or had he early on planned his exodus from his body? His elegance when he acknowledged his public was tinged with fatigue, and now that we are familiar with all his idiosyncrasies and his poignant hypochondria, we see well that this grace required an effort. The languid adolescent had already had enough; he soon embraced the world of medication and healing in the illusory hope that it would free him. But if we look carefully at his hands, we will see that they are intact. All his life, Gould had ensured that they be touched only by music.

# IV

## Air and *Sarabande*

# To Read, to Write, to Dream

### *Partita no. 6 in E Minor*

I knew if I listened to any more my illusions would be spoiled. I had managed
by degrees to reach an enchanted land from which I could look down on
the world with complete detachment, but I felt now as though someone
was demanding that I return the cloak of immortality. If, having laboriously
fought every inch of the way up that steep and twisting track, I were to be
foolish enough to allow myself to be dragged back down to the common
everyday world, the whole point of my leaving home suddenly and wandering
off like this would be lost.

NATSUME SŌSEKI, *The Three-Cornered World*

Listen – but to what? To life's petty scheming, to the banal human
comedy, to desire? This passage is taken from a novel by the Japanese writer Natsume Sōseki, whom Gould very much liked and often
quoted. How not to admire the hero, a painter who, like himself,
sets out to accomplish the task before him, turning his back on the
world's commotion? And yet, although Gould never ceased to meditate on the reasons for his own withdrawal and on what solitude
offered him that was so essential, he never tuned out the world's
hubbub; he wanted always to maintain contact with the world,
using every technical resource available to him, and, by addressing

himself to it, to make another path possible. This alliance with technology clearly sets him apart from the ascetic rupture described by Sōseki. Gould maintained an uninterrupted dialogue with the world, and he would never have propounded an aesthetic where the salvation of art required a break so radical that it would totally isolate the artist. On the contrary, he thought that the artist for a new age, for the modernity foreseen by Marshall McLuhan, ought to communicate, and to assume full responsibility for doing so. Still, like Sōseki's artist, he always felt the need to defend the logic that had led to his own isolation.

Gould read widely in his youth, and retained his love for reading out of both curiosity and a spiritual kinship he felt with certain writers. There is as yet no proper study of his reading, but the works that interested him were for the most part modern, and it is their modernity that likely appealed to him. The authors include only one poet, T.S. Eliot, and a preponderance of novelists such as Thomas Mann, whom he praised on a commemorative radio program on October 19, 1955. He read Gide, Joyce, and Kafka. He seems to have favoured the great Russian novelists, especially Dostoyevsky and Toltstoy. Among the philosophers, it is not surprising to find Nietzsche and Schopenhauer, whose radical aesthetic and attraction to the solitary life must have appealed to him. These two solitary figures also taught him something about the art of preaching. We can safely assume that much of his aesthetic of ecstasy derived from his youthful reading in the house on Lake Simcoe. Mann in particular, whose *Tonio Kröger* he liked to quote, could have inspired him in his work on Schoenberg; was Gould not a kind of Doctor Faustus who shared with Mann a fascination for music that broke with tradition and embraced an aesthetic of purity? Did Gould read Adorno? He owned a copy of his essays, *Prisms*, which he had annotated; despite the philosopher's pessimism, he must have been drawn to his austere world and welcomed his criticism of false moderns like Stravinsky.

Three writers stand out in this incomplete list: Henry David Thoreau, who inspired Gould as a naturalist and to whom he thought of devoting a radio series in the wake of his *Solitude Trilogy*, George Santayana, and Natsume Sōseki. Gould seems to have seen in each of them a kind of alter ego, as though in certain exemplary figures he could find the same ethic of solitude that he would make a precondition for his own aesthetic. The three writers have little in common, however. Thoreau wrote his memoirs inspired by a spiritual vision of retreat into nature, and Gould could well have made him a character in his *Solitude Trilogy*. But in many respects Thoreau's romanticism was a far cry from Gould's thinking; it is not likely that he would have endorsed the blessings of technology. In his letters Gould sometimes speaks of a neo-Thoreauvian inspiration; perhaps he meant a spiritual vision compatible with communications technology. Like the hero of *Walden*, Gould appreciated the richness of nature in America, and he knew that a retreat into the woods could give rise to a transcendentalist vision of the world. He could also have mentioned Emerson, whom he certainly had read.

George Santayana was a philosopher of Spanish origin, but who identified fully with American culture. His prolific output was rooted in American Transcendentalism, and Gould doubtless saw him not just as a writer but as a thinker as well. His novel, *The Last Puritan*, seems to have impressed him so much that he designated it as a kind of summing up of his own view of the world; he praised it always, and offered it as a gift to several of his friends. He particularly admired the young American protagonist, who was devoted to his community and anxious to achieve salvation by transcending individual interest. America was drawn to that essentially moral hero, perhaps seeing in him virtues it felt were already on the way out when the book appeared in 1936: generosity toward the community, a rejection of individualism. Gould's friends made fun of his passion for this no longer fashionable writer.

Nevertheless, the main character was the heroic model closest to Gould, and the most direct inspiration for his ethic. No one reads Santayana today, and his vision of a community that so moved Gould now seems to be a heritage left by the wayside.

Of these three writers, Natsume Sōseki is the only one who presents a carefully worked out aesthetic. In his novel *The Three-Cornered World*, the Japanese writer describes the torments of a painter who has embarked upon a retreat that will put him in contact with the wellsprings of creation. His pilgrimage takes him into the mountains to a hermitage where a Buddhist monk lives. This, in all spiritual traditions, is a clear metaphor for the artistic quest, and on this point Sōseki is unambiguous: the artist's spiritual itinerary is identified, as much in its approach as in its resolution, with that of the holy man. Each pursues a quest whose demands are at first beyond him: the artist, as he nears his objective, hopes the work will reveal itself to him; the saint seeks enlightenment and its serenity, even harder to attain. What is hoped for remains elusive; the work seems out of reach and everything conspires to deflect one from it. Time humbles the individual who thinks he can dominate everything; art itself is the embodiment of a patience that can only hope to disclose the horizon the artist seeks. Once visible, however, the horizon unfurls, and the work seems to have no end. This novel is largely structured like an initiatory quest, with its store of illusions, dreams, and carnal temptations, but it is above all a succession of tableaux whose precision and beauty derive from their transience. What the painter gazes upon can never be grasped; he can only consent to merge with it.

If this novel made such an impression on Gould, it was for two related reasons: first because the novel's hero, in his quest for art's absolute, embarks upon a quest that corresponds to Gould's own experience of rupture; but even more important, because Sōseki's ethic shares the same spiritual underpinnings as Gould's. To read this novel is to see how intertwined these two threads are: the artist's autobiographical account speaks of his doubts and hopes, and of the tangible consequences of a life lived apart from the world, but the story would be incomplete if it did not incorporate the artistic ethic that makes withdrawal a necessary condition for salvation. Of what salvation does Sōseki speak when he evokes the liberation from desires and passions, if not the prospect of spiritual freedom that art offers, a detachment from experience which alone can foster purity? It is possible that Gould, in time, developed an interest in Buddhism, and more generally in Eastern thought, but in the absence of clearer evidence we can view his interest in Sōseki's ethic as his response to a call voiced at the very heart of the aesthetic, a call to formulate a vision of the world free from the constraints of convention and conventional wisdom. There is nothing particularly Eastern in this idea; it can be found at the core of all artistic doctrines associating liberation with transcendence. Retreating from the world and living an ascetic life seem more essential than any precise goal.

In the beautiful portrait we have of him, dated 1912, Natsume Sōseki seems overcome by melancholy. He is wearing a black armband. His work too is infused with a sense of the world's ending. In the novel *Kokoro*, a later work than *The Three-Cornered World*, which describes the despair of a man betrayed by all but who himself betrays the man most dear to him, the author is the very model of a compassionate artist, transforming suffering into an instrument of salvation. *Kokoro* concerns a man who is moving slowly toward ending his own life after having been the indirect cause of his closest friend's suicide – an act for which he considers himself responsible. This uncompromising individual, a hieratic figure, is the perfect embodiment of moral austerity, and yet he harbours a terrible secret. His calm and reserved authority captivates a student, who approaches him, wanting to learn the secret of his apparent freedom, his complete serenity. But he is serene in appearance only. The story centres on this admiring relationship and its cathartic consequences, disastrous for the hero, each moment of the tale bringing its own store of disillusionment. But the suicide takes on its true meaning only in the context of Japanese history: entering upon a phase of radical modernization, the country saw its break with the past exacerbated by the death of the last emperor of the Meiji dynasty in 1912. This is what Sōseki is mourning in the 1912 photograph, and it is that bereavement that leads to the suicide of General Nogi Maresuke, whom the master of *Kokoro* decides to emulate in re-enacting his gesture. He is mourning authority and tradition; he is mourning a certain form of honour. But as the novel also shows, he is also mourning a way of silencing the essential, hiding an inadmissible secret behind a posture of severity.

Gould may have found some of the same preoccupations in Yukio Mishima – he possessed two of his books – whose work was an extension, both moral and aesthetic, of Sōseki's: the same austere imperative, and the same veneration of a certain kind of asceticism, which imposed an almost rigid way of leading one's life. The repression of sexuality is as important here as the aesthetic strategy for accomplishing it: to idealize art makes it a path to salvation. All of Sōseki's art is permeated by the dominance of ethics over the feeling for beauty. His work exalts the individual's power to resist corruption, and the need to forge a wide-ranging freedom for which art is both the precondition and the sovereign product. Art's sovereignty has no meaning if it is not dedicated to a lofty and spiritual life. As with Mishima, moral rigour must precede creation; it could even be beauty's only possible guise in a world of shattered harmony, ruined nature, and authoritarianism. No writing, no art can compensate, however, for the feeling of loss that pervades *Kokoro*; the master is at the mercy of an unhappy modernity; his horizon is closed and he is without succour. Whenever the admiring student voices his wish to read a work still to come, he feels himself rebuked for its tragic absence.

But in *The Three-Cornered World*, written a few years earlier in 1906, the artist is able to take an initiative, and creation does play a salutary role in a society undergoing radical change. Gould was particularly drawn to this novel, and we can understand why. The Japanese title of the work, *Kusamakura*, already refers to a journey, but not just any journey: a pilgrimage, a quest whose itinerary leads one to take leave of the world in order to acquire a truth not graspable in the turbulence of daily life. But does this ideal kindly world, free from constraint and care, exist anywhere else than in the artist's sense of hope? Is it not an imaginary compensation for the distress he senses at the heart of the modern world, and the spectacle of a triumphant bourgeoisie? In this philosophical tale, Sōseki shows himself full of boundless hope for the world he wants to escape. Another world is accessible. The artist need but imagine it to enter it whenever he wishes, for only the artist can find salvation by freeing himself from earthly desires and harmful passions; only he can bring into being, intact, this pure world, a world of incomparable beauty, of rapture, blessed in the contemplation of every passing moment. By introducing at every turn in the story the fugitive figure of a woman both rejected and out of reach, Sōseki showed that he was fully aware of the idealization whose power he was exploring. He by no means wanted to hide the impact of the world's corruption on those for whom the sexual life makes exorbitant demands and who, frightened, choose to repress it entirely. In all of Sōseki's novels the woman, poetically desired, represents an obstacle on the path toward art, and not the condition for arriving there.

Sōseki's protagonist is a painter, and he is thirty years old when he sets out on his journey to the mountain. At each stage of his ascent the landscape is revealed as pure joy, a marvel not to be missed, and the painter's meditation unfolds before us like an opened scroll:

> I wonder why this should be? I suppose the reason is that, looking at the landscape, it is as though you were looking at a picture unrolled before you, or reading a poem on a scroll. The whole area is yours, but since it is just like a painting or a poem, it never occurs to you to try and develop it, or make your fortune by running a railway line there from the city.

In this opposition between an intact nature and industrial modernity, Sōseki had long since acknowledged the tension running through all his work, but he had not yet made it the mainspring of his aesthetic; if the function of art is to reconcile with modernity, how to recognize that one must first promote withdrawal and liberation? How to see an unconditional return to nature as a form of salvation? Is nature even capable of disciplining the human heart, of purging it of all that is vile, to return it to the pure world of poetry? Without purity in the world, art would lose its powers; it too would be lost. The more the artist advances on the road of asceticism, the more conscious he becomes of the vacuity of his gaze; his descriptions of nature are perfect, they conjure a painting at the very heart of what is real, they reveal its wondrous temporality, but they have no force, no content, and they capture nothing of the dazzling surface of the world. Their only power is to repress the machinations of the world, a power Sōseki drew upon to lay the foundations for his tale.

Loyal to the literary school of his youth, the Hototogisu school, Sōseki favoured a narrative in which plot was non-existent, concentrating on his characters' thought processes within the enclosed world of their experience; this was the ideal of the masters of *Sasheibun*, one that Sōseki himself adopted under the name *Hinninjo*, a writing that was not human, that was purely contemplative. This purifying of humanity began with an effacement of the self, and it is hard not to associate it with the Buddhist sources that preached such a doctrine; but Sōseki thought he could push this effacement to its limit at the very heart of the Western aesthetic. If the work is in nature and the artist's function consists only in extracting it, we can see him exhausting himself in reaching for it; if, on the other hand, the work is within himself to the point where he can and must identify with it, then it can take shape in complete freedom.

This perspective on the world led Sōseki to a redemptive aesthetic, whose fundamentals he outlined in *The Three-Cornered World*; before even asserting the priority of art and the poetic, the artist must first attain to a moral purity, an inner state that alone will make his art possible. Such asceticism can only be achieved through a discipline that engages his entire life, and that is what makes this novel a tale of romantic apprenticeship that his English translator, Alan Turney, compares rightly with the pilgrimage of Heinrich Heine in *The Harz Journey*. If the artist's heart is tarnished by gain or troubled by sexual desire, nature cannot appear to him in all its beauty, cannot show him the path to the work he must do; on the contrary it will stand in his way. The cost of the pilgrimage is not just a symbolic one; the artist must scale the mountain that stands before him, and he must confront his demons. He must not regard his retreat as mainly a way to protect himself or to make himself invulnerable; he must on the contrary look to it for a revelation that will confirm whether or not he will reach his goal of the transparency of art. The monastic tradition that finds expression here is not exclusive to Eastern spirituality; it is characteristic of all initiatory pilgrimages, composed of encounters, struggles, and liberation.

And so Sōseki's painter reverses the traditional aesthetic formula: he must save himself before demanding anything of art, and it is within himself alone that he must seek the strength to embrace this asceticism. No support is to be found anywhere else, and art, in particular, cannot itself be the means for this ascent in search of clarity. The ordinary artist is content to describe the world of constraints and suffering. He has no idea of the need to free himself from them before winning his way to the true world of the workings and the beauty of nature. Thinking to create a representation, he only alienates himself more and more, as he incorporates modernity's troubles into art. These troubles must, on the contrary, be purged from it. Citing verses of Wang Wei and Basho, Sōseki tries to show what distinguishes sublime art from the prosaic art of modernity, pointing out the requirements for becoming an exceptional artist – the only true artist in his eyes – one who detaches himself from modernity through his own efforts and expects nothing from his art but a way ahead after this liberation. The more the artist progresses toward the heights, the more he enters into the work, and the more he himself becomes the work that he initially had the illusion and the overweening ambition of being able to produce. Plunged into a world of action and desire, he risks at all times being overwhelmed by it and losing his "cloak of immortality"; he will keep it only if he lets his life become completely disengaged, thus freeing himself, in a state of withdrawal, to enter wholly into the work. When the painter finally reaches the monastery that awaits him, where life's dramas and mysteries forever pass like shadows across the surface of screens, he knows he has only one way to free himself: to not become engaged, to renounce understanding, and to abandon himself to the ascetic idea that he himself is but a moving figure in a tableau.

What Gould might have drawn from this transcendental aesthetic, we can only try to reconstruct. Like Sōseki, he made a moral case for isolation and withdrawal; and an inner world, idealized and cultivated for its own sake, seemed to him to constitute the best hope for an artistic experience purified of all the world's dross. He found his own "grass pillow" (the original title of Sōseki's novel) on his walks through the Lake Simcoe country-side, and he embraced the resolution of Sōseki's painter: "I should like, as nearly as possible, to view people from the same stand-point as I view the world of pure poetry." Each being is a part of the poetry of the world, each moves about in the world like an element of nature, and each finds a place there that is akin to where he stands in art. The series of thirteen meditations com-prising Sōseki's text corresponds to a sequence of variations on the theme of belonging and serenity promised to the artist if, before even engaging in his art, he can develop the capacity for transparency and wonder. Once again I return to that state of "wonder" that enters in whenever we deal with Gould's with-drawal, with his own brand of asceticism, a wonder whose mean-ing is quite different from the admiration we feel in the presence of a transcendent and universal harmony. With Gould, the self remains active; it does not blend into the structured world of tonalities that reflect nature's perfection. Sōseki's narrative, on the other hand, constitutes an entryway to a realm of ecstatic con-templation that draws the individual out of himself and makes him one with an external absolute, all-encompassing and com-pelling. If we may still speak of beauty, it will not be in the sense of something concrete to be admired, but of the beauty of all that encompasses us. With no more distinctions to be made, we are spared the suffering associated with representation and a sensed distance. Buddhism seeks this epiphany in exchange for the efface-ment of all difference, all otherness. Was Gould's apprehended "divinity" perhaps this form rising out of musical wonderment, the sudden appearance of a spirit, a dematerialization? Sōseki's aesthetic would ask us to behold a divinity where the self has ceased to be, the divinity of the world with which the artist has become one.

Knowing that Gould was interested in Jean Le Moyne's thought and that he read theologians like Paul Tillich, we may ask ourselves if this spiritual detachment was for him a faith. In a 1980 interview, only two years before his death, he affirmed that he had always believed in something beyond, and that spiritual transformation was not only real but a norm that must regulate the way one lived one's life. Such a conviction does not make him a mystic, but it should be noted that he did not shy away from this way of expressing himself. For him, art must transmit something "spiritual," but beyond this requirement it would be risky to try to define it as nature or a divinity, the sublime or ecstasy.

In his novel, Sōseki introduces a woman who is as first nothing but a shadow: O-Nami. The more the painter tries to approach her, the more he hesitates, for she might just be a mirage. Yet he sees that she is the incarnation, in her person, of all he has gone through to arrive at the real: she does not act, and even if she has an unknown history, for him she is above all the bridge that unites a succession of moments, a series of tableaux. Sōseki wanted to associate this elusive and immanent personage, issuing from a strange world, with the artist's quest, with everything that might represent for him what is discontinuous but destined to resolve itself into a larger unity. The woman appears first as an absent figure, suggesting an epiphany associated with the infinite; she is another entry point to ecstasy and its wonderment, an ultimate invitation to union and the abandon of one's sense of centredness. If she remains a body, an existence, she will only act as a screen. Free from all intrigue, she belongs among the figures one must transcend, but which remain essential for one's access to the ecstatic vision. She is an apparition, a presence come from eternity into the present moment, and so she remains, deprived of any real existence until the novel's last scene, when the painter sees her at the station where he is waiting to catch the train. On her face he glimpses a feeling of compassion that allows him at last to experience her reality, but that is perhaps because he is now taking his leave of the mountain and its epiphanies. I evoke this phantom figure because it brings to mind Gould's "absent loved one" and her single appearance in a letter I will discuss further on. This oneness in absence is yet another state of being that Gould shares with the unfolding of *The Three-Cornered World*. As with Sōseki, the woman seems to have been present for him always, but always behind a screen.

If this asceticism is only conceivable in a state of withdrawal, and not, initially, in art itself, it is because it is built on a decision to reform one's life, to endow it with an essential spareness and transparency. Sōseki's artist is himself astonished at having to consider himself an ordinary person as he embarks on his journey towards detachment. It is not as an artist that he experiences difficulties; his difficulties are common to all those who want to transcend their condition, to put their freedom to the test, and only when the withdrawal has been duly achieved and this freedom has been made possible, can art reassume its place. "It is only afterwards when we tell our experiences to others that we revert to being artists. Putting it as a formula, I suppose you could say that an artist is a person who lives in the triangle which remains after the angle which we may call common sense has been removed from this four-cornered world."

This analogy is very obscure; first because of the geometry that conforms so little to the representation of space, the world being limited to three spatial dimensions but remaining open to an infinite number of moral dimensions; but above all, perhaps, because of the conundrum of communication and common sense that it is meant to illustrate. If the artist rises above common sense it is to discover beauty, but to do so he must in some sense strip himself of all that is still trivial within him. In other words, the artist does not create beauty but gives himself the means to discover it everywhere by first of all purifying himself. The new space thus created is cleansed of the everyday and is configured as a new world, that of art. What, then, are the remaining corners of this purified world?

This inquiry situates the idea of the artist on such a high moral plane that it runs the risk of separating him irremediably from the world, and in an extreme case, disarming him completely, stripping him of the desire to return and communicate what he is now able to see. The Eastern aspects of this aesthetic show through more clearly when one questions the concept of beauty; far from being a product of art, beauty is what art reveals of nature through the intercession of a purified gaze. Could Gould have recognized himself in this portrait seemingly so far removed from his formal ideal of music? The more I tried to establish this rapport – and I should state that I have no idea what importance it may have had for Gould – the more I became convinced that its basis was moral. And that is never so clear as in Gould's writing, with its spirited repudiation of inflated virtuosity. Let us go back for a moment to his letters and what we can read about his radio work: behind the over-the-top humour he injected into his dialogues to pique people's interest, we sense no arrogance, no desire to force anything on anyone, only a constant and unfailing zeal to initiate others into a sphere of thought, to facilitate their access to the realm of beauty. Like Sōseki's painter, but perhaps like Schoenberg above all, Gould would have found nothing more contemptible than a belief that he was dominating the world of others; if he wanted to remove himself from that world, it was to seek out the ideal conditions for a return bearing the gift of art. And if by misfortune he found himself believing he had attained a kind of spiritual perfection that isolated him and set him apart from others, he quickly saw how laughable that was, and realized that he had not yet arrived at the simplicity and discipline of a true artist.

Gould's writing is always friendly; that is for me the appropriate word to describe it. It communicates in a spirit of reciprocity, and places the art objects that the artist designates to save the world in a position of absolute transcendence. I have spoken of the

generous quality of his letters. Let me add that he often enclosed
with them copies of his records and the books he admired (notably
that of George Santayana, one of his favourites). This perhaps
explains why his letters were so far from the self-absorption and
obsessiveness we find elsewhere in his life; he was disciplined
enough to go beyond that. To those who claim he was incapable
of intimacy I would reply that in what he wrote he made a conscious
decision to venture beyond familiarity. In that too he resembles
Sōseki's painter, who repeatedly emphasizes that the true artist
must renounce himself. Does Sōseki not write, as if to define his
aesthetic absolutely, that art is a "blissful state of self-forgetful-
ness"? Gould's letters say so little about himself that one might
think he never respected his correspondents enough to share with
them anything important; the reality is that nothing was vital to
Gould that was not part of his art, whether a composition, a musical problem, a question of interpretation, or a work in progress. I
have gone through his correspondence with a fine-tooth comb,
and the only items of a personal nature that I have found are contained in some fragments of ethics inspired by Henry David Thoreau
and the Northern landscapes that attracted him. Like Sōseki, he
doubtless dreamt of revisiting them often, if only to reconnect
with his early experiences of detachment. I am brought back to a
passage from *The Three-Cornered World*, one among many that
reflect this call from the beyond:

> The spring breeze, which was passing drowsily through the
> empty house, came neither to gratify those who welcomed
> it, nor to spite those who wished to keep it out. It came and
> went quite naturally: an expression of the impartiality of the
> universe. I sat with my chin resting on my hands, thinking
> that if only my heart were as free and open as my room, the
> breeze would, unbidden, have found its way there too.

The artist is not only detached, in a state that already sets him apart from others, but he has reached that degree of liberty where he lets the outside world pass through him and is no longer dependent on it. Sōseki evokes an entirely inner essence, but he is quick to add that anyone can reach it, that nothing is reserved to the artist, since art represents only what is possible after the fact. The way of art, he says again and again, is there for all, and this conviction was also Gould's. He considered himself privileged, certainly, as much for his gifts as for the attention he received from his family and his teachers; he could measure the cost of the path that had opened his way to the realm of music, but for him this access was not the goal of art. Rapture can be one of life's ultimate goals, but it is nothing if it does not seek to communicate, if it does not accept its "ministry." Sōseki's aesthetic also gravitates around this process of return, a process described as the pendulum by which the world's conscience, which carries the artist off in a sort of trance, then redirects itself in a movement toward the world, a movement that is the purpose of art.

For Sōseki, idleness remained a mystery of the highest order, and if he avoids resorting too directly to the teachings of Buddhism to shed light on it, one senses in each of his descriptions that a spiritual metamorphosis is at work, along with an ongoing destructuring of the self. The painter knows that the transcendence of thought, at the instant it occurs, does not take him away from his work at all, since the artist who perseveres in his asceticism continues to move to the world's rhythm. This oscillation, this undulation that exposes the flowering branch of the cherry tree to the spring breeze, is only the simplest description of the movement by which the artist distances himself from humanity to go toward the work and then return. If Glenn Gould liked Sōseki's book so much, it is perhaps because he admired its attempt to establish a harmony with this movement in nature and identify it at the same time with art. He himself wrote nothing that would allow us to assert that this Eastern lexicon of rapture intersects with the little he had to say about it, but when we abandon ourselves to Sōseki's prose, so rigorous and yet so delicate in the translation by Alan Turney that Gould read, we at times draw so near to this rapture that it is hard to believe that this text is not its source. I will content myself here with noting this achievement, while embracing it as an example to follow.

What relationship, then, should we try to establish between this state of mind and the work itself? Although Sōseki's novel is not based on intrigue, his painter must deal with his encroaching unease at opting for idleness and withdrawal but producing no work. Gould's biographers are not very interested in the important fact that he would have liked to write music; they simply note that his published musical compositions, few in number and all minor with the exception of his string quartet, were a source of frustration to him, a kind of defeat. Nowhere do we find any expression of disappointment on Gould's part, however; on the contrary, all indications are that these rare compositions persuaded him to look to interpretation, rather, for his perspective on the world. His first opus, a string quartet, was analysed brilliantly by Bruno Monsaingeon, commenting on a letter of May 10 1960 that Gould wrote to Kurt Loebel, which Monsaingeon inserted into his edition of the crisis diary. Written when he was in his early twenties, this quartet does not entirely correspond to the modern aesthetic that Gould publicly advocated. Monsaingeon saw in it an "intense lyricism, passionate, but contained by the severity of a compositional style that is contrapuntal from beginning to end," and regarded it not only as a masterpiece but as a reflection of Gould's very soul. The description he gives is astute; he portrays the work as a search for balance between tradition and innovation. "It must be acknowledged," he wrote, "that with this quartet he took the measure of an impasse: the impasse in which contemporary music found itself, tormented by the problem of its own intelligibility."

In this respect, the quartet embodies everything Monsaingeon would have wished from such a work, and when we hear Gould introduce Schoenberg, in particular his struggle to reconcile and harmonize tonal and atonal works, from his extravagant lyricism to his pure formality in the *Chamber Symphonies* (*Opus 9* and *Opus 38*), we hear above all an injunction to himself concerning a reconciliation that was central to his rapport with music. Would he, in fact, have wanted or been able to write serial music, which he saw as the successor to counterpoint? Would he have been able to break with the ecstatic lyricism he displayed so convincingly in his interpretations of Wagner and Beethoven transcriptions?

It is doubtful. Gould had the entire spectrum of musical history at his fingertips and could not expect of himself any work that would have represented any further development. On the direct line he had traced from the English virginalists to Schoenberg, he knew exactly where he stood. That is why (and this takes us back to his admiration for Thomas Mann) I find so apt Ghyslaine Guertin's interpretation of the Schoenberg series as a self-portrait – I would almost add, as an autobiography. Gould had tracked Schoenberg to each of his extreme positions and decided to accept the tensions implicit in their profound ambivalence and not venture further – to remain poised on the crest that overlooks, from the same height, both atonal structures and the lyricism of *Transfigured Night*. He would take one step, perhaps, in the direction of Richard Strauss, or another in the direction of Webern, but nothing more. One might also suggest that his responsibility lay elsewhere, in recording, in contrapuntal documentary for radio, in everything he did to clarify the difficulties in musical composition for an era that demanded a new kind of work. But that is only too obvious.

We can already sense what this decision to move in the direction of interpretation could gain from a reconciliation of withdrawal and giving: when Sōseki introduces music in the fourth chapter of his novel, it is just when the work is beginning to be seen as an interpretation of the world, as if music – better than painting – could provide an antidote to the arrogance of representation. In that ecstatic moment, the artist's soul is like a father who has been scouring the countryside for a long time in search of his lost child, and finds him at last. Such is the encounter with the artistic work; such is the liberation made possible by spiritual progress in the state of withdrawal. It is not an encounter achieved through struggle, but has its origins on some mysteriously generous horizon, precisely because it is simply an interpretation. "Music! The word suddenly flashed into my mind. Of course! Music was the voice of Nature which, fathered by necessity, had been born in exactly such circumstances." Which circumstances, one might ask? Those of an abandon that creates the conditions for this state of wonder, for an encounter that by definition cannot be foreseen, and which issues forth in a state of grace. As for "necessity," we know what it is: it is the Platonic goddess of harmony, universal counterpoint.

We know that Gould lived in an environment that was austere in material terms, intentionally limited to what was useful, even essential. It may even have been neglected and rather run down. But when Kevin Bazzana reviews the aspects of Gould's thinking that might hint at an interest in Buddhism and Eastern thought, he notes that Gould acquired – and it seems to have been his only acquisition of the sort – a work by the contemporary painter Zao Wou-Ki. I would like to think that this austere Chinese master, whose work is a cross between oriental calligraphy and lyric abstraction, would have appreciated the fact that Gould had chosen one of his creations as the sole art object adorning a space otherwise given over to disorder, indifferent to appearances. For everything in his work, the openness, the receptiveness, reminds us of Sōseki's aesthetic. In its uniqueness, as in the spell it casts, this lithograph, whose original I have not seen, resembles Paul Klee's

didn't question his choices; neither the decision to quit the concert hall, nor his investment in a life dedicated to production (the only word that can encompass his work both as an interpreter and as a media figure) ever gave him pause. There is not a single line to suggest that he was tempted even for an instant to throw everything up, to withdraw so absolutely that he would consider no new project. No – even drained and under siege, Gould stuck to his work.

In the sarabande of a life, all sorts of people parade through, some who are close and some who have never permitted any intimacy. Gould thought of them in the solitude of his studio, he addressed them in his letters, and he talked to them on television with his trademark confidence and certitude and a generosity bordering on over-excitation: can someone love Schoenberg to the point of not only writing ten radio broadcasts to make him known but recording all his music, including the accompaniments for his lieder? If he had been devoured by anxiety, the single instance of which is contained in his 1977–78 diary, he would have been constrained to silence. He controlled this anxiety, he subjected himself to the severest discipline, and he didn't need to enter a monastery to find support; he had already made that journey, he knew the road, and had passed behind all its screens. Gould was not one of those artists the world could destroy, because the path that had ushered him out of the world led him toward a magical destination. Once again, like Sōseki's painter, he scaled his mountain and what he attained never left him. It was his only to be given back. Even if it is probable, as the crisis diary would seem to indicate, that his struggle recurred to varying degrees, it was never to the point that he became unable to achieve the moral detachment of isolation. In December 1981, Gould took part in a radio program dealing with books, called *Booktime*. He read some excerpts from *The Three-Cornered World*. To the end, the book was still with

him. This was his last appearance on a radio program, and it has
left us with a precious archive of his voice immersed in Sōseki's
writing, or Sōseki's writing engraved in his voice.

∽

Gould never stopped reading, never stopped writing. What is
available to us of what he wrote, in particular the published selections from his letters, reveals someone for whom writing played a
significant role. Gould was always a conscientious correspondent,
careful to make the proper response and to be precise on all fronts.
In his writings, we can trace the progress of several of his projects, for example the *Solitude Trilogy*, and chart the development
of his ideas as work progressed. The diary to which he committed
– often, alas, cryptically – the serious crisis when he was both
depressed and anxious about his playing, is a perfect example of
what he expected of the act of writing: it was a chronicle, a record
of his life in art, and a developmental tool to help him master a
situation. No one would go so far as to say that Gould was a tal-
ented writer, but he had a passion for writing that nourished his
passion for communicating. This life in writing went along with
his passion for documenting a subject, as we can see in his radio
broadcasts, such as his series on Casals and Stokowski; he had
an encyclopaedic knowledge of musical history and an opinion
on everything. The volume of his writing is impressive, but its
diversity impresses even more: musicological discussions, his mastery of which was evident from the start in the texts he wrote to
accompany his first recordings, are only the best-known examples.
Consider the important work he produced on Arnold Schoenberg,
for example the 1974 CBC Radio series made available to us by
Ghyslaine Guertin, well represent his aesthetic methodology and
preoccupations. And consider his many commentaries on technology and the media. Finally, there are his personal writings,

including a number of complex interviews and autobiographical fragments. All these texts have their own point of origin: Gould's apartment in Toronto, site of his isolation.

In this accumulation of writings, there is of course a wealth of artifice and complex argumentation, Gould never seeming to know what public, exactly, he was addressing, but no one can doubt the authenticity of his mission to communicate a conviction, an intensity, a comprehension of the music. I know of few performers who have written so much, and even fewer who have done so with such candour. At no time does Gould take even the most basic precautions; he doesn't worry about subtleties or the impact of a cutting judgment, he exposes his vulnerability, and always writes as if he is the only one to speak of the works, to propose a radical reading, and to experience them from inside to the degree that he does. To read him without irritation requires a confidence and a camaraderie akin to what he imagined was his own vis-à-vis the musicians and writers he admired. He received in return many objections and criticisms, and even low blows. But I do not think he was ever wounded by academic scholarship, whose pretensions he joyously caricatured, or by the judgments of the critics; he wrote as one speaks, and as Kevin Bazzana said, he was a great conversationalist. Gould, a man of conversation: this is perhaps the best way to describe this discourse that was true only to itself, and yet which sought an interlocutor imbued with the same desire to transcend conventions. Who, in the end, can fault a friend who takes risks while advancing overzealous opinions? Gould did it always, as if he were in the company of well-disposed companions, and we always hear in his convoluted prose a smiling provocation, a wanting to surprise and to be loved.

I have sometimes wondered what might have been the secret behind his endurance and his austerity, but I have come to the conclusion that there was no secret to be found other than in his commitment to reconciling withdrawal and the gift. A true secret would be a wound so deep, a tragedy so great, an impediment shutting down all of life and stifling all creation, such as, for example, the total deprivation of love. I will speak of just such a secret, which no longer exists, in the section I have chosen to present as the *Scherzo* of this *Partita*. But the secret I speak of here is none other than the mystery behind a determination so constant in its choice of austerity that we can shed light on it only when we find it expressed by others, for example in an initiatory Japanese novel.

For the moment, I am turning a page devoted to his reading, his writing, his meditation. In Gould's mind, he follows the path of Sōseki's painter; he imagines the woods of Thoreau that he sees already in a work of art and he hears the virtuous injunction of Santayana's hero. His handwriting is terrible, terrifying, hallucinatory in its rapidity and lack of care; it is laid out on the page for him alone, like an encrypted memory. One need only cast one's eyes over the pages of the diary Bruno Monsaingeon deciphered; they are veritable hieroglyphs, scattered with little coded schemas, much like a score imbued with his discipline and his asceticism. Deep into the night the lights stayed lit in his Toronto apartment, the world's hubbub drifted in, he had his agenda, he spent time on the telephone, and he wrote compulsively: all activities constituting a basso continuo for his work. One might assume that he spent hours practising his instrument, but it wasn't so; he always insisted that he almost never practised – doubtless much less than he wrote. But when we hear him play, for example the admirable *Sarabande* of *Partita No. 6*, we know that nothing of that hubbub could trouble what we hear – his grace and his "cloak of immortality." I suggest we listen once more to the air that precedes this sarabande, in the passage by Sōseki that I have so often quoted:

I knew if I listened to any more my illusions would be spoiled. I had managed by degrees to reach an enchanted land from

which I could look down on the world with complete detachment, but I felt now as though someone was demanding that I
return the cloak of immortality. If, having laboriously fought
every inch of the way up that steep and twisting track, I were
to be foolish enough to allow myself to be dragged back down
to the common everyday world, the whole point of my leaving
home suddenly and wandering off like this would be lost.

# V

*Sinfonia*

# The Importance of Being Alone
*Partita no. 2 in C Minor*

Glenn Gould's interest in Northern solitudes could suggest an affinity with the romanticism he always wanted to keep at bay. He was romantic, certainly, in the aspect of his playing that betrayed an almost Wagnerian lyricism; but this was just a concession to his masters Arnold Schoenberg and Richard Strauss – unless it was also the sign of an ambivalence that he decided not to repress. He was romantic also in his nostalgia for solitude, which alone could nourish the artist's creative endeavours. But his interest in the Northern landscape, and in the experience of isolated communities in general, must be read differently: in this isolation Gould saw the dawn of a new freedom, a freedom of communication. The North remained what it had always been for him, a spiritual home that he had longed for since childhood, but as someone who did not want to be an artist turned in on himself, the North also influenced his thinking. Nothing seems less simple than to speak of Gould's romanticism or anti-romanticism, as soon as one stops thinking of him exclusively as a genius.

Gould did not like romantic genius, its self-importance. Romanticism, he thought, would have us believe that, in the art of the musician interpreter, thought has no role to play, it counts for nothing – nothing, at least, that is measured and deliberate, and that appreciates and passes judgment. All the mediations of analysis and judgment come after the fact; the artist, if he so desires, will comment on what he has sought to do, but he will describe it as something he has produced without really intending to. Genius is not its own master, but is subject to incursions from both within and without. And so the knowledge to which it gives expression is not present when the expression occurs, and aesthetics, one's guiding light when thinking about art, can never play the role of a matrix, of a thought that shapes, or a will that organizes and puts things in context. An aesthetic is only a commentary intended, certainly, to shed light on what is heard, but powerless to influence an interpretation. The musical genius ripens in the shadows; the mystery surrounding it shields it both from the responsibility for talking about itself and from the need to acquaint others with what it has attained. Utterly alien, the artist insists on preserving the distance that safeguards his virtuosity, and on deepening the gulf that divides him from the community. So it is with romanticism and its essential silence. The artist's isolation here is as essential to him as it is chaotic and diffuse. All his life, Gould refused to identify with that kind of shadowy genius.

He liked nothing more than to make fun of artists who put on superior airs, are far too dazzling, and, frankly, are less than democratic. He opposed that model through a passionate effort at communication, whose ultimate goal could only be the deconstruction of the romantic mystique. His anti-romanticism can be summed up in one precept: for each and for all. When we reread the sum of his writings and correspondence, we can't help being struck by the constancy of his approach, its concern for equality, and its consideration for the humblest among us. Everything is there: a blunt criticism of anything that cloaks itself in inscrutability, a mordant irony in the presence of the over-dramatic, and a jolly disparagement of pretension. For him – and doubtless he had in mind a number of volatile musicians he declined to name, as well as some he roundly attacked – romanticism was first of all that: an emotion that puts on airs, and in these airs finds a means of distancing itself. But these judgments pale in comparison to Gould's ongoing discussion of his art, an art carefully thought out, whose purity must be sought in the pursuit of mastery and clarity. This commitment to discipline, manifested in an approach supported by knowledge and determined to pass on to others what it has learned, does not shy away from language. It wishes to communicate, and the type of withdrawal it advocates is completely foreign to the impetuous obscurantism of romanticism. The discussion can sometimes bog down – it has a rhetoric all its own – but Gould's model of genius will do everything it can to make accessible and to share the experience of the sublime.

Do these two traits – the egalitarian impulse and the concern to communicate perfection – have anything in common? The more we reflect, the more we are aware of their essential unity. Does one's love for Glenn Gould demand that we follow his example in embracing the media after forsaking the concert hall? Does it require that we take seriously his radio lectures on Stokowski and Schoenberg, where we find brilliant intuitions submerged in a byzantine argument? The answer to this question is not simple. We cannot unthinkingly reject a coherent aesthetic, and even less the convergence of an interpretive art and the discourse that backs it up. Our response does, however, have crucial implications; the critique of romanticism, if it is rigorous, is not without consequences. We cannot love Gould and pretend he was an artist who wanted to cloak what is sublime in music in an experience that is remote, rarefied, and unexplained. All of Gould's art is committed, on the contrary, to the conviction that what is sublime is associated with a fundamental and expressible purpose in life, to which each individual is, one might say by nature, destined. And so the act of making music has its own language; there is a wish for meaning in music as patent and as accessible as the wish for meaning in life. Ultimately, this meaning can be transmitted. All the trouble taken to achieve this end is implicit in Gould's aesthetic: for him that "part of divinity" music confers on us is meant for everyone.

In the midst of all that he produced looms a radio trilogy, an unequalled masterpiece in which Gould managed to combine an idealized contrapuntal form with an ethic of solitude as manifest in the Canadian landscape. The *Solitude Trilogy* is not a musical documentary – nor is it an aesthetic pronouncement – but it encompasses all of Gould's thinking as a musician and all of his art. When I heard it for the first time, I felt that the two worlds that everything had conspired to separate had miraculously come together in a unique and concrete form; Gould had created a vocal environment that blended the voice of the individual isolated in his quest for others, with the musical voice whose contrapuntal tension is the driving force of music itself. Voice and voice found each other in the world of experience, beyond all that separates words and music. As I will try to show, this work was the culmination of a long period of research into communication that Gould had undertaken in complete harmony with his career as a musician. I can only touch on it here, as it merits a separate, in-depth study.

Communications research is a responsibility of our time, and even the romantic genius, who dwells in nature and is effectively its creation, cannot shirk it. Gould discussed this obligation often, doubtless because it represented the flip side of self-centred romanticism but, more important, also because it became a real concern for him after his withdrawal from the world of the concert hall. His was a democratic nature – his many interviews and dialogues attest to this – and it was not easy for him to reconcile the imperatives of communication and the dissemination of meaning to the entire community with the singularity of the genius that dwelt within him. His interest in technology and communications made for a natural affinity with his Toronto compatriot Marshall

McLuhan. Gould read the writings of the great communications theorist carefully and found in them many of the principles that guided his own inquiry into technology's role in the evolution of the art of music. His preoccupation with isolated communities was inspired less by a nostalgia for their fervour and their sense of identity – although these were crucial to his project – than by a desire to guarantee their survival by giving them a voice. Gould could quote with enthusiasm McLuhan's planetary ideas or Father Teilhard de Chardin's pronouncements on the noosphere and, as we shall see, these ideas, widespread among intellectuals during the 1960s, were as important to him as his reflections on identity and community.

His primary interest lay with sound reproduction techniques, and his first challenge was to modify an interpretation by marrying a number of takes during the editing process. It has been noted, accurately, that although he was an advocate of this technique, he did not abuse it. A satisfying, even excellent, interpretation was never the perfect interpretation, by definition inaccessible, given the immateriality of music. He knew the potential of technology, but he was also aware of its limits. What was most important was the impact of technology on the sound itself: the balance, the work on voices and timbres, echo, everything a good console can do with a raw recording. We must remember that this was not the era of digital technology – only a few of Gould's last recordings drew on this process – so his enthusiasm was based on a technology we would today consider rudimentary. Gould sought from it a result nearer to the ideal he envisaged: essentially, a sound freed from the arbitrariness of public performance, a sound that lent itself to an abstract transparency true to the contrapuntal idea. A performance recorded in a studio thus had a very different status for him than a performance in a concert hall, even if it was recorded; all its constituents were entirely willed, the consequences of a deliberate decision to preserve a particular approach, which evolved from repeated listening and retakes, and nothing else. This explains why he was able to declare: "most of the ideas that have occurred to me as a performer have related in some measure to the microphone." In a 1967 CBC Radio broadcast, he confessed: "I have not been able to think of the potential of music (or for that matter of my own potential as a musician) without some reference to the limitless possibilities of the broadcasting/recording medium."

Technology was, however, just a starting point, and Kevin Bazzana has rightly said that for Gould recording techniques were ultimately, like everything else, a matter of ethics. For this assertion not to appear too vague, we must look at the implications. It is certain that Gould considered access to the repertoire through recordings to be a real advance in the dissemination of art, and in that sense technology was liberating. It made available to a wide listening public an experience that had been restricted to the concert hall. But this public was made up of isolated individuals – it was not a mass audience waiting to be entertained; and Gould, democratic as he was, shared with the Viennese theoreticians their implacable condemnation of the music market. If technology could liberate, it was because it laid the groundwork for a "creative" audience, alert to its prerogatives, and free in its choices. The individual, in his listening solitude, can recapture the conditions of the studio, and can himself assimilate the artist's work. I do not believe Gould ever quoted Walter Benjamin's "The Work of Art in the Age of Mechanical Reproduction," and I can't say if he would have agreed with its thesis on the loss of aura, a thesis referring in particular to visual art; one might presume that for Gould reproduction made it possible to recapture the aura in a solitary and privileged encounter with the work, far from the bourgeois constraints and rituals associated with live performance.

And so, to speak here of a democratization of artistic experience is not an exaggeration, but how does it constitute an ethic? In the end, and Gould did not hesitate to say it, what technology might do for art would be to support it in its pursuit of humanity's spiritual good, the consequence being that art would eventually banish itself. Did he not write, in his 1974 self-interview: "Well, I feel that art should be given the chance to phase itself out. I think that we must accept the fact that art is not inevitably benign, that it is potentially destructive. We should analyse the areas where it tends to do least harm, use them as guidelines, and build into art a component that will enable it to preside over its own obsolescence"? That can only mean the eventual completion of its task in a suffering world to which it offers succour and a language. In what world might art risk doing away with itself? When there are no more needs to fulfill, what are its responsibilities; how can it be considered essential? Perhaps we are speaking of a time when, as with Sōseki, all of life becomes art.

The answer to this paradox resides in an insistence on the value of solitude. Recording technology is a technology of distance, but it is there at the behest of a new kind of proximity. The artist can work in perfect isolation, the sum of his efforts invested in his work, in a quest for the ideal interpretation; but nothing in this quest interjects to perturb the listener's solitude. A banal assertion, but it has implications where time and duration are concerned. Works of great length that were, as experienced in the concert hall, subject to debilitating constraints, are suddenly liberated, as much for the musician as for the listener. A fine curtain descends over each of them – or more exactly between the one and the other – to make a pure listening experience possible. In 1966 Gould wrote:

> The keyword here is "public." Those experiences through which the listener encounters music electronically are not within the public domain. One serviceable axiom applicable to every experience in which electronic transmission is involved can be expressed in that paradox wherein the ability to obtain in theory an audience of unprecedented numbers

obtains in fact a limitless number of private auditions.
Because of the circumstances this paradox defines, the
listener is able to indulge preferences, and through the electronic modifications with which he endows the listening
experience, impose his own personality upon the work.
As he does so, he transforms that work, and his relation
to it, from an artistic to an environmental experience.

No one would wish to deny, as Yehudi Menuhin pointed out,
that an audience can influence the way a work is received, and I
do not know how Gould would have responded to the arguments
of a philosopher such as Hans Blumenberg, who maintained that
Bach's religious music cannot be heard properly by moderns, for
the simple reason that they no longer belong to the community
of prayer for which the work was intended. Gould had another
community in mind, isolated individuals whom he exhorted to
assimilate a work without the mediation of a listening space that
was itself a community. But this new space could generate a new
community which, through its very freedom, possessed an eman-
cipating power. I believe this is the way to understand Gould's
confidence in technology; it was a confidence predicated on a
glowing future and founded on the liberating power of art for the
individual. He seemed not to see, or grasp, the possibility that
recourse to technology might result in one's being deprived of a
living presence and in the collapse of a vibrant community. We
have no indication, for example, that he ever spoke of the destructive power of television. He saw only the emergence of another
community, more perfect for being free of the vagaries of public
performance. Thus Ghyslaine Guertin could write, aptly: "The
recording is that realm where the experience of solitude is shared."
    This hope, and one might say this ingenuousness, to which
Gould so often gave voice after abandoning the concert hall,
ought not to surprise us, coming as it does from someone who

lived the greatest part of his life in a studio, remote from others, and who created a world for himself largely through telephone conversations. One might wonder, as with the painter in Natsume Sōseki's novel, if he would ever come down from his mountain. But he compensated for this allegiance to solitude with a fierce desire for communication, and his enlistment of the media helped him to create a balance he might never have otherwise achieved. In his 1963 essay "Forgery and Imitation in the Creative Process," a text of remarkable scope that blended a philosophy of history with a plea for liberty and individuality, Gould argued for an affiliation with art marked by individual freedom; reproductive technology was to play an important role in this process of liberation. He wrote:

> Art will not become subservient to the scientific process. It will borrow its media, but it will remain independent of its aims. The communication that is art will remain indefinable as ever. It will still attempt to speak of things, to render images, that no scientific measurement can assess. But the supreme irony may be that by borrowing from the scientific world what it needs it will, far from confirming the accumulative concepts of scientific information, be able to express the agelessness of the aesthetic impulse freed from the conformity that we have permitted history to impose.

∽

I dislike the comparison that became fashionable for a while among critics, of likening Gould's style of life to that of Howard Hughes. Gould did not seek out solitude purely for phobic and paranoid reasons; he looked to it for the accomplishment of his work, and as a base from which he could address himself to others, to that perfect community he wanted to help build. This conviction was so strong that he could confess to Jonathan Cott: "To some extent or other, all of the subjects I've chosen have had to do with isolation – even the musical ones." This statement helps us understand why he viewed his radio broadcasts as a single entity that embraced both his *Solitude Trilogy* and his portraits of Arnold Schoenberg, Pablo Casals, Richard Strauss, and Leopold Stokowski. In these series, artists and solitary individuals, grouped together or not into communities to safeguard their solitude, make the case for the life they have chosen, at the same time manifesting an authentic serenity. When Cott asks the following question: "Take the idea of radio as a metaphor for solitude. It's a much more private experience. Why do you think you're so interested in this inward-turning medium?," Gould evokes his childhood and the comfort he found in the constant companionship of the radio, but he says above all that solitude is indispensable to human relationships in a way that is impossible to express. Introversion is not a flaw, it is a necessity. That he could affirm that his musical preferences were determined by solitude remains a mystery to me; we can understand that he did not privilege works designed for community consumption, such as Bach's *Passions*, but we may wonder what characterizes a piece of music as being redolent of solitude. The answer to this question seems to me beyond our reach.

Gould embarked upon this work as a Canadian artist, himself brought up in the world of the Canadian Broadcasting Corporation. This world, it must be recalled, preceded the advent of television, and was created to promote the culture of a country so vast that only radio waves could hold it together. What the great railroad lines began, the radio would complete. The first instalment of the *Solitude Trilogy* dates from 1967, the centennial year of Canadian Confederation. The CBC's FM network was in its infancy, an ambitious undertaking whose contribution to the country's culture and identity is still admired today. We, who are witnessing, helplessly, the dismantling of the cultural service on the CBC networks, both English and French, find it hard to imagine that this same CBC entrusted Gould with projects that were so demanding and so costly in technical terms. We can even note, with irony, that one of CBC Television's last great artistic accomplishments before submitting to its fate as an entertainment medium, was the impressive homage it devoted to Gould in 1998, called *Extasis*. Gould's genius was clear to all, his reputation as a performer was at its zenith, but it was no doubt his passion for communication that had the Toronto studios opening their doors to him.

Innovation was in the air, and Gould had an irrepressible desire to become involved. When we look at the radio programs he created for the CBC, we can't help admiring their richness and diversity – but also their daring and their technical complexity. First came the recitals augmented with commentary. Beginning in 1966–67, the CBC aired a series devoted to his reading of musical history, titled *The Art of Glenn Gould*, in which Gould presented his work, along with interviews with writers and thinkers such as Jean Le Moyne. The program *Anti Alea*, which dates from 1968, gives us a good sense of his aesthetic project; wanting to introduce so-called aleatory music, Gould, together with several guests, delved into the very concept of chance. I remember having seen on television, in May 1966, a program with Yehudi Menuhin presented under the title *Duo*, where the two musicians discussed, among other works, Beethoven's *Sonata for Violin and Piano, Opus 96*. It was an hour of impressive musical complicity, but also of warm friendship; each approached the other seeking a community of interpretation, and their dialogue was rooted in admiration. Menuhin, who did not share Gould's views on the limitations of the concert hall, had tender, almost paternal feelings toward him. When they played this sonata together, even though Menuhin had expressed strong misgivings about contravening the score's explicit instructions, one could sense his admiration for Gould's audacity.

To this first grouping, we must add the series of ten radio programs devoted to Schoenberg, commemorating his centenary; they were broadcast in the autumn of 1974, and the scripts reflect Gould's consummate understanding of the work, plus his desire to see it recognized for its formal and expressive richness. Gould also produced a documentary program aired in November of the same year, *Schoenberg: The First Hundred Years – A Documentary Fantasy*, which brought to a close this cycle of tributes. It makes for an exemplary companion piece to the many texts by Gould on Schoenberg. Not content with this, Gould added a program, less well known, on Richard Strauss, about whom he had already written a great deal, in particular a very beautiful text published in 1962, "An Argument for Richard Strauss." For Gould, Strauss was a genius who perfectly embodied his time, "a central figure in today's most crucial dilemma of aesthetic morality, the hopeless confusion that arises when we attempt to contain the inscrutable pressures of self-guiding destiny within the neat, historical summation of collective chronology."

In the documentary *The Bourgeois Hero*, a title that reflects Gould's ambivalence vis-à-vis all forms of conventional life, he explores in nuanced fashion the balance Strauss struck between the innovative thrust of the times and his own conservatism. In this sense, the documentary can be interpreted as a necessary complement to his work on Schoenberg. Strauss was a key player in musical history for having protected tonality; it was essential that he do so. Gould worked on this project from 1976 until its broadcast, in two parts, on April 2 and 9, 1979. I will content myself with bringing forward these examples, as the corpus of his radio work is immense, and merits a study all to itself.

Gould's television series are well known. Like most of his radio broadcasts dealing with music and composition, they are in the first instance didactic. In 1966 Gould recorded *Conversations* with Humphrey Burton, on Schoenberg, Bach, Beethoven, and Richard Strauss, an intellectual fireworks display, a bouquet of candid thoughts full of hope for the music of the future. Now that we can read his work on Schoenberg, we see how this look forward drew its optimism from a body of work that is both lucid and rigorous.

The series "Music in our Time" is the most impressive; Gould had foreseen seven thematic programs, each dealing with one decade of the twentieth century. He produced four: *The Age of Ecstasy, 1900–1910*, broadcast in 1974; *The Flight From Order, 1910–1920*, broadcast in 1975; *New Faces, Old Forms, 1920–1930*, broadcast in 1975 as well; finally, *The Artist as Artisan, 1930–1940*, broadcast in 1977. They view musical works as so many boxes to be opened, texts to be read and understood; there is no mystery, only beauty accessible to all who have prepared their minds to receive it. Gould showed himself to be an attentive pedagogue, an impassioned analyst committed to shedding light on the logic of the works and the principles one might derive from them, bearing on interpretation. His judgments are sharp, often peremptory, and we can only appreciate them if, one way or the other, we are privy to the ideals that inspire them. These few examples, selected from among his many productions, highlight an aspect of Gould's talent that confirms his anti-romantic stance; for him music can be explained, and by commenting on it, the artist endows the community with the means to assimilate it, and later to recapture it, in silence and solitude.

Gould's confidence in the media was almost boundless, and there was no technological innovation he wouldn't try; in a 1970 broadcast called *The Well-Tempered Listener*, he produced a complex document whose editing techniques were inspired by the art of counterpoint. It is in that program that he included the short film by Norman McLaren and René Jodoin, *Spheres*, a ballet of rhythmic images that turns up again in François Girard's film *Thirty-Two Short Films about Glenn Gould*. This survey would not be complete if we did not include the films in which he agreed to participate, as of 1972, with Bruno Monsaingeon. The first series, "Les chemins de la musique," was commissioned by the ORTF in France. It included four films: *The Retreat, The Alchemist, Glenn Gould 1974,* and *The Partita No. 6 of Bach,* and it remains one of our most important documents for understanding Gould's art. Gould here comes across as precise and methodical, while his playing is consummate and inspired, and he seems to have been particularly content. Bruno Monsaingeon also filmed Gould in 1979–80, in a beautiful series devoted to the work of Bach. Five parts were planned initially, but the work was interrupted after the first three, by Gould's death. *The Question of Instrument* (1979) includes, notably, the *Partita No. 4 in D Major. An Art of the Fugue* (1980) gives us the *Contrapunctus,* the work's final section. The third film was shot in New York in April–May 1980. It is devoted to the *Goldberg Variations,* and so is closely linked to Gould's work on his second recording of the work, which he produced for CBS. It was broadcast in January 1982, and the record was released the following September, just before Gould's death on October 4. Gould clearly found in Monsaingeon a collaborator in whom he had total confidence, and when we see the film *Glenn Gould: Hereafter,* a virtual testament that the filmmaker-musician made in Gould's memory in 2006, we find ourselves once more in the presence of a work whose soundness and sensitivity Gould would have appreciated. Monsaingeon was also his translator and the editor in French of much of his writing, and Gould saw in him someone who shared his goals, where communication and the dissemination of ideas were concerned. Their friendship was a unique instance, in the history of piano art, of collaboration and mutual respect.

∽

In contrast to these didactic series, the three episodes of the *Solitude Trilogy* seem in many respects to embody the essence of Gould's communications aesthetic, the range of his broadcasting principles, and the accomplishment of his social project. In this series, a triptych of radio documentaries that he produced for the CBC from 1967 to 1977 – *The Idea of North, The Latecomers,* and *The Quiet in the Land* – Gould gave of himself fully as a thinker and as an artist. These important works are little known, and their connection with Gould's thinking on art is underestimated. They are founded, however, on a number of principles that for him were deep convictions. First and foremost were the primacy of communication and the vital importance of a bond with the community. There is nothing less romantic, in fact, than the artist seeking with a microphone to capture what is at the heart of the aesthetic experience, nothing less mysterious than to want to confer on all a voice that will speak for them; in his radio work Gould found a way into more than a musical experience – he penetrated a society and its world. The *Solitude Trilogy* was a documentary on the paradoxes of romanticism, and it shed light in a crucial way on all of Gould's work for radio and television. More indirectly, it illuminated his life as an artist and the reflective process that enabled him increasingly to purify it.

Music was not the primary focus of the trilogy. It was there in the background or in the final minutes, like the last movement of Sibelius's *Fifth Symphony*, which concluded the first section, *The Idea of North*. Nor did Gould seek a sociology of solitude, although many elements in the three documentaries make a rich contribution to it. Fascinated by isolated communities as well as by the people attracted to barren lands, Gould incorporated into these broadcasts a number of narratives and accounts describing solitude in cultures that favoured it, or for which it was their fate. We can read a letter from him to Professor James Lotz, who in 1959 had published a book on Ellesmere Island, and who was preparing a research project on the North that he later published, in 1970, under the title *Northern Realities: The Future of Northern Development in Canada*. Gould invited him to participate in the program. He had already spent several months working on it, travelling and meeting people, and he had gathered material that anyone else would have wanted to exploit politically, making public, for instance, demands voiced by native people or remote communities, in their minority status and their isolation. But the central concern of the trilogy lies elsewhere, and its nature is spiritual: Gould here broaches the subject of the ethics of solitude, crucial for him insofar as it is central to our life. He conceived of the ambitious project after deciding to desert the concert hall. Like the characters in *The Idea of North*, Gould had taken the train from Winnipeg to Churchill on the south shore of Hudson Bay. On board he met a man who was to be the central figure of the trilogy's first part, a Canadian National Railways conductor called Wally McLean. It is to him that he entrusts both the narration and the broadcast's final message.

*The Idea of North* is populated by types rather than real characters, and this is consistent with the work's abstract approach: we meet the enthusiast J.R. Lotz (James), the biologist and geographer animated by a kind of utopian vision of the North; the sociologist Francis G. Vallée (Frank), a sceptic and quasi cynic, always ready to undermine the idyllic representations of others, and unimpressed by the heroism of the Northern adventurers; a pragmatic civil servant, R.A.J. Phillips (Robert), with his bureaucratic vision for development, who has been transformed by his experiences with the Inuit; and a nurse, Marianne Schroeder, working at a mission on Southampton Island and oscillating between a candid and generous feeling of hope and a kind of disabused disappointment. For her, the beauty of the North is both powerful and threatening. Gould worked from interviews with these characters, and wove them into a radio document that went far beyond their individual accounts, but in no way represented their synthesis. Even if his method had dialectic resonances, Gould did not try to override his characters' points of view in order to impose his own vision. He was content to juxtapose them and to devise a quasi-moral listening experience; it is the plurality of the voices that counts, it alone can do justice to the North's aura of purification and asceticism.

Behind the metaphors for solitude, such as limits and silence, which abound in these accounts, lies an ethic that they help to structure. Gould's questions are not abstract; they deal with the concrete direction a life takes. In his introduction to the program, Gould emphasizes the importance of the geographical dimension as a starting point for his research, but the results show that it was not given precedence. Perhaps he was inspired by the writings of Stephen Leacock, who had lived in the town of Orillia on the shores of Lake Simcoe. This great humorist, who was born in 1869 and died in 1944, also wrote several books on the Canadian experience, and in 1912 published a Northern narrative, *Adventurers of the Far North: A Chronicle of the Frozen Seas*. His little 1912 volume *Sunshine Sketches of a Little Town* painted a satirical portrait of small towns like Orillia and Uptergrove. Gould knew them, certainly, but did he share Leacock's nationalism? We have reason to think so. However, it was not so much the map of the country that interested him as the conditions underpinning the kind of life that demanded courage and tenacity daily. The virtues of the North corresponded to those he judged essential for the artist, primarily the practice of austerity. We should also note that while Gould wrote that he wanted to visit the North Pole and experience the Arctic night, the North he did in fact visit, crossing by train, on board the Muskeg Express, the 1,609 kilometres separating Winnipeg from Churchill, was not quite the Far North, which runs from Lancaster Sound to Ellesmere Island. The North that fascinated him was an idea, a geographic extrapolation of Lake Simcoe, a spiritual realm beyond the modern urban world, which he did not recognize as his own even though he lived there and even though it too offered him real solitude. Gould, after all, only reached the point from which the explorer Samuel Hearne set out.

Gould never hid his fascination for the idea of the North, which he associated variously with the Arctic landscape and the boreal forest as painted by Toronto-based Canadian artists early in the twentieth century. The light they found there, its transparency, pervades this painting Gould knew so well, in which he saw reflected both the North's desolation and its powerful beauty. The immensity of the Canadian land, as represented in Group of Seven paintings, was familiar to him from childhood. In his introduction to *The Idea of North* he spoke of the work of A.Y. Jackson, a Montrealer and a member of the group. This artist, a great colourist, took part in most of the group's outings to Georgian Bay and Algonquin Park, returning with canvases that have since become icons of Canadian culture. Along with Lawren Harris, another member of the group, Jackson, in August 1930, even made the journey Gould would have liked to take; he visited the Arctic aboard a government ship. In the writings of these painters, we see the depth of their attachment to the North, and Gould reminds us that reproductions of their paintings hung in school-rooms all across Canada. Jackson speaks in his autobiography about his discussions with the other artists in the group, and their shared fascination for the mystical landscape of the North. Gould must have known about the spiritual background to this painting, which owes much to American Transcendentalism. I have found no reference in his writings to Emily Carr, who was close to the ideals of the Group of Seven, but I presume that like her – and like Harris, Jackson's comrade in arms – Gould had read Walt Whitman, in particular his tribute to the wide-open spaces of the American landscape. And what do we see in Jackson's painting? First, a wild and tormented nature, conifers battered by the winds as in *Terre Sauvage*, a canvas from 1913, and an absorption in the landscape so complete that one seems to have been swallowed up by it. Despite the luxuriance of the colours, nothing is rich or abundant; all is starkness and severity. But it is majestic and sublime, thanks to the austerity of the rocks, the endlessness of the space. In a key book on the Group of Seven, Fred Housser wrote as early as 1926: "The tang of the north is colouring souls as it colours the leaves in autumn." Like all the painters in the Group, Jackson thought the North embodied Canada's identity, and Gould was sensitive to this mythology of Algonquin Park. I have always felt that this landscape, around Georgian Bay, is not so different from that of the Northern Laurentians, with which I associate it.

To describe it I would say that we sense a boundary, an end to things, a final threshold, almost an exhaustion; this forest shot through with conifers signals the end of the gentle broad-leaved trees, and the Laurentian lakes reflect back a sky that, without being that of the Arctic, is nevertheless open and infinite, of a piece with this desolate North. Were it possible to transcribe the light painted by Jackson or Harris into music, Gould's playing would perhaps come closest to it: a limpidity, a clarity, but above all an opening onto an endless space that is also a threshold – the perfectly defined crests at the horizon, the precision of the rocks, the encounter with a solitude of lakes and trees. In a beautiful study published in 1996, Paul Hjartarson likened Harris's experience to Gould's work, and showed that, with these two artists, the North was first of all an inner journey; and that, even if Gould did not share Harris's theosophical mysticism, he sought the same beneficial effects, a landscape that was virginal and restorative. Listening to Gould play Bach, and thinking of his fascination for this mythic North, I have often been reminded of Paul-Marie Lapointe's early poems, the magnificent *Arbres*, with their Nordic litany, their Laurentian sadness. Gould would have liked these poems, where the abstraction of the forest encounters a melancholy vision of nature.

And so there was a spiritual orientation guiding Gould's gaze; urban values, in some sense spiritually debased, seemed of less worth than those of the North. Even if he was well aware of the romantic ambiguity of his attraction to an independent and solitary life – is one not more completely alone in a high-rise apartment at the heart of an American metropolis than in a deserted locale? – Gould was still persuaded of the moral richness of his idea of North. Speaking of it as a metaphor, depicting the North's attraction as allegorical, does not at all diminish the fact that the Northern experience profoundly altered those who surrendered to it. In his introduction to the first part of his trilogy, Gould wrote:

> Something really does happen to most people who go into
> the North – they become at least aware of the creative oppor-
> tunity which the physical fact of the country represents and –
> quite often, I think – come to measure their own work and
> life against that staggering creative possibility: they become,
> in effect, philosophers.

What does it mean, to become a philosopher? To become conscious of the possibility of creating. This philosophical ideal is first of all a decision to shape one's life, and Gould took it from Henry David Thoreau, who had made it the centrepiece of all his writing. The dramatic structure he devised to illustrate this philosophy in progress was an ingenious one. Gould designed an imaginary confrontation between five points of view, ranging from a yearning for the infinite to utter disillusionment. Each was represented by the voice of a real individual; each stemmed from an authentic Northern experience, beginning with a conversation in the dining car of a train wending its way toward Churchill. This simple *mise en scène* allowed him to highlight, in a striking way, the juxtaposed philosophical attitudes, beginning with a fragment from

Pascal on diversion, and ending with Sibelius's *Fifth Symphony*. Gould often spoke of why he considered this symphony a high point in the art of solitude; Sibelius's art was profoundly Nordic, passionate without being sensual. It was in fact philosophical, because we cannot listen to his music without being conscious of what lay behind his thinking– not only Finland with its mysterious forests, but also the inner landscape of a spiritual quest striving to transcend time. Gould also confessed that listening to this symphony in a performance conducted by Herbert von Karajan in Berlin had given him proof positive of music's spiritual power. That he chose to conclude his documentary with this magical listening experience attests to the strength of this memory and what it meant to Gould, embodying as it did spiritual perfection and a state of grace suspended beyond time. In a 1974 interview, he declared: "I couldn't live without Sibelius's *Fifth Symphony*."

Gould commented at length on the technique of his triptych, as though what interested him most in the series was its form, but the listener who looks to the work for strict aesthetic principles will not be wholly satisfied with its author's introduction. Gould seemed to want to emphasize the musical analogies guiding its composition more than its moral implications. To give only one example, he presented his project as an exercise in contrapuntal radio comparable to the form of the trio sonata. In an important interview with John Jessop, "Radio as Music," published in 1971 in *The Canadian Music Book*, he spoke of his desire to work with musical forms in such a way as to avoid a too obvious linear structure. He wanted to achieve "an integrated unit of some kind in which the texture, the tapestry, of the words themselves would differentiate the characters and create dramalike conjunctions within the documentary." An example is precisely the trio sonata. Three clearly identified voices do, in fact, provide the introduction to *The Idea of North*. In this interview, Gould writes:

The scene is built so that it has a kind of ... Webern-like continuity in crossover in that motives which are similar but not identical are used for the exchange of instrumental ideas. So in that sense, it was very musical; I think its form was free from the restrictions of form, which is a good way to be, you know, and the way in which one would like to be in all things, eventually. But that took time, and in the case of "North" it started with all kinds of forbidding memories of linearity. One had to gradually grow into a different sort of awareness.

There is no reason to doubt Gould's fascination with the technical possibilities of sound editing: the montage of voices, the cutting, everything that contributes to the reconstruction in the studio of material captured in the real world – this is all profoundly musical. However, it is not long before the meaning of what is said becomes blurred due to the superimpositions. In this contrapuntal project, the technique transforms the voices into purely musical lines. And so Gould positions himself on the frontier between meaning and sound, and the music that dominates the text ends up dislocating it almost completely. No listener can be serenely unaffected by the austerity of this form, nor sustain the effort normally required to extract meaning; to keep step with Gould, one must surrender to the music of the voices. But the meaning is still there, however fragmented; an intrinsic part of the Northern experience, the voices expose its harshness, and demonstrate the difficulties involved in producing speech at all. Like the airwave interference that used to affect radio reception at a distance, this counterpoint of superimposed voices is a plea for contact, almost urging it into existence.

Moreover, as the intent of this work is to transmit a message to the listener, the director at his console emerges as the quintessentially modern artist: he orchestrates diversity and enacts the anxiety of the journey. This does not immediately make for a style, but it does dramatize the Northern allegory his characters have put together, to be deconstructed in the musicality of the work. Working closely with a technician – Lorne Tulk, who perfectly understood what he wanted to do – Gould began by establishing the form his allegory would take: a symphony of voices. The first time I heard *The Idea of North*, I thought of Stockhausen's *Gesang der Jünglinge*, a work from 1955–56, and I was not surprised to read later that Gould compared it to that composer's *Stimmung*; the fact that the choral aspects dominate made me see it as a polyphonic work. But, despite its richness and complexity, this polyphony is not there just for its own sake.

Beyond these musical analogies and the search for form, Gould is advancing a more complex proposition, clearer in the *Solitude Trilogy* than elsewhere, because it is more overt. He addresses the need for solitude and asceticism, and takes the risk of confronting head-on the paradox of solitude in the midst of a crowd, and the fate of an individual embarked on a journey that is a shared adventure. It has been suggested that the leitmotif of this journey was inspired by his reading of Katherine Anne Porter's novel, *Ship of Fools*. Tulk remembers having seen Stanley Kramer's film adaptation of the novel in 1965, along with Gould. It is possible that he drew something from it, but there are significant differences between *The Idea of North* and the book and (even more) the film, including the fact that Gould was not concerned with the dramatic interlocking of destinies; only diversity interested him, not personal adventures or the vagaries of circumstance. Fascinated by the superimposition of voices, Gould brought his five characters together for a shared meditation on the experience of North. There is no reference here to the medieval Ship of Fools, nor to the carnival atmosphere, with its attendant derision, to be found in the painting of Bosch; Gould juxtaposes spiritual attitudes toward a landscape whose redemptive powers he hopes will compensate for the evils of modernity. Wally McLean's North is one that can fulfill the aspirations of those suffering from isolation in the cities: another solitude is possible, one founded on a deep bond with nature, one that allays suffering. In a letter dated September 5, 1971, Gould wrote to Helen Whitney that the "Thoreauvian way of life" was his true *cantus firmus* in *The Idea of North* and *The Latecomers*:

> I said earlier on, that I was going to submit a non-musical proposal and, in that category, the idea which comes to mind at the moment is a look at the Thoreauvian way of life as evidenced in present-day America. You will of course, recognize this as south-of-the-border adaptation of my theme – the c.f. (cantus firmus) for The Idea of the North and for The Latecomers, et al, the relationship of isolation and solitude to ones productive capacity; in effect to one's life in the world.

Gould deeply loved Canada, and his vision of the North paid heartfelt tribute to the Canadian experience, an experience shaped by thinly populated territories coping with difficult conditions, discipline in one's personal life, and an inward and austere religious temperament. Looking back on this program, he had no reservations about what he had accomplished; Canada's Northern experience was a creative force for those who accepted and recognized its deepest meaning, its moral dimension. It was "an opportunity to examine that condition of solitude which is neither exclusive to the north nor the prerogative of those who go north, but which does perhaps appear, with all its ramifications, a bit more clearly to those who have made, if only in their imagination, the journey north ... What [*The Idea of North*] was really about ... was the dark night of the human soul. It was a very dour essay into the effects of isolation upon mankind." For Gould, we may be sure, these effects could only be beneficent.

Had he wished, Gould could have extended his research to include political repression, tackling the question of the White man's presence and the destruction of Amerindian cultures; he flirted with these issues, but his argument is set in a realm beyond politics. His Canadian landscape is not entirely metaphorical; it exists in the context of a concrete geography that is *a priori* social and political. But for Gould it offered the possibility of transcending life's strictures and limiting conditions. Freedom was certainly the primary theme; it comes into its own in the opportunity it offers for all to prevail over alienating circumstances and find themselves in a creative confrontation with the Northern solitude. The CBC producer responsible for the project, Janet Somerville, spoke of it as Canada's *Finlandia*. This notion is consistent with the fact that Sibelius is cited in the epilogue, but even more, it is an extremely acute observation related to Gould's spiritual aims; through the trilogy we are meant to experience a dimension of hope proper to the land, with its epic dimensions and its moral demands. At first glance, one might assume that Gould produced these three programs only to demonstrate the richness of contrapuntal radio and the need for an art that could incorporate complex forms, but all indications are that this form had as its goal a spiritual transcendence and the shaping of a Canadian myth.

But does this yearning for solitude not smack of romantic posturings and their evident pitfalls for the artist? Such paradoxes are disconcerting to consider: Gould the anti-romantic as apologist for solitude and withdrawal? Gould the communicator of the airwaves as the poet of Northern asceticism? Gould the fan of Petula Clark as the sublime interpreter of the *Goldberg Variations*? The path Gould chose in the *Trilogy* gives us a number of opportunities to defuse these paradoxes, define his aesthetic in terms of its give and take with the community, and so lend it coherence. I am trying to do this in various ways, and the radio trilogy, in this regard, gives us a unique perspective on Gould's non-romantic ethic of solitude. Gould had just given up performing when he produced the first part of this trilogy, and we can see it almost as a self-questioning exercise: if you have walked away from a living community, then what community can you henceforth claim as your own? If you do not want to avail yourself of anything near to you, what other closeness can you adopt? The answer is both simple and obvious: the new community available to the artist is one of distance spanned by technology, a community created by this same technology, and committed to its ascetic ideals. It is not surprising that Gould later described this broadcast as the project that came closest to being autobiographical.

This effort at reconciliation plays itself out first in the context of solitude's founding metaphors: the North, the frontier, the outer limits, the journey. There is no more beautiful image to embody all that than the one that opens and closes François Girard's film *Thirty-Two Short Films about Glenn Gould*. The artist, transported to the icy surface of a Northern lake, approaches us from an infinite distance, and moves away from us into that same vastness. If he could have seen this image, Gould would certainly have recognized the ethical vision of the North that he had tried to express in the first part of his trilogy. In fact, it is just a reproduction of a January 1970 photograph he declared to be his favourite, in which we see him walking on a frozen lake dressed in his overcoat and cap. I have earlier explained why this image bears the burden of a certain anxiety, recalling an accident from Gould's youth when the ice gave way under him. The North is not a severance from community, but the embodiment of any spiritual quest seeking transcendence; the artist, with his ascetic impulse, like any individual pushing things to the limit, does not seek separation and isolation, but a stripped down life that will help him rediscover what community really means. The North is simply a metaphor for this quest. It connotes privation and an elusive rigour; but it is not hardship that is important so much as a movement towards transcendence. The more the artist distances himself, the more aware he is of the ties that bind him. The North is the outer limit, the North is the beyond, and this beyond creates the conditions for a rapture all its own.

There is another romanticism that exalts this Northern solitude, one that reserves it for the noblest of minds and for reclusive artists with Nietzschean temperaments. Was not Glenn Gould himself just such a solitary figure? True, in his deepest withdrawal he was in constant pursuit of the sublime, but that is not to do justice to the greater scope of his activities. For this hermit never burned his bridges with society; he was never so happy as when he was in front of a microphone. His retreat from the concert hall was a great escape from the conventions of romanticism, but in the solitude of the recording studio, communication was what he sought, and of the highest order. His radio work was instrumental in that research. Here again, François Girard's film illustrates this admirably, for example in the scene where we see Gould listening in at the truckers' café to the counterpoint of ordinary voices that is intrinsic to any society, the sounds of life that are no different from music if, in solitude, one is steeped in it. Gould's radio work grew out of this listening experience, and constitutes its transcription. Through this work, he sought tirelessly to demythologize conventional romanticism. There is nothing inscrutable in the artist's solitude; it turns him inexorably back toward his community. Art is a passion for the sublime with the community in view. The North is never just symbolic; it is a magnetic north for the solitary mind. In reality the artist, like everyone, is linked, part of a society to which he will dedicate himself all the more once he has grasped the impossibility of a romantic identification with himself. Solitude ought not to see itself as a manifestation of inward-turning neuroticism; it never fulfills itself more than when it takes part in the community's song.

To express this essential link between solitude and community, Gould turned toward two isolated communities in the two ensuing documentaries. In *The Latecomers*, which deals with fishing villages in Newfoundland, and in *The Quiet in the Land*, set among the Mennonites in Manitoba, the individual's spiritual quest is inseparable from the problem of survival and an isolated group's search for meaning in life. The notion of limits or of the frontier here seems of less importance than the transposition of the hermetic ideal into an entire society. United in isolation, is this society not closer to what is truly important? But to what, exactly? It is not the boundary in and of itself that deepens one's experience, but a form of recognition and renunciation. As they face the threat of disappearance, or even the challenge of substantial change, what resources do these isolated communities draw upon?

The philosophical standpoint of *The Latecomers* is given voice by a commentator quoting Thoreau: "At least people who are removed from the centre of society are always more able to see it clearly. You know, if you go back to the nineteenth century, there was nobody in the United States who saw nineteenth-century American society with such clarity and incisiveness as Thoreau, who saw it from the perspective of a cabin in the woods, and this is till true … It is always more difficult to see anything from the centre than to see it from the outside." In his 1971 interview with John Jessop, Gould added: "I'd like to use Newfoundland to lead a life like Thoreau." This little phrase says it all. Gould travelled to Newfoundland early in autumn, 1968, and as for the first part of the trilogy, he collected voices and stories. To be a philosopher here meant responding to the challenges of isolation and insularity in a new way: with similar rigour, one had to find a way of seeing society as clearly as possible, and achieving this perspective required separation and solitude. Viewing things from the centre dooms one to a form of blindness that encourages conformity and repetition; looking on from the outside gives us a clear notion of what freedom is, and the path we should be following. Unlike the five characters in *The Idea of North*, who are all active participants in the life of the North, the thirteen Newfoundland figures, buoyed by the constant sound of the sea, focus on the demands of art: the writer's voice is central here, it articulates the blessings of a life lived far afield.

One has to admire Gould's formal research as he set out to capture this philosophical process. He himself saw it as the staging of a "journey to selfhood." The passengers on the train in *The Idea of North* perfectly exemplified this quest for a new sort of mediation; the program, in fact, juxtaposed several different ways of interpreting the journey, each sequence presenting the listener with a different brand of solitude. In *The Latecomers*, the choice has already been made, and what we hear are the justifications: "People are ecstatic about getting into the mainstream, and I think it's a little bit stupid, since the mainstream is pretty muddy, or so it appears to me." The perils of conformity, the enervation of modernity, the harsh judgment on the part of one who has backed away from the centre – it is all there. But at no point does one hear Gould's voice endorsing the overall message: the meaning here, as in *The Idea of North*, resides in the dialogue of voices, a kind of tragic counterpoint where singular lives are groping toward an ethic of solitude. Each must make contact with all the others, if the community is to be validated. There is an echo here of the meditations of Kierkegaard, another great Nordic voice in thrall to austerity.

All the documentary material relating to the lives of the native people, the culture of the islanders, the conflict between traditional ways of life and an advancing technology, takes second place to the subject of solitude. How to comprehend Newfoundland's need to see its isolation as a blessing? The style of life may vary, but each culture must look to itself for its grounds for survival. *The Idea of North* was about seeking the necessary conditions for a spiritual experience, and finding them in an acceptance of the community; in *The Latecomers* it is a matter of fighting the temptation of exile, clinging to a lonely rock, and learning that tenacity only has meaning if it is freely chosen: "If I couldn't afford to leave when I want to leave, I'd never be able to stay in Newfoundland." In every case, solitude is meaningful only when it is accompanied by a commitment to the community. The political backdrop to Gould's reflections is not given a lot of prominence, but it should be stated: recent legislation was forcing the inhabitants out of their small outports and resettling them in larger centres. Gould was outraged by this stupid and arbitrary decision, and his program offered an implicit, ethical resistance to bureaucratic power; while the inhabitants of the small village of Saint-Joseph, who make up the entire cast of characters for this part of the trilogy, protest their imposed exodus, the town itself is assailed by the ocean waves that are the work's dominant voice: insistent, dramatic, pacifying.

Almost ten years separate the first two parts of the trilogy from the broadcast of *The Quiet in the Land* in 1977. In this time Gould's broadcasting skills had greatly matured. His contrapuntal technique had evolved from the theatrical austerity of *The Idea of North* to an extraordinarily complex musical form drawing notably on the advantages of stereophonic space. The Red River Mennonites of Manitoba are now the principal actors and they are presented in several sequences, linked by a religious celebration at the church: it is Easter supper on Holy Thursday. As in the previous parts, Gould first gathered the accounts and recorded two Mennonite services, one in English and one in German, in the town of Waterloo. But beyond this enrichment of the form, Gould's reflections on solitude have passed from a dialectical presentation to a proclamatory theological exposition, an Easter gospel lacking only the organ of his *The Art of Fugue* for him to have put his

signature to it. How to see in the reserved nature of the Mennonites an essential gift for a spiritual life?

It is important not to misinterpret this religious affirmation. In
*The Idea of North*, the listener is left to determine the ethical position he considers appropriate; he is the one called upon to find his
way among the avenues proposed by the different voices. Was not
solitude just a romantic illusion, transformed into a metaphor for
a Northern beyond? Gould's response already foreshadows the need
for a symbolic redemption: neither cynicism nor romanticism can
lead to serenity. Cynicism leads to death, while romanticism, in
despair at never tallying with oneself, produces a neurosis that
makes art impossible. But the squaring off between these positions
never goes beyond a dialectic; this counterpoint in broadcast form,
especially in moments of confusion and the overlapping of voices,
embodies perfectly the philosophical difficulties involved in Thoreau's
"growing into philosophy." Everyone is thrown back on himself,
everyone has to decide what withdrawal means for him, and the
internalization of the voices, which alone can lead to a resolution,
is not provided; it is left to each individual's pondering. *The Idea of
North* in this respect represents the trilogy's Socratic moment.

The second part, *The Latecomers*, by contrast, deals with
necessity and its constraints: the freedom to remain on the island
or not, to accept that fate, only enriches one's solitude if to belong
to Newfoundland is to be free, to consent to the community. From
that point on, the artist is nothing more than the most accomplished of island figures; besieged, he must understand that his
isolation is the necessary precondition for this freedom. If from
the outset one accepts this isolation as one's destiny, then there is
no room for cynicism. Here again, thanks to the force of the community, the romantic posture is no more. This second program
marks a transition toward an ethic that is less apprehensive, less
dialectic, and more affirmative. Art here arises out of a consen-
sual solitude within the community.

This bond, the deepest of all for Gould, becomes the subject of the third documentary, inspired by Mennonite theology. This Anabaptist Christian community, which goes back to the fifteenth century, has long cultivated a non-violent spirituality grounded in the rural life its members share with another Anabaptist community, the Amish of Pennsylvania. The isolation of these communities is a function of their members' religious convictions. Solitude is willed by God, and for Him it is embraced. The citation accompanying this part of the trilogy, from Saint Paul's First Epistle to the Corinthians, is addressed as much to the artist as to the solitary ascetic: "You are in the world, but you are not of this world." One's presence in the world does not exclude one's detachment from it. Even if this ethic of separation is based on the doctrine of the heavenly kingdom, there is another remoteness at stake here: the world of art is also distinct, and isolated. For those who have elected a religious community, isolation is a sign; it affirms the identity of those who have dedicated themselves to God's service. Through this consecration, the solitude of the community becomes the solitude of all its members; they are alone insofar as the community is isolated, but are never really alone, because the community is a true community. With the Mennonites, not only is the desire to serve, as manifested in the Northern quest, assuaged but also the disquiet of people who are cut off from others by their faith and always feel the threat of being stalled, left behind, relegated to the margins of history. In *The Idea of North*, the urban individual wonders if a truth resides in a world elsewhere that would distance him from his community but reveal to him his authentic self; in *The Latecomers*, the island dweller knows that his community is threatened by civilization and its technology, but that does not stop him from being attracted by the centre to the point of wanting to return there. Nostalgia for a once perfect community encourages him to see a kind of richness in his present-day solitude, even if he knows that the fruit is already rotten. For many,

things up in such a way that she sings for them and they sing for her. And what does she sing? She prays God to give her a Mercedes; all her friends are driving Porsches and pay no attention to her; she's slaving away and deserves that God take care of her because no one else does. In that she is wrong; the Mennonites are praying for her.

Is this answer Gould's? It is hard to credit it entirely. Looking back on this trilogy in interviews and in his correspondence, we see him anxious to validate the polyphonic character of his quest, the diversity of voices. Even if serenity can be reached only through Mennonite theology, for him it was doubtless just one response among others to the injunction of solitude. Lofty, strong, it transforms all the community members into artists and philosophers; they become one single voice bearing meaning; this theology bears the modern individual's quest to its farthest limit, to the point where it might self-destruct. Anyone can in fact become an incarnation of the artist as a Christian figure: he is "in the world," since he functions there, resistant, but he is not "of the world"; he is set apart from it by his quest and by art and its aims. This is Gould's meaning when he cites Paul preaching to the Corinthians: "Come ye out from among them, and be separate." This injunction is addressed to all those for whom the quest for an inner world constitutes the essence of life. Art and religion represent two facets of this quest for sanctity; it is always a matter of fleeing frivolity, the evils of the external world, vulgar sentiment, the absurd demands of individuality. In meditating on solitude, Gould may have wanted to make abundantly clear, by interchanging them, how aesthetic and religious attitudes can converge.

He illustrates this convergence by juxtaposing gospel singing with the motets of Schütz. We know that the music that stayed with him all his life and had a special place in his heart was an ensemble of choral pieces by Orlando Gibbons, a musician of the

Tudor court, organist, and author of a number of antiphonal chorales. The negro spiritual, Schütz, Gibbons – all these forms of music aim at a transcendence of what is individual, all embody a longing for liberation. Do these preferences contradict his attraction to "solitary musical compositions"? Gould is preoccupied with the paradox of community: how can the artist conform to the demands of community life, such as that of the Mennonites? He can only take inspiration from it, echo its call. Janis Joplin would no longer suffer if she could blend into one of these choirs, where the sublime consists in the fusion of solitary individuals with the community. But in this fusion, is the artist's solitude, his entry point to creation, still valid? Has the dwindling of romanticism not done away with the individual? It's not at all certain that Gould would have endorsed the views of one of his Mennonite interviewees on the dangers of philosophy and the banning of television. In a world of relinquishment and loss, fusion with the choir is perhaps just one more illusion. "The North," says the character Wally Maclean, "is a place where you can be faithful to yourself." With the Mennonites, that challenge would perhaps be impossible.

The quest for solitude and the ethic on which it is founded, if it is to involve the community, has no choice, ultimately, but to blend in with it. The *Solitude Trilogy* proposes to stretch this quest to its limit to show that it is not paradoxical, that it implies no contradiction that would compromise creativity, but that it provides no solution other than the need, itself, for the quest. Here again, the image of the artist moving away and coming forward on the surface of the ice can guide us as we listen: he will never reach us, yet he will never remain entirely separate. Gould's anti-romantic convictions could not take him anywhere else. I look at the familiar *Terre Sauvage* painted by A.Y. Jackson, a canvas that could serve as an emblem for the *Solitude Trilogy*. There I see trees pointing like arrows to the sky, and rocks giving onto chasms, and the raw hues that are the hallmark of the Group of Seven. In this symphony of feral colours there is a counterpoint to *The Idea of North;* this is the landscape that called out to Gould, beckoning him to solitude, this is the world that had embodied it for him since his early youth. Neither Janis Joplin's voice nor the Mennonite choir troubles the silence.

# VI

*Scherzo*

# Music and a Life's Shape
## *Partita no. 3 in A Minor*

What is the shape of a life? For the Greek thinkers it was clear-cut: lives were shaped according to recognizable types drawn from an established repertoire. However, we are no longer certain of being able to see ourselves in the hierarchy they proposed and which Plato outlined in his *Republic*. Why, we wonder, should we assume that the life of the mind is superior to a life in business or the life of a politician? Hannah Arendt, although critical of the precedence given to the *vita contemplativa* over the *vita activa*, still thought that dislodging it from that rank was not a simple task. Those who withdraw to find in the leisurely life of the *otium* the sort of peaceful liberation that only retreat can offer, are they truly disengaged from political concerns? Can they put out of mind the injustices and sufferings that weigh down those plunged in the thick of action?

When we reflect on this traditional hierarchy and ask ourselves whether a contemplative withdrawal is the only path to genuine happiness, it seems to me that Hannah Arendt's criticism is incomplete. How can we not see that art and creation are given no place at all in this pyramidal model? In Plato's happy city, poets and artists are not really welcome, the philosopher hesitating between their forcible expulsion and the temptation to give them some healthy advice. But would Arendt herself have approved of their withdrawal? Or would she have seen in their artistic commitment, in their asceticism, a kind of life compatible with being active in the world? To shape one's life is to make a fundamental and irrevocable choice, and the gulf separating those who back away from those who throw themselves into the flow of things was for the Ancients an unbridgeable gap; withdrawal meant a complete absorption in the life of the mind. The omission of art from this model, in which the political always takes precedence over the poetic, brings to light another paradox, for even if the artist retreats as completely as the thinker, he remains active on the world stage. His solitude, as I have tried to indicate in a number of ways, does not exclude the world. The choice to be made is never as radical as the Ancients thought; devoting one's life to thought or art cannot silence the world to the point of our ceasing to know anything of it and forgetting the gift we owe it. Contrary to what Arendt says, to choose a life from which thought and art are excluded would be all the more radical and exclusive, because amnesia would be built in.

The choice Gould made shows how impossible an absolute withdrawal is; there is always an inherent opening onto the world, an implicit gift. His dedication to music and the asceticism it required of him ruled out only one thing: an ordinary, conformist existence. But do ordinary lives really exist, lives so orderly that they lack transcendence and are completely untroubled by demands from an always improbable elsewhere, another world wanting more than a simple response? Gould chose a form of life in which renunciation became, over time, a prerequisite for art. The improbable was thrust on him along with his talent, and he had to accept its consequences just as he had to live a solitary life.

At the core of this life, glowing with a dark light, is a hearth where life and art are fused. Every artist is illuminated by it; therein lies his authenticity. For Gould, I repeat, all of life is in art, all of art is in life. These are matters that preoccupy all those captivated by his art. It is not just a question of developing a heightened appreciation of the direction his life took; having recognized it, we need to see how this form of life, which involves a very particular ethic, can illuminate his aesthetic. These two realms are sufficiently distinct that we may study them separately; like superimposed transparencies, neither predominates over the other. Gould's aesthetic is all there in the word "ecstatic," the sense of wonder that informs a luminous reading of music history and the philosophy of art. His references to a "part of divinity" bear the marks of the transcendental tradition with which counterpoint is as much associated as was his broadcasting art. Ethics is intrinsic to the shape of his life, it is the specific *bios* of a man who was never tragic, however many things he renounced. To know what "the good" meant to him we must look again at his particular form of asceticism, and at his withdrawal.

What we risk in doing so, given what we know about the artist, is to call into question the way we assimilate his art, the art of an interpreter. Many pianists have lived rich and fascinating lives, but for most the connection between their art and their life seems unimportant: Horowitz was doubtless as brilliant as his playing, Pogorelich very impetuous, Richter fiery and justifiably angry, but these descriptions are still perfunctory, as we have no access to the substance of their personal ethic. On the other hand, when we confront Gould's art – and this Thomas Bernhard clearly demonstrated – all of life comes into play. Bernhard's novel *The Loser* was the first to attempt a moral description of Glenn Gould. Even if the description is largely fictitious, modelled on the lives of a number of anguished writers – in particular the austere and anxiety-prone Ludwig Wittgenstein – it has the significant virtue of going to the heart of Gould's perfectionism and asceticism. I raise the subject again to describe how this personality type in its state of withdrawal is constituted.

We consistently encounter solitude, withdrawal, problems with the outside world, a rich inner life, a deepening immersion in books, an unrelenting search for the ideal interpretation, a desire for transcendence. As with Wittgenstein or Joseph Beuys, we are in the presence of a thinker and artist whose existence, stretched to the extreme, is entirely given over to sublimation and its transformative power. I would not hesitate to speak of the sanctity of art, even if I cannot with precision enumerate its virtues. Are we, as beneficiaries of Gould's art – of the genius of his readings, of the courage underlying his many provocations – correct in seeking an understanding of it in the life itself, where his aesthetic and ethic were so deeply rooted, and to which the art gave expression? This complex question has its mirror image, not to be forgotten: an entire life may be informed by the dictates of art, by its strictest demands, to the point where it may fall entirely under art's sway. To explain art through life can only enlighten if we at the same time seek a single generative wellspring beyond art and life – a source that has authenticated the quests of all great artists, and has shaped their lives according to models whose meaning can only be understood through their art. The problem here is linguistic: what language could possibly do justice both to the art of an interpreter and to the life he has chosen?

We would not be so interested in Gould's life if we were not persuaded that we had a chance of finding there what was most vital to his art – and if we had not seen that he himself played with high stakes, risking potential pitfalls, as in 1955, for example, when, in revolutionizing the interpretation of the *Goldberg Variations*, he laid out its aesthetic framework as well. Who was this person who dared to scale such heights and take such a gamble? Once we recognize a life so shaped, in its steadfastness and its intense asceticism, then we can anticipate its providing us with insights on art that an aesthetic discourse could not muster on its own. The problem with descriptors that try to capture a performance in and of itself is also the problem of all approximations; "buoyant," "clear," "rigorous," "sublime," these qualifiers can only express our own desire to get a grip on the aesthetic by hoisting ourselves to the ethical threshold of the artist's risk taking. By turning toward the life an artist has led, one hopes that these approximations might clarify themselves, to the degree that descriptions of performance will be grounded in a moral language inherent in the life itself.

Gould himself encourages us in this. Very drawn to the score of the *Goldberg Variations* as a young pianist, he presented them first in a Toronto concert on 16 October 1954, just a year before the recording that made him famous. In his interviews with Jonathan Cott, speaking of Rosalyn Tureck, he had already made the connection between his aesthetic research and his interpretation of the *Variations*.

> I was fighting a battle in which I was never going to get a surrender flag from my teacher on the way in which Bach should go, but her [Tureck's] records were the first evidence that one did not fight alone. It was playing of such uprightness, to put it in the moral sphere. There was such a sense of repose that had nothing to do with languor, but rather with moral rectitude in the liturgical sense.

The terms he uses in this recollection are clear: "uprightness," "moral rectitude." But how to understand this association of moral rigour with the liturgical meaning of a performance? It is just at this juncture of the moral and the aesthetic that biographical writing begins; it would have no particular interest otherwise. A biographer as sensitive as Kevin Bazzana does not shrink from this challenge; he reveals the life through the art. From his child-hood, Gould's life was ruled from within by the demands of art, and all those who are interested in what made him unique – as much his precocity as his singularity – face the fact that nothing in this life was without meaning in relation to the art it made pos-sible. Evoking his neurotic syndromes, recalling his phobias and idiosyncrasies, highlighting the stereotypical aspects of an excep-tional human being, documenting his failed romances – none of these makes sense unless it can be related to an appreciation of his art, where genius is reconciled with life. We find ourselves in the same situation as when we look at the many portraits of Gould that we love; we look for traces of the art to be confirmed by the life, but if the details are baldly presented, whether via an anecdote or an obsession, their relationship to art risks being obscured. Gould's gaze, the movement of his body in performance, the flu-idity of his gestures, even his posture at the piano, cannot be reduced to idiosyncrasies; rather they open the way to questions about the shaping of a life. This applies also to François Girard's beautiful film, which proposed, on the model of the *Goldberg Variations*, thirty-two icons designed to capture a life's shape.

In order to clarify this relationship between life and art, we have to show what makes it possible and demonstrate its internal coherence. Despite his constant quest for transparency, as much in his playing as in his life, Gould could well remain a mystery to us, and this transparency could remain a kind of illusion, an inacces-sible ideal. Why? Simply because in dealing with this relationship we must take the necessary risk of including a moral consideration of the artist's experience and, in Gould's precise case, we must include the quest for the absolute and for solitude that character-ized his entire life. In drawing on the concept of "a life's shape" to come to terms with this experience, I am distancing myself once more from its Wittgensteinian usage, which relates to the role the outside world plays in the understanding of an act, a gesture, or a

listening to those hidden, inner voices that are the warp and woof of counterpoint, and whose articulation Gould seemed able to absorb physically.

But if we hope to comprehend the relationship of art to this form of life, we must dare one more step. In documenting so much that is unique – a destiny so exceptional, a relationship to the world marked by so many phobic features, to cite only one recurring motif in the accounts of those who knew him – do we come any closer to an aesthetic that was the culmination of the artist's quest? We have no hesitation in affirming that we do: what was uncompromising in Gould's life was his pursuit on all fronts of a total coherence with the aims of his art. I have spoken of it as a perfectionism that affected all aspects of his life. To detect the operative sublimation here, and to relate it to what was sublime in his interpretations, is what an aesthetic view of his life ought first of all to achieve. What is the sublime? Kant associates it directly with what is solemn, while ordinary parlance, paradoxically, has us gazing at it obliquely from below to on high. But one could also interpret it as the boundary we cross in moving from one state to another, the alchemical sublimation to which Freud introduced us. It is the level we attain that matters, and this search for a state of ecstasy relies on our essential need to reach higher; it plays itself out in such a way that what is chemical and material, one's very unconscious, is elevated, transformed, idealized. It is language that resists any elevation that, whether through pure solitude or complete withdrawal, would cut itself off from the solid ground that made it possible.

A comparison with Joseph Beuys's art can be of help to us here: an unconditional search for perfect solitude reconciles art with poverty and leads to freedom from attachment. Beuys's art always sought the sublime in what was poor and depleted, and his stripped down life is not only the crux of his art – its matrix – but also the key to its interpretation. What we see, and what is proposed to us as a possible experiential language, is just what the artist lives out in his quest – a life that is destitute, vulnerable, willingly impoverished, and almost ravaged on every level. The depiction of experience stripped bare and, in certain cases, the enactment of this poverty in solitude, are thus a fulfilment of life. Beuys refused to let his art and his genius be divorced from his vulnerability; he made this the condition for the political and social commitment that bore the signature of his generosity. It was the same for Gould in his renunciation of glory and worldly pleasures; to know the life he chose for himself is to devise, where indications converge, a description that will enable us to fuse the aesthetic with the life. How indeed to evoke art and life as one entity, without the separate treatment of an aesthetic position on the one hand, and a life, its shape and style, on the other? In modern aesthetics these two realms are rarely considered together – it is deemed inadvisable to do so – and yet they are profoundly interconnected.

Gould was extremely prolix where his aesthetic positions were concerned – often to the point of confusing matters – analysing in detail his preferences in the repertoire, his aversions, his interest in serial music, his criticisms of others' interpretations. Gould wrote a lot, talked a lot, and seemed never to tire of giving reasons for his positions; this prolixity denotes a kind of confidence in the rational exercise of an aesthetic which was nourished in him by a precise and comprehensive knowledge of musical composition and the history of the repertoire. Mind you, in the end, these positions, even taken together, do not yield an aesthetic system, and they contain a number of paradoxes that Gould happily fuelled. I have noted his admiration for Schoenberg's ambivalent music, and even of Richard Strauss, but I have not spoken – to give only one example of his lyrical preferences – of his work on the transcription of *Siegfried's Idyll*. His writing was rich in idealizing proclamations supported by lively and insoluble contradictions. This is how I take his declarations of love for the music of Gibbons: a call to follow exclusively a path that, however, can never be singled out from others ... in other words, he yearned for the impossible.

Although solitary and retired, Gould was, as I have said, intensely active as a communicator and worked busily in the media as a host and as a popularizer of the repertoire. Although critical of the concert hall, he valued his work in the studio to such a degree that he drew increasingly on technology in order to arrive at a perfect interpretation. Despite shunning intimate contact with others, he could talk to them for hours on the telephone. All of this is well known and if I come back to it, it is in the attempt – keeping everything in balance – to designate a constant and common point of reference for all his positions: the quest for the sublime, embodied most notably in his severe criticism of romanticism and his veneration for a perfect, ideal music, Bach's works for the keyboard being the most accomplished example. Did this search lead him to an aesthetic ideal independent of moral stands, an ideal whose formulation was clearly expressed? His declarations on this question are isolated and rare, reminiscent of the phrase I have introduced here as a refrain, the cantilena of this *partita*, the recurrent theme of a fugue. If the quest for ecstasy is the end point of the sublime, can it show the way to an objective reality, or can it only designate now and forever the "state" of one who, like Sōseki's painter, is en route toward the ultimate summit? Gould talked of the purpose of art, but he never defined it; I would like to associate it with the quest for the inner voice, the supreme manifestation of song – born from harmony – that always accompanied his playing. Might we characterize it as a fusion of the artist and his inner life with what was central to the music? But this definition still cannot account for his aesthetic if it implies a disconnection between his solitude and his acting in the outside world; there is a paradox implicit in my questioning.

Some interpreters of Gould's aesthetic thinking have wanted to contrast what they viewed as the torments of the artist's life with the transcendental serenity of his work; but that does not, it seems to me, accurately describe what lay at the heart of Gould's experience. If ecstasy, in a state of detachment and withdrawal, leads to an experience of the absolute, with nothing of the senses ultimately being engaged, we should not be speaking in concrete terms of suffering, but rather of an ongoing pathos associated with his concentrated quest for the sublime. Gould was not a tormented individual prey to perplexing afflictions or to unconscious forces beyond his control. There was nothing gloomy about his genius; he was not a dark figure, and his aesthetic confirms that absolutely. His correspondence attests to a constant joy, and unless we suppose him captive to a deliberate strategy of camouflage, we must accept this joy at face value as one more aspect of his search for serenity. His voice on his radio broadcasts, his body language on television, all lead to the same conclusion. Glenn Gould was an ascetic, his renunciation was genuine, and he was committed to an elevated vision of the sublime, to which he was determined to dedicate his life. When he describes himself as an experienced hermit, we have to believe him. The sublime had as much of an impact on his life, for which it was an emblem, as did his art. And so it was the same silence, the same ineffability, that he embraced both in his aesthetic quest for the sublime and his quest for an ecstatic life.

Were we to try to determine his aesthetic principles purely in terms of repertoire, we could start with two affirmations, each eccentric and extreme: a distaste for the music of Schumann, and the veneration of English virginal masters such as Gibbons or Byrd. Gould's letters and interviews are clear: these choices were consistent, precise, meticulously argued. We are familiar with the pedagogical virtuosity of his radio and television appearances. His preferences were not simple opinions or tastes, but stylistic positions whose perfect incarnation was to be found in his revised reading of Bach. By introducing the notion of perfection into what an interpreted musical work has to offer, Gould was insisting on the fact that the pianistic aesthetic resides as much in the choice of repertoire as in the reading. A detailed analysis of the programs he chose, both for concerts and for recordings, reveals an exceptional concern for rigour. We owe their exhaustive reconstitution to Otto Friedrich and Peter Ostwald. The presence of Webern and Schoenberg in his early solo recitals is evidence enough that, from the start, Gould chose to trace a very precise route through the history of piano music, a route that led directly to himself and bore on his desire to compose, even if he did not devote himself to composition as much as he would have liked. This analysis shows that the criteria he applied were founded largely in a reading of the history of compositional form.

This itinerary always favoured structure, which he tried to make transparent and perfectly visible in performance; it sought also to isolate the clarity and lightness that could alone bring out the lyrical purity beyond the workings of the counterpoint. Finally, it set aside any superfluous emotion, all sentimentality that was too obviously pianistic. Gould was often torn between his judgments and his playing. So it was with his reading of Brahms, which was impossibly unfaithful but perfectly rigorous in terms of the abstract and idealized history he was trying to reconstruct. His knowledge of musical composition was prodigious, so sophisticated that he was able to rewrite works, to cite all the measures from memory, and to justify points of view that were radically critical.

When he thought it necessary to deviate from a score, it was the result of a decision that substituted a general interpretation of music history for the authority of the work. He felt thoroughly authorized to do this. His criticism of ornament was consistent with his criticism of romanticism, and that is what made his relationship to Beethoven so ambivalent; everything in Beethoven that was susceptible to a classic reading was luminously interpreted by Gould, while everything that resisted such a reading received an interpretation that amounted to a rewriting. That was the case, for example, with *Sonata No. 29, Opus 106,* the *Hammerklavier,* whose slow movement Gould could only see as a prelude to the fugal conclusion. And so he played it without feeling and claimed not to like it. A remarkable example of the tensions inherent in the choices he made was his recording of Schoenberg's *Lieder.* What remained of the romantic in the young Schoenberg, Gould rendered with a great deal of respect, but with a sort of resistance that lent his interpretation an overwhelming inner strength. He accepted its ambivalence as the reflection of his own hesitation vis-à-vis any lyricism that was overly assertive.

The dismissal of romanticism did not at all imply a rejection of lyricism, in other words of everything that in his favoured repertoire embodied a purified version of it. We learn from his biographers – and have ourselves seen – that the technique in which he was schooled by Alberto Guerrero required a form of "tapping," on the finger tips, a technique that perhaps explains how he so quickly mastered his interpretations of Bach; eschewing all *legato*, Gould learned to favour the workings of rhythm. He soon developed a touch that allowed him, in striking the keys, to isolate each note and produce a transparent clarity never before heard. This special training also helps explain one much observed detail: the wearing of gloves and mitts. Gould thought he had developed a kind of tactile sensitivity at the ends of his fingers that was essential to his playing, and he was always afraid of losing it. His performer's memory depended on this sensitivity; to lose it would be to be deprived of the inner rhythm he identified with his personal aesthetic. His unique punctuation served in effect to isolate this pure lyricism, an inner and quasi-material song that permeated his entire body – even his voice – when he was playing.

I only bring up this behaviour, already dealt with in earlier sections of this book, because it helps us understand the aesthetic implications of Gould's rejection of romanticism and his quest for the sublime; contrary to what has often been claimed, there was nothing paradoxical in this position. I hope to have demonstrated that these seeming paradoxes can be resolved. People were surprised, for example, that, whereas Haydn was in a sense the perfect embodiment of non-romantic music, Gould did not reinvent the interpretation of his sonatas before Rudolf Buchbinder, even though he played them magnificently in his last years. But Haydn lacks what Gould found in Bach and what lent his interpretations their strong affinity with Bach's music: the combination of sublime lyricism and a perfectly crystalline counterpoint. Haydn often remains captive to an aesthetic of entertainment, whereas Bach never strayed from that state of rapture that Gould sought. I would like here to recall Ostwald's description of the first Gould concert he attended in 1957, when Gould played Bach's *Concerto in F Minor*, a vivid illustration of the strong connection between his playing and his aesthetic stance:

> His playing was remarkable, sculptured, three-dimensional; each phrase seemed to have a life of its own ... Gould became ecstatic, his expression one of rapture, his eyes closed or turned inward ... His interpretation of the slow movement ... was truly a revelation. He projected the soulful melody like a silver thread by articulating each phrase with immense deliberation ... The result was so songlike that it was difficult to believe one was listening to a piano.

Are we now in a position to propose a clearer link between style and the shape of a life, and if so, might it be Ostwald's "silver thread"? What I like in his description is the emphasis on deliberation as a necessary condition for lyricism. Have all the variations on Gould's art and life finally found a common theme? Have we found the common denominator that can bring together an engagement with life and an engagement with the work? If a critique of romanticism entails a quest for clarity just for its own sake, then it risks being hollow or abstract. Let us compare, for example, Schoenberg and Bach: at both ends of the musical spectrum, sadness and joy are conveyed without any reference to the individual who is their bearer; on the contrary, musical feeling is detached and assigned to an absolute and idealized dimension.

I must be careful with my terminology if I want in my turn to maintain a certain rigour: one needs both clarity, which is the essence of interpretation and performance, and a form of the sublime, which is the essence of a work when it is interpreted transcendentally. Rapture is the sublime, attained and embraced; it is also its home, its destination. The sublime is in a sense the abstract ideal of music, a transcendence that makes itself felt first in the act of composition and in the ethereal harmonies envisaged by the philosophy of counterpoint. Rapture begins when one is carried beyond musical expression to the realm of beauty, when the artist is released from his starting point, delivered from all physical constraints and transported to a place beyond – outside – language, free of limits. This existential immersion, which one expects from music, can also occur in life. Perhaps this is where we will find the ultimate meaning for our *aria da capo*, now become almost an axiom for life: a wisdom that pervades every moment on this longed for and transcendent horizon of wonder and serenity.

And so we see that we can only conceive of this connection to life if we introduce an ethical dimension, a consideration of the moral choices that enter into Gould's interpretations beyond a purely aesthetic position. Whereas aesthetics is limited to a concern with style in its pursuit of a perfect interpretation, a moral position transforms the interpretation because it affects the relationship to the body and to life. Pianists of excess, such as Sviatislov Richter or Ivo Pogorelich, are certainly very different from discreet or modest pianists such as Alfred Brendel. Their work, like that of Gould, demands that we recognize how style may be affected by the shape of a life and how it is defined by its goal of ecstasy. Kevin Bazzana recalls how Gould admired ecstatic interpreters, those whose "idiosyncratic" commitment to the music guaranteed a transcendent and spiritual interpretation. Pogorelich's limpid renderings of Scarlatti have been much celebrated, and yet we can only wonder what in the shape of this exalted pianist's life, in his relationship to joy in particular, makes possible such a gentle levitation from his instrument and transforms it into a paradigm for interpretation. Similarly, in Mitsuko Ushida's readings of Schubert, her affinity with the melancholy of his last sonatas allows her to convey – through the juxtaposition of a holding back and an urge to move ahead – a particular tension that we also find in her interpretation of the *Impromptus*. But here again, and despite many attempts to define it, this relationship remains obscure, and the very notion of expressivity and its relationship to ethics is conspicuous by its absence. In Gould's case, we know almost too much. This is not because every detail in his performance can be interpreted in terms of his life's compliance with the demands of art and the sublime, but because he bestowed on us, as his most generous gift, his own paradigm for the convergence that made his art possible.

If we are to understand this gift, we must look again at Gould's ethic in its simplest terms: the notion of solitude as a necessary precondition and the end point for interpretation, and the notion of rapture as a quest for the sublime. Biographical details are of less interest here than the constancy of the moral commitment, but it too is biographical – it informs every act, it inscribes the shape of a life into the life itself. And so I will try another direction, and look at how this gift was first experienced by Gould before being returned to the world once he entered his withdrawal. The biography places us in the presence of an artist who suffers from a void he is trying to fill, and even if this void had its origins in his childhood, when his mother's demands and his extreme vulnerability isolated him and set him apart, it was not necessarily this vulnerability that made the expression of his genius possible. I do not deny that serene geniuses exist; what interests me, rather, is the coincidence I spoke of earlier between the sublime and a life in retreat, a solitary withdrawal in the interests of all that is widely considered essential to life, and which we might call love. Of what love, one might ask, is the interpreter's gift a sign and irrefutable proof?

Gould wanted to give, but he did not give in order to fashion his own identity. His life was concentrated in solitude and monopolized by his artistic vocation, and the only constant love we can attribute to him was the love of his art, the love of music, and, through this love, an indisputable love of the world, to which he made a constant gift. The intersection between his aesthetic ideal of the sublime and his solitude brings us to the point where we can now try to reconstruct the terms of his life in the context of his aesthetic. From the sublime to sublimation, however, the way is not so simple. I have sidestepped it so far, but now it must be dealt with. As I go over some of the same ground as earlier, and speak now of the gift and love, I can no longer keep my distance, by circumventing it, from this ethical paradox. On the contrary, I would like to draw as close to it as possible. The idea of a life's shape becomes very tangible here, as we take a concrete look at how it relates to Gould's personal experience. Solitude and the quest for rapture are what stand out in this style of life, and it is the stable moral position they represent that inspires the aesthetic. But if I propose to take another look at them while introducing the concept of the gift – a gift received, a gift offered – it is so that the kind of life for which I am trying to find expression can come into focus. And the same may be said for love.

This gift was first of all a gift received – an enormous gift, its dimensions those of a childhood immersed in art. Without embarking on a hasty psychoanalytic investigation, I believe one can make some comments on the maternal relationship. Because she recognized these precocious "gifts," Glenn Gould's mother, herself a musician and piano teacher, decided to take the fullest possible advantage of their potential. But to put it this way does not do justice to the gift that Glenn's birth itself represented for his mother. Florence Greig had experienced great difficulty in trying to have a child, and had undergone several miscarriages. During this final pregnancy, at the age of forty, she opted to expose her unborn child to a constant stream of music, either from the radio, or playing it herself. From the very first months, she saw that Glenn neither cried nor screamed, but only murmured in singsong. Her desire for a child and her desire that this child be a consummate musician were one and the same. In a photograph, we see Gould as a baby held by his maternal grandmother at the keyboard of the family piano. Peter Ostwald, in his efforts to associate Gould's solitude with his behaviour as a withdrawn child, helps us take full measure of the gift he represented for his mother. His youth was lived in symbiosis with her, and this is only confirmed by the pale figure his father made. Robert Fulford, a close childhood friend who was sensitive to Gould's precocious musical talent, recounts that the father had agreed to give up his place in the conjugal bed to his son, at their Lake Simcoe cottage, every other day, an arrangement that lasted several years. Gould himself is said to have confided to a friend that he thought he had disappointed his father, not being the ordinary offspring he would have preferred. That his father disappointed him is another story, one that would come to a head after the death of his mother. I will not delve further into this Oedipal triangle that is almost too obvious to be true; I will simply let it rest where it began, with Gould on his mother's lap as she teaches him to play.

As far as Gould's mother is concerned, we could follow in Ostwald's footsteps and discuss the attempts at psychological analysis in the course of Gould's life, attempts he vehemently resisted. His contacts with doctors were infused with an irony that systematically masked his suffering. Still, it is clear that all the behaviour patterns noted by those who knew him include a moral component that Gould may well have chosen to assume as part of his artistic destiny, not as a neurosis or illness. The fear of certain objects, the love of animals, the aversion to cold, the departure from social conventions, the ritualized gestures, the self-referent conversations, the nocturnal lifestyle, even his fasci-nation for the radio voice and the intimacy of the studio, all that derived, doubtless, from an almost total absorption in the body of the mother. Ostwald goes so far as to affirm this, by describ-ing a life lived in a cocoon. His narrative is substantiated by that of his colleague and friend, the psychiatrist Joseph Stephens, who came to know Gould very well but did not write about him. Ostwald interviewed Stephens, and spoke of him as someone Gould particularly liked. The account interested me, especially since Ostwald had given Stephens the daunting task of encour-aging Gould to undergo analysis.

Gould himself, as he confessed to Geoffrey Payzant, liked to compare the studio where he spent most of his time to the mater-nal womb. Charles Riley, who wrote eloquently about Gould, suggests that the studio was like a glass bubble that he needed in order to replicate his life in front of a screen that would protect him from the presence of others. It's an interesting formula, though somewhat exaggerated. Let us not forget that this mater-nal body was also that of music itself, that his mother passed on to him musicality and discipline at the same time, and that it was she who saw that at the age of three he had perfect pitch. She was herself inclined to identify strongly with the Mozart family, a notion that her husband, a man of limited depth, did not oppose.

To have done so would have meant seeking for Glenn a more ordinary, more balanced life, and forcing him onto a path as a more conventional student. Rather than that, young Glenn attended school irregularly while being entrusted to music teachers who, as soon as he was admitted to the Toronto Conservatory of Music, predicted a brilliant career for him. And so the body of his mother was, as it were, entirely transposed into the body of the music he inhabited from childhood. The studio was but a transparent envelope, like the glass cabin from which, spellbound, he watched Herbert von Karajan conduct Sibelius's *Fifth Symphony* in Berlin. He could have sat in the hall, but he chose to place a wall – always the same wall – between himself and Karajan.

Florence Greig Gould's death at the age of eighty-three, on July 26, 1975, came as a painful shock to Gould. He had remained very close to her over the years, much more than to his father. The account of his cousin, Jessie Greig, who became his confidante in the ensuing years, is clear: this death was traumatic for him. He was devastated, especially since, despite his affection for her, and perhaps because of the unusually deep nature of this filial love, he couldn't bring himself to visit his mother in the hospital during the days leading up to her death when she was in a coma. For Ostwald, the death of Gould's mother, and the guilt it caused him, might have had some bearing on the crisis he chronicled two years later in 1977–78, after experiencing some difficulties in his performance. It does not seem likely, as the time gap is rather long, but it cannot be denied that his mother's ongoing support had provided him all his life with much-needed protection against anxiety, and in particular against the loss of the image that guided his playing from within. Once she was gone, he was left in a state of affective solitude he had never known. What followed only made the situation more difficult: his father remarried a woman Gould never accepted, to the point that he opposed the union in childish fashion, and did not attend the ceremony.

Solitude and the quest for rapture also bring us back to the last puritan I spoke of earlier, and what he represents. The gift, once received, was transmuted into a generosity driven from within by demands so great that they affected all the relationships Gould undertook with others. Ostwald has made a point of how hard it was to talk to Gould, who was always prolix, but always self-involved, and almost indifferent to his interlocutor. Deprived early on of normal contact with other children because of the number of hours he spent at his instrument, Gould communicated first with himself. Ostwald notes that behind his perennial courtesy and ami-ability, he cultivated a form of detachment, a stance that isolated him. Kevin Bazzana speaks of narcissism and a lack of empathy, but he also balances the portrait with his account of Gould's invari-able generosity to all. Gould expected nothing of others and was doubtless easily bored, but he always and irresistibly wanted to create and to give. His idiosyncrasies and his hypochondria went back to his early youth – Robert Fulford was witness to that – but it does not explain the palpable reserve behind his unfailing jovi-ality. A generosity that asks nothing in return is often suspect, and yet Gould was never shy to call those he wanted to talk to, even in the middle of the night, again and again; they all understood that he was asking for a different call to be heard – a call beyond the projects, the readings, and the discussions.

Andrew Kazdin, the producer with whom he worked for a long time, and whom he greatly respected, had his own story. There were tensions in their relationship over the years – inevitable in the close collaboration of making recordings – but Kazdin recalled in his memoirs that he never had a truly warm and friendly rapport with Gould. When CBS ended Kazdin's contract, Gould drifted away from him as if those fifteen years had never existed, express-ing neither regret nor gratitude. Kevin Bazzana associates his resistance to close friendships with his puritanism, and feels that although Gould desired physical contact, his anxiety stood in the way. Gould was sure of his need for solitude and convinced that it represented the only kind of life that could enable him to reach the goals he had set for himself. He was aware of what contact with others might offer him, but he didn't want to depend on that or think about it in any other context than this boundless gift for music that possessed him absolutely. We can see what friendship represented for him in the immediate present; Kazdin's account shows that it had no place in the longer term.

This resistance to close relationship was exemplified in a complex episode that I have kept in reserve until now. I could have spoken of it in the context of Gould's illnesses and his relationship to his body, but that would have risked limiting it to his hypochondria, when in fact much more was involved. To trivialize it would be to hide something important, while to exaggerate it would betray an ethic of solitude that might have necessitated his going that far. I present it, therefore, with caution. It is perhaps the only event comparable in importance to his decision to abandon the concert hall, the only one that put his ethic to the test so directly; it can only be understood, in fact, in the context of that world of moral austerity he had evolved for himself, and it is revealing both of the constraints of this austerity and of its dictates. Another gift was at play, another love perhaps, but also a rejection that one can only comprehend in the light of a relationship with the body predicated on a refusal of all proximity, a resistance to any physical contact, to every intimacy. The importance Gould lent it in his correspondence shows that for him this was not a banal or trivial episode. On the contrary, it came closer to being something of a drama.

On December 8, 1959, Gould met with Steinway's head technician, William Hupfer. In the course of the meeting, Hupfer placed his hand on Gould's shoulder, most likely giving him a friendly tap, perhaps even forceful and manly. What followed is well known: in the succeeding days and months, Gould complained of serious ailments, consulted a number of doctors and physiotherapists, and accused Hupfer of having grievously injured him. Through his lawyers, he even registered a complaint with Steinway, already foreshadowed in a letter to Edith Boecker on January 21, 1960, in which he confessed, "I cannot speak of it without wincing." Very concerned, he spoke of consequences that might "become permanent," but he had the candour to admit that no one seemed to take him seriously. On February 5 he announced that he had cancelled all his concerts and he then consulted a Doctor Sherbok in Denver, Colorado, about the quality of a Boston clinic, Brigham Hospital, doubtless in the hope of surgery. On March 10, having received a cortisone treatment, he reported "miraculous" progress. But a few weeks later, he met with Doctor Epstein, a well-respected orthopaedic surgeon in Philadelphia, who placed him in a cast for four weeks. The results were disappointing and Gould subsequently gave up his search for surgical solutions.

As I noted when discussing his hands and his relationship, as an artist, to his body, Gould's youthful injury on Lake Simcoe had likely left him with a weakness in his back. The injury was treated, but he constantly resuscitated the memory as if the consequences had been permanent. Following the Hupfer incident, he was, like a surgeon concerned with his manual dexterity after having received a shock of this sort, extremely anxious about anything that might compromise the equilibrium he had been able to muster, especially when it came to his performance at the keyboard. No one should underestimate an artist's anxiety when it comes to his body; Peter Ostwald has indicated that in Gould's case it was "massive." But beyond the conflict, doubtless latent for some time, with a technician he faulted for being inappropriately familiar, this incident must be viewed in the context of all Gould's difficulties on tour, leading up to his 1964 decision. One might have suspected him of capitalizing on his muscular problems, and exaggerating them, to justify cancelling his concerts, but as Bazzana notes, these troubles disappeared as if by magic when he was faced with a different sort of engagement, such as for example a recital for American television on January 31, 1960. Was the injury real or imaginary? How serious was it? Gould, as usual, consulted a number of doctors and therapists – he was certainly in pain – and he was doubtless very concerned at the thought that this injury might provoke new troubles. In short, he clearly somatized a real malaise, certainly superficial, while exaggerating its severity out of all proportion.

This episode, recounted in detail by all Gould's biographers, echoed a youthful occurrence when he was making music with friends; complaining of problems with his shoulder blades, Gould asked each of them to probe the surrounding area. Anxiety about his body, noted Ostwald, reached a phobic dimension with the Hupfer episode, one that affected his human relationships. I am not ruling out the possibility that his rapport with Hupfer indicated a repressed desire for physical contact, to the extent that, in the text of his legal proceedings, Gould made reference to a series of "unduly strong handshakes and other demonstrative physical acts." For someone who felt easily threatened, even attacked, familiarity quickly became "excessive" and physical contact "demonstrative," but what sort of demonstrativeness was it, since Hupfer's intent, as he attested, was likely no more than simply an expression of workplace camaraderie? Gould's masseur, Cornelius Dees, accompanied him on a number of tours, and his constant presence did provoke rumours of homosexuality. Ostwald reports that between January 8 and October 22, 1960, Gould received Dees at his home, where he had a massage table, 117 times – almost every day. Ostwald's friend Joseph Stephens, who saw Gould from time to time, was present at a number of these sessions and remarked: Gould "obviously enjoyed being massaged and I sometime wondered, considering the sexually inhibited person he was, whether maybe this gave him some erotic pleasure. Ordinarily, Glenn had an aversion to physical contact."

I do not believe that this reading is correct or the only one that is plausible: what the Hupfer episode reveals is not repressed homosexual desire – though one need not exclude that possibility; it is rather the absolute repression of all desire of this nature, homosexual or not, including any "demonstrative" act, whatever Gould meant by this typically puritan turn of phrase, so critical, in its expression, of excess. The photo of Gould encased in his cast is like none other: for once he looks like any other young Canadian after a rough and tumble hockey game. His gaze is that of someone who is saying, you'll never see me like this again. The injury, real or imagined, served subsequently as the ideal excuse not to have to endure physical contact with most people. Those tensed shoulders would belong only to his art, no one was to touch them. We may assume that Hupfer or Kazdin might often have wished to embrace him, but who would have dared? He sued the first and showed no gratitude to his most faithful collaborator in the recording studio. Between them and him there was the glass wall of the studio, and there was no question of its being breached.

The relationship to the body is only the most visible manifestation of one's relationship with feeling and with one's affective life in general. Embarrassed by any show of emotion he considered excessive, Gould gave no indication that he suffered from his isolation. Perhaps, as I have suggested, he might have wished for more contact, but he could not tolerate it. His friend Robert Fulford associated this feeling with the fear, inherited from his mother, of anything erotic or sexual. Apart from the one letter to an idealized fiancée – doubtless fictive, but expressing a dream, a desire for absolute love – his correspondence makes no reference to any intimate relationship, male or female. But this absence, which has given rise to many suppositions, in no way signifies that his life was devoid of such relationships, only that none are reflected in his writings. I see this as a telling sign of Gould's idealization of love, and I will show in due course how this tardy idealization has obscured certain facts.

Recopied into Gould's diary, this text had no known recipient, but has been dated by his editors as being written in 1980. It could derive from an unidentified source and be addressed in fact to an unidentified recipient, on the subject of an absent loved one, as in Beethoven's six-lieder cycle based on poems by Aloys Jeitteles, *To the Distant Beloved, Opus 98*. Here is the text:

> You know.
>
> I am deeply in love with a certain beaut. girl. I asked her to marry me but she turned me down but I still love her more than anything in the world and every min. I can spend with her is pure heaven; but I don't want to be a bore and if I could only get her to tell me when I could see her, it would help. She has a standing invit. to let me take her anywhere she'd like to go any time but it seems to me she never has time for me. Please if you see her, ask her to let me know when I can see her and when I can ...

The fragment ends on this "I can." That bit of prose, whose every line exudes a youthful romanticism worthy of Schubert, is surprising coming from Gould, and I see it as the expression of a desire dreamed, but repressed. It could, however, be related to his memory of an early love, a real one, and through it to an incapacity and a refusal that destined him for lifelong solitude. Kevin Bazzana also quotes a tormented passage from a notebook of this same year, 1980, concerning a confused relationship. Gould was determined to put an end to it, and set out his reasons for not engaging himself further. Like the letter, I believe the conversation was imaginary, even if it revived painful memories of a past love. Coming late in his life, this text explores the dangers to the artist of uncontrolled emotionality, and, especially at this date, it can be linked to no one. Preoccupied with the end of his pianistic career, which he feared would take place as of his fiftieth birthday – he claimed to have foreseen its demise and to have virtually decided on it – Gould had thoughts of renewing his life. But as his harsh judgment of his father's remarrying shows, it was never possible to start over; there was no question, even, of dreaming about it. The letter, like the diary fragment, revived the impossible dream of a new beginning, a dream about what had not happened and Gould knew never would.

Gould remained a bachelor and was easily offended when people asked him about his private life, as Andrew Kazdin learned to his chagrin. It was not hard to believe he was homosexual, or simply indifferent to any kind of sexuality, but as I said, these were never more than suppositions, and gratuitous at that. The rumours could only displease him, just like the frequent insinuations associating his playing with a kind of feminine grace and lack of power. Even if no one today would lend any credence to this sort of criticism, it was doubtless wounding to the artist, and for good reason: such insinuations were based on an assumption whose negation was central to Gould's ethic. Art, he thought, is a form of release, of freedom, and this freedom may require a total withdrawal, even from a sexual and emotional life. The gift that was to result would otherwise be impossible. No one can say to what extent Gould wanted to develop this principle, but he conformed to it totally.

Still, it cannot be forgotten that he carefully hid, even from those close to him, a love to which several of his biographers have alluded, without wanting to name the person involved. Given the absence of any reference to it on his part, Gould would certainly have considered it unseemly that one pry into his personal life. After many years of silence, Cornelia Foss told the story to the *Toronto Star* journalist Michael Clarkson in August 2007, and again in the documentary film by Michèle Hozer and Peter Raymont. A painter, Foss was the wife of the composer and orchestra conductor Lukas Foss, who died in New York on February 1, 2009, and it was in some sense their shared admiration for Gould the pianist that led them to him. They met him around 1956, when he was only twenty-four, and they heard him in concert in Los Angeles, where they were then living. In 1963, when they moved to Buffalo, Lukas and Cornelia Foss found themselves within hailing distance of Toronto. Gradually, the relationship evolved, and according to Mrs Foss, in 1966 Gould eventually proposed. An episodic relationship then became more serious; Cornelia Foss left her husband some time in 1968 to settle in Toronto with her two children, not far from Gould's apartment on St. Clair Avenue.

It might come as a shock that Mrs Foss insists on the sexual nature of their relationship, and it is even more troubling that Hozer and Raymont's film is intent on cataloguing the women Gould might have loved, as if it were necessary to rescue him from an unhappy fate – the solitude he had chosen and imposed on himself after his relationship with Cornelia Foss had proved unworkable. This is indeed what happened, as she herself recounts with forthright honesty. She was barely installed in Toronto when she had to admit the truth: Gould could not sustain a lasting relationship, and she was privy to a number of paranoid episodes that made her fear for the future. Without ever living under the same roof with Gould, she nevertheless stayed in Toronto for four and a half years, returning to Buffalo on weekends to see her husband. Mrs Foss claims that during this period she had to take care of her children, of Glenn, and of Lukas Foss. The final break, in 1972, was difficult. Gould did not resign himself to it easily, and for a long time tried to keep Cornelia near him. It may in fact have been his memory of this painful period that inspired the diary fragment referred to earlier.

As we see in the film *Genius Within: The Inner Life of Glenn Gould,* Foss's children cherish the memory of a man who was joyful and attentive, an ideal big brother. As we consider these years, we may wonder why Gould kept them so secret. Andrew Kazdin wrote that this relationship was very special for Gould, even though he only saw the two lovers together on one occasion. Would Gould not have nipped many wounding rumours in the bud if he had agreed to make their relationship public, and perhaps even found a way to strengthen it, to make it last? Greta Kraus, a friend of Gould from whom he separated rather harshly, claimed that Gould could not tolerate love: "I have the feeling that any expression of affection would cause him to panic." Notes from the end of his life show that this tendency had roots that went very deep, and that he did not want to commit himself. All accounts of his emotional life show that even if a life with love existed for him – and his relationship with Cornelia Foss proves that it did exist, and most beautifully – it had no deep or lasting importance: in the most fundamental way possible, Gould's choices were absolute, and excluded any engagement that might interfere with another kind of goal entirely. That is why I have serious reservations about Cornelia Foss's insistence that, from a very young age, Gould was very sick. This relationship, like every other, was impossible for him. Why talk of sickness?

In any case, the critics' interest in Gould's sexual life seems to me symptomatic of a complex resistance to his personality; it is as if his ethic associating art with the gift were to be enthusiastically espoused by those drawn to his artistic accomplishments, but to have no tangible consequences on the spiritual plane, especially where withdrawal and its uncompromising demands are concerned.

This withdrawal and its truths would seem to be more substantial and above all more consequential than any hints of supposed relationships, however well founded. None were real enough for him to have made them public, or even written about them. The loved one, real as she may have been, was forever absent, relegated to a discrete reality. And so I prefer to speak of a form of abstention, of an austerity imposed by his commitment to art – something like a moral abstinence.

In this light, the mind boggles at the tactlessness of Leonard Bernstein, who is reported to have said to Gould, after one of his concerts, "You played so beautifully in the cadenza that I almost came in my pants." The story is told by Peter Ostwald, who makes no bones about Bernstein's sexual attraction to this angelic figure, and it shows what different planets great artists sometimes live on without their being aware of it. Knowing who Leonard Bernstein was, knowing his exuberance and his unsettling lack of reserve, we can only imagine how Gould reacted to what came close to being a proposition. Bernstein was a far cry from Salzburg and its ceremonies – he stood for another kind of life altogether – but if Gould abhorred Salzburg's bourgeois circus, he certainly disliked just as much the vulgarity of New York. Bernstein's admiration ran very deep, however. He never missed an opportunity to express it, and he wrote later, regarding the Brahms concerto, "I never loved him more."

We have several direct or second-hand accounts of the episodic friendships Gould enjoyed with women in his entourage, but again, nothing that would attest to Gould's emotional involvement. It was as if this realm was foreign to him, a realm that his mother, who had awaited him for so long, monopolized during his childhood and all through his youth, and that he later sublimated entirely into his music. After Cornelia Foss's departure in 1972, Gould's withdrawal was complete, and his life, which one might describe as a form of spiritual virginity, became a kind of emblem for his ethic; more consented to than ascetically sought after, it worked in favour of the project of solitude that nourished his aesthetic. That this ethic may have been supported or motivated by an anxiety that forbade him all closeness to others, we can only suppose; his correspondence bearing on complex relationships shows that he feared them and always opted for distance, even breaking them off when they exacted intimacy and commitment. He could talk passionately about a woman, as Peter Ostwald noted, but he would make no effort to approach her.

In his 1980 note, the same year that he recopied the letter relating to his "absent loved one," Gould observed, not unwisely, that clarity and rigour were essential to him in human relationships. On this occasion, as if he were revisiting an ancient and weighty decision, so weighty that it influenced all he did, he commented on the sort of life he had chosen for himself: "Years of prepar[ation] for this way of life. Change would be destructive and produce the kind of resentment that would rather quickly cause our relationship to flounder. Therefore: no change is contemplated." This inner monologue took the form of a dialogue with an imaginary loved one whom Gould wanted to respect his commitment to solitude. He also had to assume himself the psychic challenge this commitment represented. Perhaps, as Bazzana suggests, with the relationship taking on a sexual colouring to which he would offer strong resistance, he was sketching out a draft for a difficult conversation. And perhaps as well he was reliving the pain he had harboured ever since Cornelia's departure.

Gould outlines here in no uncertain terms the destructive effects of sexuality. He writes schematically, as if consigning something to memory: "Theories of physical relations = psychic deterioration," and, as in an ascetic exercise to strengthen memory, he repeats a demand out of the distant past. Moreover, when he notes that most people fail in the transition to an intense physical relationship, he seems to be exorcising in advance this reality or this threat. Margaret Pacsu, a friend of Gould who worked with him at the CBC, once said, according to Otto Friedrich, that Gould "was one of those people who take vows." "Buddhists do this," she went on. "Gould made a conscious decision to concentrate entirely on his art." Here is Bazzana's response:

> But he did not necessarily take vows for moral reasons, to remain pure in an impure world; more likely he meant to avoid the problems he seemed unable to avoid in sexual relationships. Given his inflexibility and self-involvement, but also his genuine desire not to hurt others, the demands of his art, and his one, failed long-term relationship, he must have been tempted, in his forties, to leave behind the whole business of romance.

This judgment certainly makes sense, but it minimizes the exigencies Gould always advocated and defended. Rather than dismissing them as untenable idealizations, I prefer to think that Gould, in this area, was as free and sovereign as elsewhere. To speak of "self-involvement" is to view Gould's withdrawal more as a function of narcissism than of the gift. An overview of Gould's life would indicate that he saw things differently. The gift came first, and remained so; but I would not quibble if it were claimed that I too am in thrall to the idealization of the artist.

This attitude, where principle is all, finds confirmation in Gould's relations with his father after his mother's death. While his father was engaged in a new relationship with a woman called Vera Dobson, Gould undertook to dissuade him from it, and he entrusted to his notebook some arguments to this end. They date from the beginning of summer, 1979. Gould first expresses a kind of moral condemnation of remarriage, especially at an advanced age; to him it appears inappropriate. He would like to counsel a peaceful life. And so in his notes we find instructions addressed to himself long before: all love stories create dependence, the need to be with the other; they impose an impossible burden of communication, even if the exercise is rich and challenging. And then he writes this: "and while that may be a fasc[inating] exercise in com[munication?], it's also exhausting and it has one other, gr[ea]t disadv[antage] to wit – that it distracts you from contemp[lation], from looking inward." In a later entry, we read again: "to really meditate upon the shape of your life – one doesn't do that, because one thinks one is starting one's life."

But that is just it; we cannot begin our lives again; we can only try to respect the demands of the kind of life we have chosen, and Gould could respond only in terms of the discipline he had imposed on himself. It is astonishing that he could have thought, even for an instant, that he could lay down the law to his father, and that he could even conceive of talking to him in this moralizing tone. But not to do so would have meant forgetting the deep bond with his mother that he was never able to set aside, or even less betray, in drawing near to the troubling equation he identified with love. That his father wanted to replace his mother with another woman must have seemed to him as unthinkable as if he were to have done so himself. There exists the draft of a letter, never sent, but dated December 2, 1979, and recopied into Gould's diary. In the letter the son refuses to be a witness at his father's wedding, and when he recopied it in 1980 he scratched out the final salutation, "Love," and replaced it with "Sincerely." Nothing could be clearer, nothing more painful than this farewell to his father. He certainly resented his having sold the house at Lake Simcoe early in 1975, even suspecting that this decision had played a role in the decline of his mother's health, and he had reproached his father for it. This final rupture confirmed a kind of void that had existed since his childhood – an unspoken absence.

We must, however, draw attention to a factor I have already mentioned, which has elicited little interest from his biographers.

Among his favourite books, perhaps the only one he read and adhered to unconditionally, was *The Last Puritan,* by the Platonic American philosopher, George Santayana. In the novel, which describes the education of a young man from a New England family raised outside the conventional norms of the industrial bourgeoisie, the philosopher presents the model for an ascetic upbringing and a creative solitude placed at the service of a community. The puritanism he presents is austere, demanding strict moral standards, and when we read that Gould told many people that he saw himself mirrored in it and was totally committed to this ethic, we have good reason to believe that the effort of sublimation he made in his art found in Santayana an expression he judged to be accurate. Ostwald recalls that he used to make fun of Gould's "Santayanism," and tried at times to get him off the subject. Its message was that to distance oneself from society, to reject its worldliness, to accept chastity as a condition for art and not as a pathology, to transform solitude into a realm of creation and autonomy, all represented a higher form of wisdom. What we know of Gould's childhood Protestantism tends to support this view of his ethic. Santayana's Platonism lent these positions an elaborate metaphysical foundation, but to my knowledge Gould never expressed himself on the subject. Perhaps he associated metaphysics with feeling and preferred not to embark on a path where convictions other than those that were moral or aesthetic might be demanded of him. His reading of Thoreau, as he spoke of it in his correspondence, confirmed for him the importance of a simple life devoted to nature, and the spiritual affinity of Santayana and Thoreau makes that all the more credible. Ostwald suggested he read Emerson, which he undoubtedly did.

Gould never saw these two constituents of his life – the symbiotic relationship with his mother and a puritanism committed to solitude – as problematic; nor did he consider them obstacles to the practice of his art. His entire life experience was transmuted into music, as his biography confirms without question. When Gould's hypochondria began to interfere with his career as a soloist, with the slightest symptom leading him to cancel a performance, his friends such as Peter Ostwald or Joseph Stephens diplomatically suggested he consider analysis. Gould always derided the idea. As I have said, his physical afflictions may have been entirely initiated by the faulty posture he inherited from his first teachers. For him the problems were identifiable, could be localized, and required no psychosomatic explanation. Very soon he undertook to cure himself, consulting dozens of specialists; he abused his prescriptions, treated one with the next, and played the doctors off against each other, in a kind of tragic autosuggestion that contributed in no small way to his death.

How to explain that Gould, going against the current of the times, resisted any form of analytical approach? Not only did he not believe in it, which to a psychiatrist represents only the most elementary sort of resistance, but we have to accept the possibility that none of the behaviour that everybody who came into contact with him noticed posed any problem for him. It did not make him suffer. In any case, by the time analysis looked like a possibility it was already too late, as Gould had long since put together an elaborate pharmacopoeia he thought he could control. This rejection of – or indifference to – an analytic cure does not mean that Gould had no insights into himself as an artist committed to a solitude that isolated him from normal contact with the world. The collapse of his relationship with Cornelia Foss seems to have left no trace, and the few notes that remain to us indicate that he was perhaps, in the end, relieved. On the other hand, his cordiality and his desire to be listened to, especially on the telephone at night, show that his inner life and his restless meditation were inhabited by musical form in its purest state; and to no one, it must be emphasized, did he complain about being alone. His language, like everything he loved, was permeated with music.

He always had something to say to others, to give to them, to have them discover in and through music, all sorts of music. And so these manifestations of solitude – as much his relationship to his mother as his flight from sexuality – were simply aspects of his resolve to assume, as his artist's destiny, the constraints he saw as moral choices. The anxiety he recorded in his secret diary, none of which made its way into his correspondence or anything ever said about him, shows to what degree he controlled both his inner life and the way he was seen from outside. When Bruno Monsaingeon edited the text in 2002, he remarked that the tortured life described in the diary had been invisible to all those around him.

Much in Gould's life after his abandonment of the concert hall seems consistent with this view. His commitment to a moral realm, and his idealization of the puritan life – whose last representatives, in America and even in Ontario, Gould certainly knew, if only through the radio and newspapers – constituted a paradigm for his musical quest, the ethical context for his entire life, and the necessary conditions even for his art. We can trace all of that in his own words: he uses ethical language from the outset in speaking of his 1955 interpretation of the *Goldberg Variations*, proposing terms such as moral rectitude, elevation, and liturgical meaning. This position resembles that of Wittgenstein, and it suggests a very close connection between the aesthetic of the sublime and the ethic of solitude, which is precisely what I see as emerging in his interpretive art. He also draws on ethical language in his famous *Solitude Trilogy* for the CBC, certainly the most extraordinary series of musical programs produced for Canadian public radio. I have spoken earlier of its capital importance on all levels, musical, formal, and moral. We need only recall how these three programs associate the purity of listening and song with the existence of puritan, sacred, ritualized communities, or groups protected by their insularity from modernity's corruption; and of how Gould transposed onto them, for the sake of the greater community of

Canada and the United States, his experience of solitary life on Lake Simcoe. In this Northern ideal shared by three marginal communities, and representing a life that was protected and purified, he found an angelic paradigm, free from obligation and sentiment, dedicated wholeheartedly to the community through the medium of music. He thought of himself as being deeply Northern, through his love for Sibelius's forestland and the hues of the countryside around Georgian Bay. In time, with his life in the studio and on the radio, that his how he came to view his art's role and his life's destiny: as an absolute gift of music, itself an elevated form of life dedicated to the good of the community and the world. And so in him, through a constant dedication to communications technology and the quest for the ideal form of a musical work, Santayana's puritan ideal found its most exemplary incarnation.

Where Gould is concerned, only the adoption of an ethical language, which brings together concepts such as authenticity, a mode of life and its demands, and ultimately the unconditional gift of love, can help us reconcile the art and the life. It also can help resolve the paradoxes of a withdrawal from the world and a passion for communication, the sublime and the trivial, asceticism and eccentricity. Too many discussions of Gould's eccentricity unnecessarily attribute it to neurosis; too many descriptions of his idiosyncrasies and symptoms ignore the central fact that determined his life and art, and which is strikingly present in his playing and in all his photographs: the absorption in music and the desire – the will – to give back as much as possible of what he had received.

I return one last time to the expression "wonder and serenity": was it not presented with "edification" in mind as an ideal? I would not want to follow too closely in the steps of a philosopher like Richard Rorty regarding the importance of edification for the construction of the self, as what edifies does not always come to us from the outside; nor does edification always result from the endless cultivation of human friendship. However, if to edify is first of all to elevate and to build – to have the power to exalt – then art is crucial to it. This is the definition Gould might have given for his ethic. Because the artist's destiny is to isolate himself in order to create, the interpreter embraces the solitude of his creation only so as to go beyond it toward a community that welcomes his art, and which, through this gift, finds itself "edified" in turn.

Peter Ostwald writes that Gould was concerned that his public be as conscious of his genius as it was of his vulnerability. When I reread this sentence I think of Joseph Beuys's fox, I think of Gould's love for animals – I think of everything in him that called out for protection, everything that appealed, voicelessly, for affection. Gould did not try to hide the troubles he inherited from his childhood, or to camouflage anything that in the eyes of ordinary society might pass for pathology or represent a kind of madness, any more than he cared for his appearance. He tried, rather, to integrate it all into an ongoing moral project, infinite in scope; and to that project he gave the name wonder, serenity, rapture. He made it the very substance of the gift that was his art. He trusted the synthesis that would epitomize, through his art, all the elements that had come together to shape his life. Those who do not like Gould's art, or not enough, criticize him for having imposed himself on it too much, for being too visible and extravagant. I hope to have shown that on the contrary, for those who continue to love him, the transparency of his life illuminates his art, revealing it as a spiritual destiny fully assumed, in harmony with a moral ideal proposed in and by the music. The spiritual and moral language that gives us access to his experience is the only one that can help us to describe his art, and it is in this way that the ethical sheds light on the aesthetic.

# VII
*Gigue*

# On the Road, at the Lakeshore, in the Forest
*Partita no. 6 in E Minor*

In an autobiographical essay written toward the end of his life, Gould recounts a dream. He evokes the trees that haunt his early childhood memories ... massive, magnanimous, without number. Trees inhabit this dream, nothing but trees, and the dream itself is an enduring afterimage of his childhood and all the music associated with it. Reigning over the grandiose natural beauty of the Ontario lakes, the centenary maple forests reddening in autumn were a comfort to this childhood and protected it. This is not just one memory among many; it incorporates all the depictions of nature that provided sanctuary for the artist, where he later sought refuge, where he looked to find peace. They are there in François Girard's film, and again in Bruno Monsaingeon's final homage, where, following in Gould's tracks, he travels once more the enchanted roads of the countryside north of Toronto. Gould's parents owned a summer home on the northwest shores of Lake Simcoe, near the small village of Uptergrove. This lake, like all the lakes of the Canadian boreal forest, offers its visitors an enclosed space, a place of peace, and a chance to meditate. I will let a short gigue keep us company as we take this homeward path, following that road on an imagined summer's day. Thoreau speaks to us as we stroll. But we need to make room for other voices as well.

Glenn was a joyful child, and loved taking a boat out on the lake, alone or with his dog. According to his father, he was never so happy as when he was in the water, and he swam like a fish. The last light of day filters through the windows of the little wooden cottage, and the lake has calmed. Peace descends; it is five in the afternoon. His mother has called him from the dock; she is preparing hamburgers. Around the lake, all the families are assembling. Young Glenn has placed a score on the piano, the *Inventions* perhaps, or he has turned on the radio. He is tired from swimming, but it is a gentle fatigue.

This spontaneous and longstanding love of nature, as one finds it in the tranquil countryside, is the dream of all industrious Canadians, as though it were given as a token of thanks for their labours, as though it embodied some truth about living in Canada. In his little tale of Orillia and Uptergrove, Stephen Leacock describes the improbable encounters between an innocent rural population and the city dwellers who observe them. A gallery of picturesque characters bustles about, but benignly, without much fuss. We hear their voices, we see them polishing their cars on Saturday, and going to church on Sunday. I don't know how to explain it, but in imagining these Lake Simcoe summers I have often thought of Gabrielle Roy's memories, perhaps because they evoke Manitoba, perhaps because of the refuge she found for herself in Petite-Rivière-Saint-François, where she had a few friends, and where she found the peace she needed in order to write. A conversation on the veranda, a stroll by the edge of a field lying fallow. The succession of seasons, so marked in this landscape, the eruption of cold following on the autumn colours, the silence of the snowy spaces – all part of the climate that marked Gould's thought and the blossoming of his art. Nothing was more remote from his nature than those

Bahamas beaches to which he set off, to his mother's delight, on a trip he made with Jock Carroll. When we look at the pictures Carroll brought back, we see a slight tension, and already, a withdrawal. At the piano Gould is swept along, but elsewhere he seems awkward, turned in on himself. His strength came from another world, from his musical childhood and its idyllic setting, the cottage retreat where his mother watched over him at the keyboard and they annotated scores together.

It was only natural that Gould, emerging from adolescence and taking leave of his teacher Alberto Guerrero, decided to move on alone and began to spend long periods of time at the Lake Simcoe cottage. There he found the solitude and the isolation he needed for his work, and was able to re-establish contact with his childhood and his piano. His neighbours remember him playing late into the night. Making his way there was always a joyous experience. In time, his childhood home became a kind of sanctuary, and the accounts his biographers have assembled from among the nearby residents are unanimous: Gould loved talking with them, he appreciated the company of the children, and he frequented the simplest restaurants where, without establishing close ties, he was very cordial. When he left the city, which happened less and less as the years passed, it was to reconnect with the sites of his adolescence: Manitoulin Island in Georgian Bay, where he dreamed of establishing a refuge for abandoned animals, and a number of other small locales scattered north of Toronto. Gould loved to drive the roads that wended their way through these still sparsely populated areas, often in a big American car. I particularly love, among François Girard's short films, the one where we see Gould as a truck stop habitué listening in on the conversations of local inhabitants and straining his ears to hear a song by Petula Clark. Gould was no longer an adolescent but an adult returning to the scenes of his youth. Listening to Petula's songs, he reconnected with something that had once been there – but time had passed.

What songs? Probably "Downtown," to which he offered an affectionate tribute in his 1967 essay "The Search for 'Pet' Clark." While remembering Highway 17, which follows the northwest shore of Lake Superior, he imagines the immense territory running from the Montreal suburbs to the Manitoba prairies: the Canadian Shield, all the land painted by the Group of Seven. A.Y. Jackson's *First Snow, Algoma,* a canvas from 1919. The fishing villages, the lumber camps, the names: Michipitcoten, Batchewana, the Indians pushed back by colonization. This simple world calmed him because it was the world of his childhood, just as it was that of so many who loved Gould, whether they lived in Toronto or Montreal. In this Laurentian universe the monster of wealth had not yet put in an appearance; wooden porches prevailed, the mosquito screens of July, the seven o'clock plunges into the lake. But this world also harboured traces of another more repressed world, and just as, in preparing *The Idea of North,* he had measured the impact of the territorial grid introduced by the railroad, Gould could not help but divine here other signs, other solitudes. How not to sense, behind his caustic description of the little town of Marathon, with its accumulated pulp and the small leavings of industry, Thoreau's dream of a nature intact? To contemplate Lake Cognashene was to imagine the land before it entered modernity.

It was in a truck stop along Highway 17 that Gould discovered Petula Clark's songs: first "Who Am I?," then "Sign of the Times," "My Love," and finally "Downtown." He stayed in a motel in Marathon and listened to them all. I am attracted to this memory of Gould's, because this song was in the jukebox at Terrasse Foisy, where my family spent the summer near the Rivière des Prairies. The song played from morning to night, and we heard it everywhere. Gould had met a Dutch tourist who told him that "My Love" reminded him of a congregation singing in church. But what did Gould himself think? What love might he have been dreaming of?

Once I thought that love was meant for anyone else but me
Once I thought you'd never come my way
Now it only goes to show how wrong we all can be
For now I have to tell you everyday

It was not only, or even primarily, popular culture that these songs
stirred in him, and even less the evangelical memory of love in the
community; it was their message, and the message was the following: "detachment" and "sexual circumspection" – his words.
But what detachment could Petula Clark be promoting, she who
was an idol of modern suburbia, of the new mass culture, during
the glorious years when the middle class could fulfill its dream of
a cottage "up north"? Why would this dream of a love always in
the offing be a mistake? "Downtown," Gould wrote, is an adolescent daydream, a song that intoxicates, precisely because it
makes one dream of the availability of love in the heart of the city.
As usual, he embarks upon an intricate explanation – a learned
analysis – and proposes a deep structure for four songs; but in fact
his resistance to what he has perceived is so persistent that he turns
himself inside out to bring it under control. But in vain, and the
puritan in him is annoyed:

There's an inevitability about that quartet with its relentless
on-pressing to the experiences of adulthood or a reasonable
facsimile thereof. To a teenage audience whose social-sexual
awareness dovetailed with their release dates, Petula with her
well-turned-out Gidgetry would provide gratifying reassur-
ance of post-adolescent survival.

Gould was not certain himself of having survived adolescence.
His "well-turned-out Gidgetry," a term that contracts "girl" and
"midget," stems from a novel by Frederick Kohner that was very
popular in the 1960s. Who can forget Sally Field in the 1965 tele-

vision sitcom *Gidget*, showing everywhere at the time? The landscape of Highway 17 was not only populated by miners and
truckers; it also exhaled a perfume that Gould, then thirty-three
years old, was not yet able to breathe. In this music he senses a tension between rebellion and a middle-class pressure to conform.
His analysis peters out – the subject has become too highly
charged – and he drifts into a dissertation on tonal popular music,
a scholar once more. Despite this shift in direction, the essay tells
us something important: even in this idyllic countryside where he
sought peace, Gould could not easily find it. Petula Clark, even
heard through the filter of Schoenberg's and Webern's music, had
only to begin singing, and something went awry. "Who am I?"
Petula repeatedly asked, and Gould didn't know what to answer.
Who, indeed, was he, who returned to the scenes of his youth and
let a dream carry him away? He did know, however. The song
gave its own response: "I close my eyes, and I can fly, and I escape
from all this worldly strife. ... "

The final answer belonged to the vastness of this space infused
by music, a space he came to and tried to merge into, and where
he wanted nothing more, perhaps, than to recapture Gidget. But
Gidget was as inaccessible as the loved one, absent or distant, in
his dream letter of 1980. In all these truck stops there were the
same aluminium-rimmed green Formica tables for four with
matching leatherette benches and small individual jukeboxes
where, for a few cents, one could order up the latest songs on the
hit parade. Gould also used to listen to them at full volume on his
Chevrolet Monte Carlo car radio. If he suddenly had to find
refuge, he would get back on the road, turn off the radio, and
make his way to that spot on Highway 17 where it hits the high
ground, somewhere north of Lake Superior. From there, Gould
noted, all the waters flow toward Hudson Bay and the Arctic
Ocean, and one had the feeling of being able to dominate the
Northern spaces, the entire boreal forest. On this promontory one

could meditate, dream, think of the idea of North, envisage its limits. One could graft onto the infinite horizon the need to strip everything down. It is there that radio reception was at its best.

All the accents of the continent are spread across the band, and, as one twiddles the dial to reap the diversity of that encounter, the day's auditory impressions with their hypnotic insularity recede, then re-emerge as part of a balanced and resilient perspective.

One wishes that Gould had taken a photo, but François Girard did it for him, depicting so well that encounter with the truckers, the ordinary people of Highway 17.

Even if some inoffensive songs heard in the North triggered low-level fears, Gould's love for the countryside and all it offered was essentially soothing, inducing a mystical feeling for music that called for silence. Petula was not everywhere; one could escape her – escape the noise, try to recapture music that was not so bewitching, the music Gould always needed. If the musical experience was to end in the contemplative state that oneness with nature can alone provide, then it would have to distance itself from everything that, in the concert hall or elsewhere, makes this impossible. For Gould, even Petula Clark invited detachment, and he thought of her exhortation to sexual circumspection as a lesson addressed to a generation that wanted to free itself too quickly from the constraints of puritanism. But was that really the case? When we listen to "Downtown" and its refrain, we hear something else: "When you're alone and life is making you lonely, you can always go downtown" is not an invitation to withdraw. Gould heard it differently; he heard it as an ironic refusal of the city's sexual dream, of the casual encounter, of the end to care. Nothing of that sort would just happen; one had to learn to give it up. One had to pursue an authentic detachment, one that left the city behind; what he wanted was Highway 17 and the forest.

This countryside was tranquil, even with different voices vying to be heard. For Gould, there was no conflict. Early on, Gibbons's antiphony and Bach's keyboard music presented themselves as the "subjects" of these solitary and silent landscapes; they belonged to them. Petula Clark's songs were certainly not there in the 1940s, but he heard many others then and afterward, fitting them all into his musical spectrum, that he might return to them later in his radio work, as he did to Janis Joplin's despairing lament: "Oh Lord, won't you buy me." How, to mention just one example, could the music of spiritual composers from Tudor times accommodate what seems such a noisy contradiction? It is not too difficult to imagine, in fact: the silent land of Lake Simcoe resembles in many respects the world Gould evoked in the *Solitude Trilogy*, and all music comes into its own when it can reach its listeners in a contemplative manner. When Gould entered the immense universe of scholarly music, he had to accept the isolation such a commitment demanded of him, and what he heard in this other music was what he had given up without a second thought. Could there even be any question of his going "downtown"? His essay on Petula Clark gives us the answer: he had to avoid it at any cost.

It is hard to believe that Gould's contrapuntal radio programs, prepared with such care, were broadcast on the same station as Petula Clark, and Gould saw the humour in it: thanks to the CBC, thanks to its "ministry," truckers could listen to Pierre Boulez. This concern for equality, this democratic passion that so consumed Gould the communicator, was perhaps not apparent to all; he himself may have had an impact not unlike that of Boulez drifting onto a truck radio somewhere in the countryside. I try to imagine the impression he left in the places he visited to prepare his trilogy: how did these complex reflections, grounded in a

refined spiritual quest, stand up to Petula's songs, especially given
that they were broadcast in the same years?

To speak here of spirituality is to recall all the passages in
Gould's writings lauding an inner life that lifts one toward the sublime. In Natsume Sōseki's novel *The Three-Cornered World*, Gould
reconnected with the directive to think of art as a spiritual itinerary guiding one into the world, a journey that reached its destination thanks to an absolute detachment. Just as the painter in
the novel takes his self-searching quest to a distant monastery,
Gould never stopped seeking, in the countryside around Georgian
Bay and in the Northern solitude he imagined, a place where this
detachment would be available to him. If he speaks of A.Y. Jackson's painting, it is less because the painter depicted the Georgian
Bay landscape he so loved, than because he supported his dream
of an idealized nature. He had to struggle, as his encounter with
Petula confirms. And he never stopped. Like all artists, he favoured
a contemplation that would provide the conditions for this spiritual rapture; removing himself from the constraints of action and
routine, freeing himself from desire, was not for him a flight, but
a commitment to another way. What does contemplation mean, if
not to inform one's vision of the world with an intensity and a
concentration that merges us utterly with this gaze, and detaches
us from everything else? That Gould succeeded in this at the
Formica tables of the Marathon truck stop on Highway 17, I have
no doubt. It was possible to meditate there, listening to music chosen by others; at the same time, one could spend an entire evening
in silence.

In a 1962 article, Gould asserted that applause spoiled the
musical experience, and at a concert-lecture at the Stratford Festival, he requested that, after *The Art of Fugue* had been played,
the lights remain dimmed and the audience refrain from clapping.
That same text included his vision of what art should be: an undy-
ing quest for a state of serenity and wonder, an enlightenment, the

setting free of what is divine in each of us. There was little need to follow up these self-effacing demands; after leaving the concert stage in 1964, Gould never had to repeat them. He could find silence in his studio and he could recapture it at Lake Simcoe. However, these injunctions do teach us something about the way art and life commune in nature, freeing the spirit in silence. *The Art of Fugue* is the most persuasive example, in that Bach inscribed therein a poetic and religious testament upon which Gould liked to expound, and in which he found an affinity with the church of his childhood that made a strong impression on him, especially when he was playing it at the organ. I don't know if he played the organ or harmonium in the village church; it is possible. We can imagine Petula Clark in this church, or even imagine her praying; the Dutch visitor was perhaps right. This is what Gould makes credible in speaking of her, however defensively, with such affection. Everyone is looking for a love that will help him define himself and answer the question, "Who am I?" Seated in front of his score for the *Inventions*, Gould already has his answer. On the porch, his father puts his fishing tackle in order, while Glenn says again that fish ought not to be sacrificed. Night falls, and we hear the first crickets.

I have often wondered why Gould had so little to say about Bach's religious works: the *Passions*, the cantatas, the *Mass in B Minor*. A likely reason was that he was not that attracted to vocal music, but this would contradict his predilection for Gibbons. Perhaps the passage from pure, strict counterpoint to the dramatic expression of prayer was for him already an obstacle to transparent contemplation. Here too, Petula can help us: voices create a screen; they can intoxicate, especially if one must pray. If we must talk theology, Gould's would be a kind of mysticism infused with nature and harmonizing with counterpoint's aura of grace, and not the symbolic doctrine found in Christian music. The only notable exception would be his work on the Mennonites in the

*Solitude Trilogy*; how not to recognize, as the hymn recurs again and again, the same childhood memory that haunted his *Art of Fugue*, the image of the stained glass in the church on Sundays. Here, and perhaps only here, Christianity left its mark.

In a letter dated April 19, 1962, to his former English teacher, Miss Harriet Ingham, he made clear, however, that this outlook did not represent a deep conviction. To his correspondent, who seems to have reproached him for not having given enough importance, in a program devoted to Bach's music, to the religious compositions – even though he had included one such work, *Cantata 54, Wiederstehe doch der Sünde* – he replied by pointing out the fundamental link between this music and the composer's experience of faith in a faithless age. Bach, he wrote, opposed the "galant theatricality" of his sons' music, and was deeply imbued with the spiritual values of the Reformation "in a world which at that time was becoming increasingly hostile to the sanctity of spirit." In an intriguing parenthesis, he explained that if he did not say more on the subject, it was because the program was to be broadcast in French in Quebec. This remark makes one smile, in its presumption of hostility on the part of the Catholics toward Protestant spirituality. I do not want to give this too much importance, other than to show that Gould assumed his Protestantism, and that he defended its values to the point of embracing Bach's resistance to worldly theatricality. In the Toronto area, more reformed religious music would have been acceptable, but in Montreal, no.

When Gould speaks of the process through which every human being is urged to liberate that part of him that is divine, he is simply drawing on the spiritual heritage of the American transcendentalist tradition: the effort to purify oneself, to go beyond oneself, to arrive at a pure transcendence for which nature is both a likeness and an unfailing sign. Intrinsic to Emerson and

Thoreau's tradition was a mystical view of nature, and it was a perspective Gould almost certainly shared. Petula Clark's song made it clear that detachment was his only option; it demonstrated, not without tenderness, how hard it was to resist suburban conformity. All these "suburbia," then in their ascendancy, thought they had found salvation along the roads bordering Georgian Bay. Purification demanded something else, an opening onto a vaster space, and that, Gould knew from childhood, only art could provide.

Many landscapes merge together in the boreal landscape of Lake Simcoe – those of the Group of Seven paintings, those of a Canada dreamed and imagined, but also those of the Scandinavian forest with its wealth of mythologies, and those that resonated for him in his mother's name: Greig. Florence Gould was in fact born Greig, and she was related, very distantly because her great-grandfather was the composer's cousin, to the illustrious Norwegian composer Edvard Grieg. Gould recorded his *Sonata in E Minor* in homage to this mysterious filiation that had crossed continents to reach him. He greatly respected artists who, like Grieg and Sibelius, were successful in integrating the Northern spaces into their music. When we reread his letters, we come upon an enigmatic figure from time to time: Fartein Valen, whom Gould affectionately called "the hermit of Norway." His music is little known, but it includes two beautiful piano sonatas, and as of 1971 Gould included them in his radio recordings. And so on July 18, 1972, he played the *Sonata No. 2 for Piano, Opus 32* along with Grieg's *Sonata in E Minor, Opus 7*, for the program "CBC Tuesday Night." In playing them, Gould no doubt pictured this hermit's retreat on the shores of a Sunnhordland fjord, where he lived from 1936 until his death in 1952, in a solitude protected by the presence of his sister. We learn from his biography that he was the son of missionaries, spent a large part of his childhood in Madagascar, remained a bachelor, spoke nine languages, composed thousands of exercises for the piano and a magnificent concerto for the violin, and cultivated roses. In the gallery of characters Gould might have run into in his walks around Lake Simcoe, could he have found another that so resembled him?

Gould continually returned to the mystery of the fjords, their depths, their mystical silence – all that Sibelius's *Fifth Symphony*, in its succession of metamorphoses, represented to him – as a vital metaphor for the North. But this North was no longer that of the *Solitude Trilogy*; it was closer to hand and more spiritual, the North of Georgian Bay, Highway 17, the scenes of his childhood. Its horizon was accessible, less rough and less wild; and rising out of it, strong, like the great symphonic waves that form the beauty of Sibelius's music, was an enduring call toward the infinite. And, at any moment, a call from those other voices that he loved – voices from which he had learned to disengage.

# Bibliographical Note

I have brought together in this note all references to sources that I have used directly, or have quoted. Many studies are worthy of our attention, and I have read them extensively over the years. The fact that I may not mention all of them here does not mean they are of no interest; I have simply limited myself to what I thought was essential. In their article in the *Encyclopedia of Music in Canada*, Kevin Bazzana, Geoffrey Payzant, and John Beckwith have included all the useful references to Gould's recordings, writings, and films, as well as an important research bibliography. It is an essential starting point. My book owes much to the work of these scrupulous scholars, and I thank them warmly.

Among the essential sources, we must first count Glenn Gould's published interviews: for example, that with Jonathan Cott (1984), and those assembled by Bruno Monsaingeon (1986) and by John P.L. Roberts (1999), as well as his various writings, brought together by Bruno Monsaingeon in two volumes (1983 and 1985), Tim Page (1984), and John P.L. Roberts (1999). These texts are the most accessible direct sources for Glenn Gould's life and thought. We must also include the correspondence, of which we still have only a part, edited by Ghyslaine Guertin and John P.L. Roberts (1992–). The French translation includes an interesting introduction, different from that in the English-language edition. There is also the selection of letters published by Bruno Monsaingeon, as an appendix to the crisis diary (2002). The crisis diary of 1977–78 is an interesting source; it has not been published in the original English, but is available in French translation (Monsaingeon 2002). A volume of interviews with people who knew Gould was prepared by Rhona Bergman (1999).

Gould's discography was compiled by Nancy Canning (1992). Glenn Gould's archives have been deposited in the Library and Archives Canada. They may be accessed on the following internet site: www.collection-scanada.gc.ca/glenngould/index-e.html. An inventory of the indexed documents was prepared by Ruth Pincoe and Stephen C. Willis, and published in 1992. Much information may also be found on the site of the Glenn Gould Foundation, www.glenngould.ca, as well as in the magazine the foundation has published since 1995 (vol. 1, 1995–vol. 13, 2008). Sony has re-released the complete collection of Gould's original recordings on CD (*The Original Jacket Collection*, 80 CDs, 2007).

The biographies available to date are varied and complementary. They draw on very diverse sources. I have relied primarily on the work of Kevin Bazzana (2003), which draws on all the available documentation, and proposes a nuanced moral and aesthetic reading. This work is indispensable for any study of Gould. Even if its bibliographical notes do not always enable one to retrace the documents it relies on, I have chosen to trust it. I also very much respect the work of Peter F. Ostwald (1997). Deceased in 1996, Ostwald saw Gould on numerous occasions after meeting him following a concert in California in February 1957; this long friendship greatly enriched the book's narrative. The biography by Otto Friedrich (1989) was officially commissioned by the Glenn Gould Foundation; it includes, notably, a detailed chronology of the concerts and a discography.

The radio broadcasts and the television films are available in part on DVD, and it is regrettable that there is no complete, codified catalogue. The *Solitude Trilogy*, a series of three radio programs directed by Glenn Gould in 1967, 1969, and 1977, and produced for the CBC is available on compact disc: *Glenn Gould's Solitude Trilogy: Three Sound Documentaries* (CBC Records, PSCD 2003–3, a three-disc set with a booklet containing Gould's introductory texts). An interesting film, *The Idea of North*, a co-production between the CBC and PBS, was made from the first program in 1970 by Judith Pearlman. It has recently been restored. Bruno Monsaingeon's films are among the most important documents available to us. They include essential material, especially that devoted to the recording of the *Goldberg Variations* for its quasi-testamentary value. Among the other available films, one of the most interesting is that of Yosef Feyginberg, *The Russian Journey*, produced in 2003 and based on documents relating to Gould's tour of Russia in 1957. There is also David Langer's program *Glenn Gould: Life and Times*, directed for the CBC in 1998. The homage produced by the National Film Board under the direction of Jocelyn Barnabé, and presented in 1994 under the title *Extasis*, is also interesting; it consists of a montage of excerpts from the book by Michel Schneider. François Girard's *Thirty-Two Short Films about Glenn Gould*, now available on DVD, is a vibrant and inspired tribute. Gould recited an excerpt from Natsume Sōseki's novel on the CBC in 1981; it is available on the site Ubuweb. The CBC Archives site provides some excerpts from Gould's programs and interviews: http://archives.cbc.ca/IDD-1-74-320/people/glenn-gould/. Finally, we must note the publication, under the direction of Michael Stegemann, of a biographical documentary presenting the life and work of Glenn Gould (*The Glenn Gould Trilogy: A Life*. Sony, 3 CDs, 2007). Using the collage technique so dear to Gould, this work reproduces several excerpts from his radio work and recordings. It also gives access to a number of selections from his writings, through the mediation of a narrative voice.

Gould's playing of works that were for him both paradigms of what he preferred in the repertoire and an opportunity to demonstrate his approach has been given little formal analysis; there is, however, one important exception, Kevin Bazzana's indispensable book (1997), which includes a detailed study and examples on an accompanying disc.

There are many books of Glenn Gould portraits, including Malcolm Lester's album (2002), which includes photos from Gould's childhood and concertizing period. Jock Carroll's photo collection (1995) boasts a wonderful selection of youthful portraits, as well as a lively account of the trip they made together to the Bahamas in 1956. Don Hunstein has brought together a number of his portraits exhibited at the Canadian Embassy in Washington in 2005: *The Hunstein Variations: A Photographic*

# Bibliography

*Glenn Gould's Writings*

Cott, Jonathan. *Conversations with Glenn Gould*. Boston: Little &
Brown, 1984.

Gould, Glenn et al. *Glenn Gould: Variations*. Edited by John
McGreevy. Toronto: Doubleday, 1983.

– *The Glenn Gould Reader*. Edited with an introduction by Tim Page.
Toronto: Lester & Orpen Dennys, 1984.

– *Écrits. Tome I. Le dernier puritain; Tome II. Contrepoint à la ligne.*
Compiled, introduced, and translated from the English by Bruno
Monsaingeon. Paris: Fayard, 1983–85.

– *Non, je ne suis pas du tout un excentrique. Un montage de Bruno
Monsaingeon*. Paris: Fayard, 1989.

– *Selected Letters*. Edited and compiled by John P.L. Roberts and
Ghyslaine Guertin. Toronto: Oxford University Press, 1992.

– *Glenn Gould's Letters to… (1957–81)*. Selected and edited by
Ghyslaine Guertin. Montreal: Momentum, forthcoming.

– *Lettres réunies, présentées et annotées par Ghyslaine Guertin et John
P.L. Roberts, avec la collaboration de Valerie Verity et Jean-Jacques
Nattiez*. English translation by Annick Duchâtel. Paris: Christian
Bourgois, "Musique/Passé/Présent," 1992.

– *La série Schönberg*. Text edited and introduced by Ghyslaine
Guertin. Translated from the English by Caroline Guindon. Notes
by Ghyslaine Guertin and Stéphane Roy. Paris: Christian Bourgois,
"Musiques," 1998.

– "Bach's Keyboard *Partitas*: A conversation with Glenn Gould." *Glenn Gould*, vol. 4, 2 (fall 1998), 47–55.

*Glenn Gould: Journal d'une crise, suivi de Correspondance de concert.* Introduced by Bruno Monsaingeon. Paris: Fayard, 2002.

### Biographies and Studies

Bazzana, Kevin. *Glenn Gould: The Performer in the Work.* Oxford: Clarendon Press, 1997.

– *Wondrous Strange: The Life and Art of Glenn Gould.* Toronto: McClelland & Stewart, 2003. (French translation by Rachel Martinez. Montreal: Éditions du Boréal, 2004).

– Payzant, Geoffrey, and Beckwith, John. "Gould, Glenn." *Encyclopedia of Music in Canada/Encyclopédie de la Musique au Canada*, 2nd edition, 2002; new revised edition available on line, 2007.

Bergman, Rhona, *The Idea of Gould.* Philadelphia, Lev Publishing, 1999.

Canning, Nancy. *A Glenn Gould Catalog.* Westport, Connecticut: Greenwood Press, "Discographies," vol. 50, 1992.

Carroll, Jock. *Glenn Gould: Some Portraits of the Artist as a Young Man.* Toronto: Stoddart, 1995.

Clarkson, Michael. *The Secret Life of Glenn Gould: A Genius in Love.* Toronto: ECW Press, 2010.

Friedrich, Otto. *Glenn Gould: A Life and Variations.* New York: Random House, 1989.

Fulford, Robert. *Best Seat in the House: Memoirs of a Lucky Man.* Toronto: HarperCollins, 1988.

Guertin, Ghyslaine, (ed.). *Glenn Gould: Pluriel.* Montreal: Louise Courteau, 1988; 2nd edition, revised and expanded, Montreal: Momentum, 2007. (English translation, *Glenn Gould: Universe of a Genius.* Compiled and presented by Ghyslaine Guertin. Translated by Denis G. Coupal. Montreal: Momentum, 2007).

– (ed.). *Variations sur des thèmes de Gould.* Montreal: Momentum, 2007. (English translation, *Gould and Variations.* Compiled and

presented by Ghyslaine Guertin. Translation by Judith Terry.
Montreal: Momentum, 2007).

Hafner, Katie. *A Romance on Three Legs: Glenn Gould's Obsessive Quest for the Perfect Piano*. New York: Bloomsbury, 2008.

Hjartarson, Paul. "Of Inward Journeys and Interior Landscapes: Glenn Gould, Lawren Harris, and 'The Idea of North.'" *Essays on Canadian Writing*, 59, 1996, 65–86.

Kazdin, Andrew. *Glenn Gould at Work: Creative Lying*. New York: E.P. Dutton, 1989.

Kingwell, Mark. *Glenn Gould*. Toronto: Penguin, "Extraordinary Canadians," 2009.

Leroux, Georges, "La représentation du génie." In Guertin, Ghyslaine (ed.), *Glenn Gould: Pluriel*. Montreal, Louise Courteau, 1988, 23–39.

– "La nécessité d'être seul. À propos de la *Trilogie de la solitude* de Glenn Gould." In Melançon, Benoît, and Popovic, Pierre (eds.). *Miscellanées en l'honneur de Gilles Marcotte*. Montreal: Éditions Fides, 1995, 197–210.

– "Les mains de Glenn Gould." In Calabrese, Giovanni (ed.). *Prodige de la main*. Montreal: Éditions Liber, 2006, 135–40.

– *Style et forme de vie. L'art de Glenn Gould dans sa vie même*. Montreal: Momentum, 2007, pp. 73–98. (English translation, "Music and Form of Life." In *Gould and Variations*. Compiled and presented by Ghyslaine Guertin. Translation by Judith Terry. Montreal: Momentum, 2007, 69–102).

Lester, Malcolm. *Glenn Gould: A Life in Pictures*. Foreword by Yo Yo Ma. Introduction by Tim Page. Toronto: Doubleday Canada, 2002. (French translation by Robert Macia. Montreal and Paris: Flammarion, 2002).

Marcotte, Gilles. "Glenn Gould, la grandeur, le Canada." *Liberté*, no. 168, December 1986, 32–7.

McFarlane, Matthew. "Glenn Gould, Jean Le Moyne, and Pierre Teilhard de Chardin: Common Visionaries." *Glenn Gould*, vol. 8, 2 (fall 2002), 70–7.

McNeilly, Kevin, "Listening, Nordicity, Community: Glenn Gould's 'The Idea of North.'" *Essays on Canadian Writing* 59, 1996, 87–104.

Nattiez, Jean-Jacques. "Gould singulier: Structure et atemporalité dans la pensée gouldienne." In Guertin, Ghyslaine (1988). *Glenn Gould: Pluriel*, 57–82.

Ostwald, Peter F. *Glenn Gould: The Ecstasy and Tragedy of Genius.* Foreword by Oliver Sacks. New York and London: W.W. Norton, 1997. (French translation by Christian Dumais-Lvowski and Lise Deschamps Ostwald. Arles: Actes Sud, 2003).

Payzant, Geoffrey. *Glenn Gould: Music and Mind.* Toronto: Van Nostrand Reinhold, 1978 (French translation by Laurence Minard and Th. Shipiatchev. Paris: Fayard, 1985).

Roberts, John P.L., (ed.). *The Art of Glenn Gould: Reflections on a Musical Genius.* Toronto: Malcolm Lester Books, 1999.

– "A Pianist's Hands: The Implications of the Secret Diaries of Glenn Gould." *Glenn Gould*, vol. 9, 1 (spring 2003), 28–35.

Schneider, Michel. *Glenn Gould, piano solo. Aria et trente variations.* Paris: Gallimard, "L'un et l'autre," 1988.

### Other References

Beach, David W. *Aspects of Unity in Bach's Partitas and Suites: An Analytical Study.* Rochester, New York: Rochester University Press, "Eastman Studies in Music," 2005.

Bernhard, Thomas. *The Loser.* Translated from the German by Jack Dawson. New York: Alfred A. Knopf, 1991.

Blumenberg, Hans. *La Passion selon saint Mathieu.* French translation by Henri-Alexis Baatsch and Laurent Cassagnau. Paris: L'Arche, 1996.

Brendel, Alfred. *Me of All People: Alfred Brendel in Conversation with Martin Meyer.* Ithaca: Cornell University Press, 2005.

Davis, Ann. *The Logic of Ecstasy: Canadian Mystical Painting 1920–1940.* Toronto: University of Toronto Press, 1992.

Girard, François. *Thirty-Two Short Films about Glenn Gould*, 1994.

Housser, Frederick B. *A Canadian Art Movement: The Story of the Group of Seven*. Toronto: Macmillan, 1926.

Jackson, Alexander Young. *A Painter's Country: The Autobiography of A.Y. Jackson*. Foreword by Vincent Massey. Toronto: Clarke Irwin, 1958.

Kivy, Peter. *Music Alone: Philosophical Reflections on the Purely Musical Experience*. Ithaca: Cornell University Press, 1990.

Menuhin, Yehudi. *Unfinished Journey*. London: MacDonald and Janies, 1976.

Riley, Charles A. *The Saints of Modern Art: The Ascetic Ideal in Contemporary Painting, Sculpture, Architecture, Music, Dance, Literature and Philosophy*. Hanover: New England University Press, 1998.

Santayana, George. *The Last Puritan: A Memoir in the Form of a Novel*. New York: Scribner's Sons, 1936.

Scheler, Max. *Le saint, le génie, le héros*. Translated from the German by E. Marmy. Lyon and Paris: Emmanuel Vitte, 1958.

Sōseki, Natsume. *The Three-Cornered World*. Translation by Alan Turney. London: Peter Owen, 2002. (*Kusamakura*, 1906; *L'Oreiller d'herbes*, French ranslation by René de Ceccaty and Ryōji Nakamura. Paris: Éditions Rivages, 1987).

Spitta, Philipp, *Johann Sebastian Bach: His Work and Influence on the Music of Germany, 1685–1750*. Translated from the German by Clara Bell and J.A. Fuller Maitland. New York: Dover, 1951; original German edition in 2 volumes, Leipzig, 1873–79.

Wittgenstein, Ludwig. *Culture and value*. Ed. G.H. von Wright, translation Peter Winch. Chicago and Oxford: Basil Blackwell, 1980. (*Remarques mêlées*, French translation by Gérard Granel. Paris: Flammarion, 2002).

Yearsley, David Gaynor. *Bach and the Meanings of Counterpoint*. Cambridge: Cambridge University Press, 2002.

# Index